PUSHING THE LIMITS

by JOHN HOWARD
with PETER NYE

WRS
PUBLISHING

A Division of WRS Group, Inc.
Waco, Texas

First published in the United States of America in 1993 by WRS Publishing, A Division of WRS Group, Inc., 701 N. New Road, Waco, Texas 76710
Book design by Kenneth Turbeville
Cover design by Talmage Minter and Joe James
Front cover photo credit: Albert Gross
Back cover Photo credit: John Howard Collection

10 9 8 7 6 5 4 3 2 1

Library of Congress Catalog Card Number
John Howard
Peter Nye

ISBN 1-56796-015-4

Dedicated to our parents:

Mary and Harry Howard
Charlotte and Abner Nye

Acknowledgments

Writing is labor-intensive and notoriously lonely, and along the way it's helpful to get support and encouragement. Family members, racing rivals, teammates, race officials, friends, and industry representatives of John's were consistently generous with sharing their time and experiences.

Especially instrumental in putting this story together were Ray and Louise Blum, Ann and Gust Svanson, Gerry Ives, Steve Brunner, Al Federowsky, Martin (His Incorrigibleness) Meletio, Ron Smith, Ann Page, Russell Mamone, Lloyd Feldman, Lisa Rothmund, and Joan Claybrook. Pete Ehrmann was always good for a well-timed shot of wry.

Neil Sandler was a prince who made it possible for me to move up from a manual typewriter to an electric typewriter.

Thanks to a few good friends: Trever Igor, Karen Naylor, and, especially, Valerie Rice.

Peter Nye
Arlington, VA.

Foreword

I was the one who first tagged John with the title "The Incredible Human Machine," but the thing I really like most about John is that he is far more human than he is machine.

I'll never forget my first meeting with John Howard. It was in the spring of 1983 while I was in the process of developing the world's first gel bicycle saddle pads. I sought out John to ask his advice based on his experiences in riding the grueling, 3,000-mile Race Across America (then the Great American Bike Race). He told me he actually had not suffered severe saddle soreness in what has been called the toughest bicycle race in the world, but ever since the competition, he had had a numbness in both hands in his ring and little fingers. I immediately diagnosed his problem as ulnar nerve damage caused from prolonged handlebar pressure at the base of his palms. (He had ridden ten days, over 20 hours a day.) I told John I would like for him to test some experimental gloves with protective gel pads in the palms. He was my first guinea pig for a product which has since been sold to millions of riders around the world.

Our friendship was further sealed in 1984 when John took the time and effort to bring a team of racers to a bicycle race I sponsored, called the Spenco 500. This was a 500-mile race from Waco, Texas, to Comfort, Texas, and back. John's team won the race, which I used as a testing ground and promotion for the gel saddle pads, and today, almost 20 percent of all saddles around the world have incorporated the gel concept.

Since the Spenco 500, John and I have worked together on numerous sports medicine products, and I have learned to know John as an innovative thinker and teacher—not just as a world-class cyclist. He has the rare, uncanny ability of a champion to focus his energy on his current goal with a burning intensity, like a magnifying lens concentrating the sun's rays onto a spot the size of a pinhead. Nothing can divert his attention from that goal until he conquers it, at which time he sets a new, more challenging goal.

When one looks at John Howard's athletic achievements, the title of this book seems almost an understatement. He seeks to do the impossible with no regard for fear or pain and today, as a master's champion, gains little more reward than a deep personal satisfaction that in turn drives him to push his limits another step. Today's competitive cyclists and tomorrow's champions owe an incalculable debt to John Howard, "The Incredible Human Machine."

Wayman R. Spence, M.D.
Founder, Spenco Medical Corporation
Chairman, WRS Group, Inc.

Introduction

Heat and intense brightness corrugated off the flat, pristine white Bonneville Salt Flats, creating such visual distortion from light bouncing off the salt that mirages formed and stacked up double and triple—artificial images reflecting one another. The salt flats in July—or any time of year, for that matter—are a surreal plane uninterrupted for 12 miles in one direction and six miles in the other. To the north are the Silver Island Mountains, which loom rough and gray against the horizon, on an otherwise vast expanse of the Great Salt Lake Desert. Its uninhabitable landscape provides natural protection from voracious real estate developers. Visitors are few, but those who make the trip, about 100 miles west of Salt Lake City, tend to come for one reason: speed. The flatness, desolation, unrelenting summer heat, and brightness offer the ideal private setting for man and machine to wreak havoc in the name of a new world land speed record.

For three years, John Kennedy Howard had been aggressively stalking the world speed record on a bicycle. One night he had a dream in which 152 MPH appeared in computer letters. That became his goal. Nearly all adults have driven a car in their life. Few, however, have driven a vehicle more than double the U.S. legal speed limit of 65 MPH. Yet Howard felt he could push the limits and pedal a bicycle 152 MPH.

Of course, such awesome speed is impossible for a cyclist to pedal alone. An intrepid cyclist, on the right kind of bicycle, can pedal at phenomenal speed behind another vehicle that pushes air aside and vastly reduces wind resistance for whatever is tucked closely behind.

Howard arranged for a low-slung rocket car that packed a 540-horsepower engine in the front and a five-foot fiberglass shelter on the back where he rode in the vehicle's slipstream. Added to his campaign was a muscle bicycle unlike anything available anywhere: a hybrid of motorcycle and bicycle parts. The chain he pedaled rose diagonally to a sprocket behind his seat, and that sprocket was fixed to another chain that descended to the rear-wheel hub. A regular one-speed bicycle typically has a gear of 76 inches, a measurement that refers to riding a wheel 76 inches in diameter. Howard's innovative reduction-gear system gave him a gear of 390 inches, equivalent to riding a wheel 32^1/2 feet in diameter. Each revolution of his pedals carried his bicycle 111 feet, just shy of the 120 feet that Orville Wright, a bicycle racer and bike shop proprietor, went in his first successful flight at Kittyhawk. Howard would pedal his bicycle more than 140 RPM.

His plan was to usurp the 138.671 MPH record that Allan V. Abbott, a Los Angeles physician and motorcycle racer, had set pedaling behind a 1955 Chevy on August 25, 1973, at the Bonneville Salt Flats. Howard's campaign was more than a daring physical act behind a rocket car. The enterprise was expensive, time-consuming, and required the help of a crew of mechanics and engineers with specific talents, as well as officials and photographers to certify the record.

Howard prevailed on industry contacts to raise $100,000 in corporate support, then assembled a full-scale operation to go after the record in the summer of 1982.

What led Howard there in quest of his world record was a restlessness that drives artists of many different disciplines. In another month, Howard would turn 38. His cycling career already had made him well-known. He had competed as America's premier road racer in the 1968 Mexico City Olympics, 1972 Munich Olympics, and 1976 Montreal Olympics. He had won the gold medal at the 1971 Pan American Games road race in Cali, Colombia, and six national cycling championships. He had helped inspire another generation of American riders, one of whom was Greg LeMond, who got into bicycle racing after watching Howard closely in the 1975 Pan American Games trials in Nevada. As the 1970s concluded, Howard was generally regarded as the rider of the decade.

A characteristic common to champion athletes is the continual desire to push boundaries, and Howard faced the new decade with a broader athletic portfolio. He set out to accomplish a modern endurance version of the Labors of Hercules: to win the Ironman Triathlon in Hawaii (a 2.4-mile ocean swim, a 112-mile bicycle time trial, and a 26.2-mile run); to win a 3,000-mile race across America (from Santa Monica to New York City); to set a new distance record for 24 hours (517 miles in New York's Central Park); and to set the new land speed record.

Chapter 1

"Get your kicks on Route 66."
—Lyrics by Bobby Troup

In 1947, when John Kennedy Howard was born in Springfield, Missouri, the focus of local talk was Red and Julia Chaney's hamburger stand. The Chaneys' restaurant was a popular place, renowned for home-brewed root beer, dill pickles, and, of course, hamburgers. Savvy travelers took a road spur on Business Route 66 to the restaurant, called Red's Giant Hamburg—because the word "hamburger" had too many letters to fit on the sign. Since travelers and locals in a hurry liked to shout their orders into the kitchen through an open window, Red and Julia decided to respond to demand with what is considered the world's first drive-through service window. This, however, was not the only claim Springfield had to fame.

Missouri's third largest city, Springfield has considerable local color. During the Civil War, Confederate troops had held it after the bloody Battle of Wilson's Creek, which took place 11 miles south of the town. On August 10, 1861, some 2,500 Confederate and Federal soldiers were killed there. Six months later, Federal troops routed the Confederates. One of the scouts for the Federals was Wild Bill Hickok, who lived in Springfield. In 1865, Hickok settled a gambling debt by shooting Dave Tutt in the town square. Acquitted of murder, Wild Bill later ran for town marshal, but was outvoted.

John K. Howard's parents, Mary Kennedy and Harry Howard, grew up in Springfield. In their early teens, they had witnessed one of the most grueling endurance sports events ever held. Billed as the First Annual International Trans-Continental Foot Race, the 3,422-mile run from Los Angeles to New York City was called the Bunion Derby.

The organizer of the race was C. C. Pyle, a promoter whose initials alternately stood for Cash and Carry, Cold Cash, or Corn and Callus. His reputation had been made when he persuaded

University of Illinois football star Harold "Red" Grange to turn professional and join the Chicago Bears. Grange was a junior halfback who, in 1924, scored four touchdowns in 12 minutes against the University of Michigan, thereby attaining sports immortality.

Football thus gained its first superstar, and Pyle had his official starter for the transcontinental footrace.

On March 4, 1928, Grange set off a bomb (Pyle would not settle for something as small as a starter's pistol) to start 275 runners off on Route 66 before a crowd of 500,000.

Mary Kennedy was 14 years old when she watched the runners trotting past her home in the country on Route 66. "I remember they were pretty weary when they went by. It was such a crazy thing to do. We gave the runners some water. Sometimes they even stopped and talked with us."

Harry was 13 when he saw the race. "Springfield was a stop on the way. By the time they got to Missouri, runners were strung out [along the road] for five days. They were coming into town on Route 66 at all hours—morning, noon, and through the night."

Records show that Andy Payne of Claremore, Oklahoma, ran ahead of 55 finishers to win. He ran into New York City in 87 days—573 hours of actual running—to win the $25,000 grand prize. C. C. Pyle failed to garner the media attention he expected.

Despite being billed as the first annual, the transcontinental footrace was never repeated. But within a year, Route 66 entered the American vocabulary as a special American road. And the recollections that Mary, Harry, and others in Springfield had of watching the runners trot across America helped feed their son's imagination of what physical limits could be pushed.

Mary Kennedy grew up on her parents' apple orchard and chicken hatchery. In 1931, she was an honor graduate of Springfield's Central High School.

Mary's older sister, Virginia, attended Southwest Missouri State Teachers College (now Southwest State University), but there wasn't enough money to send more than one child to college at the same time. So after high school, Mary briefly attended Draghon Business School, where she learned secretarial skills.

"I went to work as a secretary at radio station KGBX, the first radio station in Springfield, for the sum of $5.00 a week. KGBX broadcast some of the first hillbilly acts on radio—what we call country and western music today."

Working in the radio station had advantages. Mary worked

her way up to writing, and when a television affiliate was subsequently established, she started writing scripts. She worked for the radio and television station for 23 years altogether.

Harry Howard had a tougher time growing up in Springfield. His father, Albert, had died when he was young, as had two older sisters. "That was very hard on my mother, Katherine," he says. When he graduated from Central High in 1933, attending college was not even a consideration.

"It was the Depression—jobs were scarce, and what jobs there were didn't pay much. I would crowd two or three jobs at a time. I worked at the Red Cross. I worked as a lifeguard and taught swimming. I worked nights at the *Springfield Leader-Press*, in the mail room. I was always doing something, staying busy. We had to in those times."

In 1939, he passed the federal civil service examination, which qualified him for the Public Health Service. There he found permanent employment and worked until his retirement in 1973.

Harry and Mary met in 1940 through mutual friends. They married that November 27 in Kansas City. A little over a year later, the United States entered World War II, and Harry enlisted in the U.S. Air Force, becoming one of 14 million Americans in the Armed Forces.

"I was in a training command and remained Stateside during the war. I was a cargo-carrying glider pilot and made thirteen landings, including two at night. I was stationed in Biloxi, Mississippi, when the war ended in 1945 and I was mustered out. I went home immediately. Mary and I had postponed having a family during the war years. Then we had three children in four years."

First came John Kennedy Howard, born August 16, 1947. Next was Harry David, on March 24, 1949. Elizabeth Anne was born October 13, 1951.

The Howards enjoyed an extended family. Visits with Mary's parents, Harry and Maria; Harry's mother, Katherine; and with cousins were frequent, especially on holidays and birthdays. The only exception to this was when the Public Health Service transferred Harry and his family to Atlanta for three years. When his Atlanta tour was up, Harry moved his family back to their hometown. They settled in a new country farmhouse which an architect friend of the family had designed. It had basement wood paneling that had been cut from St. Louis waterfront beams riddled with bullet holes.

"[In the 1930s], gangsters used to fire into the waterfront wharves for target practice," explained Anne. "The timbers were [later] sliced into boards for paneling, which had lots of texture. Our neighbors thought the bullet holes in the paneling were neat."

In the late 1950s, young John Howard rode around neighborhoods with other kids on a red balloon-tired Schwinn. From a Schwinn dealer, he picked up a comic book the company distributed and it made a big impression on him. Published in four vibrant colors and called *Bike Thrills*, the comic book's illustrations showed how Schwinn bicycles were made at the company's factory in Chicago, depicted some famous bicycles in history, and told the stories of two remarkable cycling daredevils who captured the public's—and Howard's—imagination.

One was Charles M. Murphy, who had startled the world back in June 1899 by pedaling 60 MPH. Murphy, of Brooklyn, New York, had ridden a standard racing bicycle—designed for the track, with no brakes and just one gear—on a special board surface laid between rails of train tracks on a stretch of the Long Island Railroad. He had paced closely behind the back of a train fitted with a wooden frame hood over the rear to protect him from the wind. A group of newspaper writers, who made up the media in those days before radio and television, had watched closely from the back of the train and reported what they saw. Murphy sped through the mile in 57^4/s seconds. From then on, he was known as "Mile-a-Minute" Murphy. One of his cycling rivals was Barney Oldfield who, four years later, switched to car racing and became the first to drive a car through the minute barrier.

Murphy's landmark ride led the way for "drafting"—that is, riding behind another vehicle—at great speeds. As car engines improved, a Frenchman followed in Murphy's wheel marks to become the subject of the other daredevil story illustrated in *Bike Thrills*. In May 1941, Alfred Letourner rode 108 MPH behind a racing car in Bakersfield, California. Letourner's new world record was a feat of daring and athletic talent. Letourner wore no special clothing for the event—just regular black wool cycling shorts, a long-sleeved jersey, and a leather helmet. Schwinn had built Letourner's bicycle and published *Bike Thrills* to direct attention to American cycling's glorious past, Schwinn's product line, and Letourner's accomplishment.

As with other sports legends, Letourner had a nickname—Red Devil—and such a long list of achievements that many were overlooked. A native of Amiens, France, he liked to defy tradition by wearing the number 13 boldly across the back of his red, silk jersey in races. He excelled in the grueling six-day races of the 1920s and 1930s, which enjoyed great vogue in European and North American cities. In these races, 15 two-rider teams would compete for 144 continuous hours around a steeply banked indoor board track measuring 10 laps to the mile. One rider would be on the boards while his partner was in the infield eating one of eight meals a day or taking a nap. Crowds delighted in watching the riders' bright, silk jerseys speed around the right turns on the saucer-like tracks.

Letourner arrived in the United States in the golden age of American racing, when cyclists were among the best-paid athletes. He was 20 when he entered the March 1928 six-day race in New York City's Madison Square Garden, the Super Bowl of international racing. In March and December, the Garden hosted "sixes" that served up $75,000 in prizes. (At that time, National Football League franchises, including the Chicago Bears, were selling for only a few hundred dollars each.) The Red Devil's brilliant riding made him a crowd favorite. He won six of the Garden's "sixes" and followed the sport's migratory flow to win others in Philadelphia, Chicago, Detroit, Cleveland, and Buffalo. For three years in the 1930s, Letourner reigned as national champion in motorpace racing, another popular but now forgotten event. In this, cyclists rode at speeds topping 60 MPH by pacing behind motorcycles.

The outbreak of World War II effectively ended the international six-day circuit, and with it professional cycling in America. Letourner took up a new challenge—the world's motorpace speed record. Schwinn sponsored his ride and made him a Paramount bicycle. His original plan was to pace behind legendary cowboy Tom Mix, but Mix was killed in a car crash in 1940. Letourner spent some time looking around for another pacer before he teamed up with well-known racing driver Ronnie Householder.

Officials from the American Automobile Association timed Letourner's ride on May 17, 1941. It took him three miles to get up to 100 MPH, then he officially clocked 108.92, dashing through the mile in 33.05 seconds. He needed four miles to slow down.

"When I read that comic book, I was really inspired," Howard recalled. "I was just a kid, and I thought what he did was so terrific. His record went from being an inspiration for me to [being] a dream. Then, as an adult, I held onto that dream and found a way to do it."

When Howard read *Bike Thrills*, professionals like Letourner were retired. Six-day races were revived fitfully but failed to draw attendance. A career in sports typically meant either baseball, football, or basketball, and rewards in those endeavors were long on glory but short on financial returns. Free-agent negotiations and corporate sponsorships were still decades away. Rules governing amateur athletes were so strict that track-and-field athletes were disqualified from trying out for the Olympic team if they worked in a store that sold running shoes.

American cycling was limited to amateur competition. Virtually an underground sport, it was rarely reported on, and the new generation of cyclists knew little about the sport's roots or traditions. Once every four years, the U.S. Olympic Committee, located in a townhouse on Park Avenue in Manhattan, New York, issued athletes flight tickets to go to the Olympic Games. For U.S. cyclists, making the Olympic team was the peak of their career. But Europeans dominated the cycling events, and used their victories as stepping stones to turning professional.

The most celebrated bicycle racer in America was Ezio Pinza, the basso of Milan's La Scala and Broadway's musical stage. In his youth—when Letourner was still a child—Pinza had been a professional cyclist in Italy. He rode long road races, some lasting 12 hours, during which he ate from a bag of food tied to his handlebars. After finishing second in a race, Pinza sang in the shower. Other riders told him he would make a better opera singer than cyclist. After he had stayed in cycling long enough to realize his fortune was elsewhere, he listened to their advice.

At age 14, Howard was six feet tall and weighed 135 pounds. Football became his sport, and he played it in the seventh through ninth grades. "My father said he had played football, and I had to play football, too."

One hot July Fourth, Howard was with his family blasting firecrackers on the Wilson's Creek Civil War battleground, when he saw a cyclist pedal up on a Schwinn Varsity 10-speed bicycle. Ten-speeds were new on the American market, although they were commonplace in Europe. (Americans were still riding heavy but durable balloon-tired bicycles with upright handlebars and one speed.) The cyclist stopped his machine by pedaling backward to engage the coaster brake, an invention the Wright Brothers had patented. Howard saw the derailleur that hung from the rear hub of the Schwinn Varsity to transfer the chain to one of five rear sprockets and two front chainrings, for a total of 10 speeds. The bicycle also had dropped handlebars and brake levers, a radical departure from those Howard was accustomed to seeing.

"I had read about this cyclist in a newspaper feature that told how he had completed 700 miles riding across the state with a friend," Howard said. "I felt he was as free as a bird on his bicycle. He also arrived with a bag full of cherry bombs that made our firecrackers sound like little caps. He made a big impression that day."

Soon the two Howard brothers were saving the money they made from mowing lawns to buy bicycles. They bought Schwinn Continentals, which featured 10-speed derailleurs and cost $84.95 each. "H. D.'s bike was copper [colored] and mine was blue," Howard said. "The bike shop proprietor tried to talk us out of the bikes, using negative psychology. 'No,' he said. 'You don't want them. They're racing bikes.' That clinched it for me. The next day was cold and bleak, but that didn't matter because I wanted to go riding."

Howard and H. D. began riding with local American Youth Hostels Sunday recreation rides. "They were low-key and fun. My first associations with riding were touring and the esthetic reward that came out of that experience. We were riding in small groups up and down the Ozark foothills. I got to where I could ride 100 to 120 miles in one day on the weekend. Back in school on Monday, my classmates would say, 'Wow! I was riding in my car and I saw you riding your bike.' That was positive reinforcement. I was pushing my limits, building new ones."

Cycling opened new vistas to Howard, but it was still an extracurricular activity in his school. For one year at Glendale High School, he ran the mile on the track team and swam. In May 1964, his sophomore year, he won the Ozark Mile in a time of 4 minutes 44 seconds.

Bicycle racing was still ahead. His track coach cautioned against mixing running with cycling. "At that time, coaches felt that riding a bicycle ruined your legs for running. I liked riding a bike, though. Out there under the blue sky, breathing the fresh air and seeing a change in scenery were things I liked doing."

He discovered that equipment for lightweight bicycles, especially tires, was in short supply. Howard's tire treads were wearing thin. He went back to the bicycle shop, A & B Cycles, for a pair of narrow tires. All the shop manager had was a pair that obviously had some miles on them. Young Howard was disappointed.

"The manager said he would let me in on a secret," Howard said. "He told me they were special tires. Pat Murphy had ridden them." The shop manager told Howard that Murphy was a legend in North American cycling. A two-time Canadian national cycling champion from Delhi, Ontario, Murphy had competed for Canada in the 117-mile road race in the 1956 Melbourne (Australia) Olympics. He had then gone to the world championships in Europe and turned professional, a huge undertaking. Continental professionals were the giants of the road, but Murphy held his own against them in strenuous 150-mile road races. He also rode in six-day races. In the early 1960s, he retired from racing and joined Schwinn as vice-president for sales in the Midwest.

"I bought the tires because they were special—Pat Murphy had ridden them," Howard said.

When he returned home and showed H. D. his new tires, telling him what he'd learned, the younger brother scoffed. "You mean you bought used tires from a fat old man?"

Skepticism didn't deter Howard. Equipped with Murphy's tires, he hit the roads for more miles. "He was considered odd for riding a bike in high school," says his sister Anne. "Riding a bicycle was something that little kids did back in the 1960s."

All the miles made Howard's legs strong, developed his stamina and confidence, and improved his heart and lungs. In the summer of 1964, he was among millions of Americans watching broadcasts of the Tokyo Olympics on black-and-white television sets. While today's television coverage of the Olympics is a multibillion dollar operation, the Tokyo Olympics were covered on a low budget. Jim McKay of "ABC's Wide World of Sports," itself only three years old, did the voice-over on video tapes that were flown on jet planes to his studio in New York City. Some of the coverage included Jack Simes III, of Closter, New Jersey, who was wearing the Stars and Stripes jersey. America's premier sprinter, he competed against European champions on the banked outdoor velodrome.

"Watching Jack Simes racing his bicycle on television really excited me," Howard said. "Here was a sport that I enjoyed, and a good cyclist could go all the way to the Olympics. Watching television that afternoon in our living room, I was absolutely convinced that by 1968 I was going to make the Olympic cycling team."

Chapter 2

"No psychic reward would ever be so powerful
as winning a dare with yourself."
—Norman Mailer, *The Executioner's Song*

The work ethic runs deep in Missouri, whose early nineteenth-century settlers stubbornly declined to take someone's word for anything. They insisted on being shown, and thus earned Missouri the "Show Me State" nickname.

In northeastern Missouri on the bank of the Mississippi River is Pike Country, where tight-fisted farmers were called "pikers." This term crept into the vocabulary as a reference to frugality. Growing up in this area, with parents who worked full-time jobs, and with an extended family whose older members raised children in the depths of the Depression, helped instill in Howard the feeling that achievements are gained through hard work.

"Dad would come home from work at the end of the day and ask us, 'What did you do today?'" Howard recalled.

Yet hard work had rewards. Harry Howard appreciated fine cars and always, even back to his first automobile, a 1929 Ford roadster, drove a convertible. His sons inherited a love of cars. "They were inoculated with the car bug," he says.

While Harry bought cars from Detroit, his sons developed a fascination for European sports cars, in which they indulged with money they earned from seasonal enterprises. In winter months, they chopped black oak and sycamore trees for fire wood—cutting, splitting, and stacking a cord an hour, a rate that full-grown men would be hard pressed to match. When the weather warmed, they mowed lawns.

"Our dad helped set us up in business with a 1946 Ford 2-ton, flatbed truck," Howard explained. "We would load mowers in the summer, and head out to service our customers. Because of the money we earned, we had great toys."

Their first was a 1955 Jaguar XK140 roadster, which they bought cheap because it needed considerable repairs. Howard was 16 and could drive it legally, and was deft at body work and painting. His brother, H. D., performed minor miracles on the engine. The brothers restored the car to mint condition. Because of the Jaguar's low sweeping body lines and yellow finish, the family called it the "Speedy Banana."

In Springfield, the Speedy Banana was an anomaly. Springfield is heartland America. Muscle cars from Detroit—Ford Mustangs, Chevrolet Corvettes, and Pontiac GTOs—were what young Americans who could afford them were driving. "Foreign cars were unheard of in the Midwest," Howard notes with pride. The Jaguar was as unique as his cycling, which also attracted attention when he pedaled his bicycle to school.

After school, high-school drivers liked to show off their cars by drag racing on city streets. Oversized engines in the Mustangs, Corvettes, and GTOs could power ahead of the Jaguar on straight stretches. But out of the city, on twisting, hilly Ozark Mountain roads, Howard and his brother took on all challengers.

"On the Ozark Mountain roads, we never lost a race," Howard said. "We took a lot of risks out there, driving at speed and flying around turns. I'd never do that again."

After the Jaguar was restored, the brothers acquired a 1958 356-A Porsche coup, which they also fixed to its original condition. (Today H. D. has a business in Austin, Texas, where he is a broker for expensive imports like Jaguar, Ferrari, and Alfa Romeo.)

By 1965, young Howard had earned letters in football, track, and swimming, but he left those sports for cycling, which, at the time, created friction between father and son. "Cycling was not a big sport in Missouri in the 1960s," the elder Howard explained dryly. "You had to live in Europe to get into bike racing back then. I was upset that he wasn't going to play football."

With the extra money Howard earned in the business he ran with his brother, he bought a Schwinn Paramount, a handmade steel frame that Schwinn made in limited numbers, in keeping with the heritage of the bicycle that the Red Devil rode. Howard's yellow Paramount, with chrome fork tips, was a road-racing bicycle fitted with the best components from Europe. Included was a 10-speed Campagnolo derailleur made in Italy.

Dedication, particularly to daily training and 100-mile Sunday morning rides with the American Youth Hostels, was understood by the family, but Howard's speed training, when he paced behind trucks in town, created some trouble. "One time a police officer in a patrol car accompanied John home on his bicycle and told us he had been drafting behind a truck," his father said. "John didn't get a ticket, but the officer didn't want him to do it again.

All the riding and occasional speed-work behind a truck helped to prepare Howard for racing, but information about upcoming races was hard to come by. "One day I was out on a training ride, when a car went past and the driver stopped, got out, and flagged me down," Howard recalled. "He said I must be brave for being out like that, and I said I was going to be a bike racer. He told me he was the promoter of a race called the Olathe-Council Grove Classic in eastern Kansas. He took my telephone number and later called me. That was how I learned about my first race."

That was in late May 1966, when Howard graduated from Glendale High School. He had been accepted for autumn admission to Southwest Missouri Sate University as an art major, and had secured a summer job as lifeguard at Meador Park pool. Following his father's example, he was a certified lifeguard and a water-safety instructor. The lifeguard job left his mornings free for training.

Harry Howard overcame the disappointment caused by his son's decision not to play football, and volunteered to drive his new blue Mustang convertible the approximately 200 miles to Olathe for his son's first race. At 18, Howard was competing in the open division, with none of the five categories there are today that let riders maximize their talent and skills. He signed up as a member of the Amateur Bicycle League of America, which was referred to as the ABL and was the sport's governing body. (The ABL in the mid-1960s had about 1,500 members, considerably smaller than the 35,000 who were in the ABL's successor, the U.S. Cycling Federation, in 1993.)

Equipment was in short supply, but through the American Youth Hostels, Howard learned he could order much of what he needed by mail from a business in Cadillac, Michigan. He ordered his wool jersey and black wool cycling shorts from a mail-order catalog. When the jersey arrived, Howard discovered it was a track jersey, which lacked the road jersey's pockets across the back for packing food to eat on long rides.

"My jersey was blue with red and white stripes," Howard said. "Mom sewed red pockets on the back."

The Olathe-Council Grove Classic was 102 miles, from Olathe in a southwest arc to Council Grove, on the bank of the Council Grove Lake. Ten riders entered. "Most of them came from St. Louis and Kansas City," Howard recalled. "One rider was 35. I remember him as being ancient."

The weather on that early June morning was sunny and pleasant as the pack of riders pedaled over gently undulating farmland with fields of wheat, herds of cattle, and grain silos. Bicycle races are characterized by cyclists pedaling closely together, as the leaders block the wind and create a protective shell of air for those behind. This cohesion keeps everyone moving at the same speed. As riders tire and falter, they trail off the back and generally don't regain contact because it is harder to ride alone than in the group. Howard kept up with the experienced riders as they worked a pace line in which the leader took a turn blocking the wind by riding at the front for about 200 yards, then dropped back to the end of the file as the next rider took his turn towing the others in his draft. At 6'2", Howard was the tallest rider in the race, which also made him a convenient windshield for others to draft behind.

"In the second half of the race, the sky clouded up and it started to rain. Then it came down in buckets," Howard said. "We kept on riding. That's bike racing."

Howard's long training rides up and down the Ozark Mountains had strengthened his legs. He was still in contention to win as they approached Council Grove. But there was no finish banner, only a small number of cars parked along the road, and scattered people standing under umbrellas in the rain to indicate where the finish was. Howard naively asked the other riders where the finish line was. Just ahead, he was told. He promptly wound up his sprint.

He was at peak speed at what he thought was the end, leading out the other nine riders. They were quick to take advantage of his draft and neatly lined up behind him like teeth on a comb. For a moment, Howard felt he had won. He eased up on the pedals and started to relax as he gasped for breath at the end of four and half hours of continuous riding. Suddenly one rider, Rich Dawson, burst past for the real finish, another 200 yards farther. Others were swarming around him in their dash for the end. Howard realized he had made a mistake and summoned all he had left. He recovered and chased hard enough to keep anyone else from overtaking him.

"I was pretty excited to finish second," Howard said, recalling his first race with renewed enthusiasm a quarter of a century and more than a thousand races later. He still has the trophy he won that day.

It was a good introduction to racing. The commute and the

race took up the whole weekend. He was exposed to the elements, including a chilling rain. At the end, he nearly blew his chances when he went too early for his finishing sprint. And his reward was a trophy which didn't come close to covering his expenses, for gas, motel, and food. But in the excitement of doing well and proving himself in his first real test in the wheel sport, none of that mattered. He was a bicycle racer.

"He went home and told his mother that he sure had found his sport," Harry Howard said. "I didn't know he was going to be so good at cycling."

Howard learned there were more races in St. Louis, 225 miles northeast of Springfield. St. Louis is steeped in cycling tradition. The St. Louis Cycling Club was organized in 1887, making it the oldest continuously active cycling club in the United States. The club's most renowned member was Carl Schutte of Kansas City, who won the bronze medal in the individual road race at the 1912 Stockholm Olympics. The event was a rugged 200-mile race that also counted in the team competition. Following Schutte in were Alvin Loftus of Providence, Rhode Island, in 11th place, and Albert Krushel of Buffalo, New York, in 13th. They scored for a bronze medal in the team classification. The two bronze medals remained the last that U.S. cyclists brought back from the Olympics.

St. Louis was also the home of the Nelsen family, which had produced three generations of Olympic cyclists. Chester Nelsen, Sr., went to the 1928 Olympics in Amsterdam, Holland, and competed in the road race. He was coach of the 1948 Olympic cycling team that included his son, Chester, Jr., who rode in the London Olympics road race. Grandson Donald was on the four-rider, 4,000-meter (2.5-mile) team pursuit on the velodrome in the 1964 Tokyo Olympics. Donald also set the national 100-mile record in July, 1965, when he won the Missouri state championship in 4 hours, 23 minutes, 45 seconds.

Other Olympic cyclists over the years from St. Louis were Walter "Peg" Martin, James Freeman, and John Boulicault. Another distinction that St. Louis held was that one-third of the 12-member American contingent going to the 1956 Melbourne Olympics was from the city: Joe Becker, George Van Meter, and Erhard Neumann rode their way onto the team, and Chester Nelsen, Sr., was the manager.

When six-day races had been in vogue in the 1930s, St. Louis was a regular stop on the winter circuit. "Sixes" were held downtown in either the city coliseum or Kiel Auditorium. The ABL held four national championships in the city between 1925 and 1962.

The St. Louis Cycling Club, whose slogan was "Headquarters in the Saddle," helped keep cycling active. "We had a limit of 100 riders in the club," said Chester Nelsen, Jr. "But we always had more than that."

Howard's second race was the 50-mile Tour of Florissant, an old French community in north St. Louis County. The two-mile circuit wended through Florissant's streets, past late eighteenth-century homes that the French fur traders who settled the city had built. The Tour was an established summer event, with drawing power in the Midwest. Howard commuted there, with his father driving the Mustang, top down, along Route 66.

"It was a big field, with 60 riders," Howard said. Riding in a pack like that means cyclists are elbow to elbow and wheel to wheel as they speed along, with little margin for error. It was his first time in such close quarters, and he found it a terrifying experience.

Keeping up with the best riders in the Midwest as they coursed through Florissant had a heady effect on Howard. "I got cocky, thinking I was going to do well," he said. Then he was forced off the side of the road by another cyclist and fell. "The crash destroyed my front wheel."

It was a hard lesson. He had commuted some 450 miles round trip with his father across the state for a race in which he fell, suffered abrasions, wrecked his front wheel, and went home empty-handed. Yet he was undeterred in his Olympic quest. "I had tasted battle and enjoyed it," he said.

As the summer ended and he prepared to enter college, Howard lined up for his third race, a local 25-mile criterium—a term referring to a short circuit of streets closed to car traffic—that Ed Morton organized around a grid of streets that embraced Parkview High School. "Three Kansas City riders came to the race and rode against John," Morton recalled. "John won."

Howard's initial racing season had consisted of a modest program of three races, hardly an Olympic-caliber schedule. But his enthusiasm ran high, and his victory in the third race, while small, gave him a boost. He felt encouraged enough to keep training for the Pan American trials coming up the next year, as a step toward the 1968 Olympic cycling trials and the Mexico City Olympics.

Life on campus with 15,000 students held many distractions for a freshman who had just turned 19, but Howard dug into his studies as a full-time student and kept up his cycling. "I wanted to keep training and stay on course to make the Olympic cycling team. I had two years to get ready. I was determined to make it."

An early influence on Howard's road to success was Ed Morton, who left his job as math teacher for a career in the retail business. In 1966, Morton opened The Bike Shop on Kimbrough Street, near the Southwest Missouri State University campus.

"Everyone in cycling in Springfield was involved in the American Youth Hostels," explained Morton, who now lives in Kent, Washington. "Everyone looked up to John because he was such a strong rider. I met him at an AYH meeting. He was quiet and unassuming. It took a few years and a few successes to make him come out of his shell."

Morton helped found the Springfield Racing Club, which had its headquarters in his bike shop. Other founding members were Morton's son, Scott, Howard, and Tim Mullikin. "We started out as a small club, with four members the first year," Morton said.

Morton, 32 when he opened The Bike Shop and formed the club, was new to cycling, but had international athletic experience as a runner. He had grown up in western Canada—in Minnedosa, Manitoba—and represented Canada at the 1954 Commonwealth Games in Vancouver, British Columbia, in the mile event—the centerpiece of the British Empire competition.

Morton didn't win a medal, but he earned a track scholarship to the University of Arkansas in Fayetteville, Arkansas, where he made the All American Cross Country Team in 1955 and 1956. In 1958, he represented Canada again at the Commonwealth Games in Cardiff, Wales, where he ran a lifetime best of 4:07 for the mile.

"At the Cardiff Commonwealth Games, I began hobnobbing with the cyclists, including Pat Murphy, who had competed in the Vancouver Commonwealth Games four years earlier. Cycling sounded like a more fun sport than running. I thought about cycling for a while, and my son was interested in the sport. In 1966 I decided to leave running for cycling. That's when I opened The Bike Shop in Springfield."

A bike shop is more than a retail business where customers buy products. It is the essence of the local cycling community. What a new customer typically sees upon entering is neat rows of new bicycles with gleaming frames and spokes that scintillate in the light. Available wall space is decorated with photos of heroes and posters advertising new products. The back, where new bicycles arrive in cardboard boxes for assembly, and where bicycles are repaired, is where the telephone and cash register are. Smells of grease, oil, and rubber mingle in an odor indigenous to bike shops. Seasoned cyclists know that the place to go for learning what is going on in the cycling community—from upcoming rides to what products are good and what are bad—is a bike shop.

When Morton opened his shop, the only cycling consumer magazine in the country was *Bicycling*, which was struggling to find its niche. His shop became the center for the Springfield Racing Club and the source for regional cycling-related news. Morton's shop was small—3,000 square feet—and had a personal feel to it. In addition to his inventory of new bicycles, chiefly for recreation cyclists, there were photos of Missouri state champions framed and mounted on the walls. Racing bicycles were in short supply, a situation he remedied by carrying the Peugeot PX10 racing bicycle from France. Peugeots were distinguished by their white frames and trademark black-and-white checkered trim on the down tube and seat tube. Leading racers in Europe were riding to victory on Peugeots.

"At that time, half of the bicycles ridden in American races were Schwinn Paramounts," Morton said. "Most of the others were Italian bicycles like Frejus, Bianchi, and Atala, and some French bikes, like Peugeot and Gitane. The Peugeot PX10 sold for $142.50, weighed 21 pounds, and was ready to race right out of the box. They were more affordable than the Schwinn Paramounts and all the others, which cost $200 each. Riders began buying the Peugeot."

Howard bought one, but preferred to keep it as a second bicycle, with his Schwinn Paramount as his primary bicycle. He rode the Peugeot when the weather was bad.

As a college freshman, Howard took classes in English composition, algebra, history, and art appreciation. "I wanted to major in art, preferring sculpture and art history." When he wasn't attending classes or studying at home, Howard was out riding miles on his bicycle. "I trained through the winter. Sometimes Tim Mullikin went out riding with me. Winters in Missouri are tough. One time we bundled up and went out riding at 10 degrees below zero—just to say we could do it."

By the next spring, Howard was fit and ready to hit the road for more races. An early season event was a 50-mile criterium in

Kansas City, where he learned there is more to training than just the number of miles covered. The course was flat, about a mile around on downtown streets, and the pack of more than 40 riders remained intact as they surged to the finish. This favored the riders who had worked the least at the front to stay fresh for the finish—a philosophy of "stick-and-kick" that often works in criterium races. The race came down to who had the most speed over the final 200 meters.

"I had no sprint speed," Howard said. "That taught me an important lesson in bike racing. Afterward, I practiced my sprinting on training rides—really worked on sprinting. I didn't have a good jump, but I did develop a fast top end."

When daylight savings time took effect and the days had longer light, Morton organized 10-mile handicap races for local riders, in which riders are given head starts in proportion to their descending abilities, with the slowest riders going first and the fastest going last, on scratch. Howard rode scratch and chased everybody—the hound in pursuit of the hares.

"We had a hilly course on the east side of Springfield that went around a loop," Morton explained. "John rode his Schwinn Paramount in races until one Tuesday evening when it was raining and he left his 'good' bike at home. He took a minute and a half off his best time. From then on, he rode his Peugeot."

That summer Howard resumed working his lifeguard job at Meador Park and went back to his routine of training in the mornings before going to work. He raced on weekends, alternating the commute to the race with Morton or his father driving. Morton had a 1967 Chevrolet Impala with a trunk so big it could fit three bicycles—the entire collection of Springfield Racing Club's bikes. Morton, who didn't race, also took his son, Scott, 12, and Mullikin, 13. Most often they went to St. Louis, a four-hour drive.

"The races were usually a weekend trip," Morton said. "We would drive up the day before the race, spend the night in a motel, get up early for the race, and afterward eat and go back to Springfield. It cost a little money, but it was a lot of fun."

Other races Howard went to were in Kansas City; Marion, Indiana; and Moline, Illinois. Prizes were most often trophies, but sometimes there was merchandise like a gallon of house paint, a bicycle chain, or a pair of wheel rims. With the local Tuesday evening time trials and weekend races, Howard was often riding in two races a week. He was gaining important experience in handling his bicycle at speed around corners, improving the way he rode in packs, and perfecting his timing in breaking away from them. He was also getting faster and stronger.

"John was becoming a mean competitor," Morton observed. "Most of the races we went to were criteriums of 35 to 50 miles. John was consistently a good finisher. He wasn't a sprinter, but he could ride hard up the hills and really put the pressure on the others. He would go out for a training ride in the mornings and have 100 miles done by noon, so he could go to work as a lifeguard at one o'clock. He was riding 500 miles a week. We used to call him 'The Ironman from Missouri'."

One of the state's important races of the season was the Missouri state cycling championship, held in St. Louis. Finishing in the top three qualified a rider for the nationals. The 100-mile state championship road race was held on a 15-mile course along Riverview Boulevard, adjacent to the Mississippi River. Most of the course was flat, with a steep quarter-mile climb about 600 feet up into the bluffs overlooking the river, then a swoop down to the flat flood plain.

Howard rode strongly, but others with more experience took advantage of his strength. He finished fourth. He was paying his dues to learn some of the wheel sport's finer points.

His riding brought him to the attention of Ray Florman, Sr., Missouri state cycling champion in 1936 and 1937. Florman characterized Howard as "a rough, tough rider. He pedaled a big gear and didn't have the bike handling finesse that a lot of St. Louis riders had, because he trained most of his miles alone. But he had a lot of brute strength. The Ozark Mountains where he trained much of the time are steep and long. Riding them made his legs strong."

As young Howard commuted to weekend races around the region, his consistently good finishes drew brief reports in the two local daily newspapers. Mickey Cohen followed them closely in the sports section to keep track of Howard's progress. Cohen was probably familiar with the glory days of American cycling, which had occurred in his youth, before he left New York for Hollywood. During those days, six-day races were held at the Madison Square Garden in December and March. New York's 14 daily newspapers published the latest race reports, and WMSG broadcast radio coverage. The sixes were a cash cow for the garden. It was sold out for the entire six days and nights, with more than 15,000 spectators filling the Garden to standing room only. The fire chief ordered a detail of firemen to form a cordon around the cavernous building to keep people from sneaking in.

"I remember Mickey Cohen as a small, meek, and mild-mannered man who used to follow my racing career," Howard said of the former West Coast mob chieftain. "He used to write me notes and letters. He kept telling me to get a fresh haircut."

The biggest competition in the northern and southern hemispheres in the year before the Olympics is the Pan American Games, our counterpart to the Commonwealth Games. The two-week 1967 Pan American games began July 23 in Winnipeg, Manitoba, Canada. Howard's earlier cycling inspiration, Jack Simes III, made the team and went on to win a silver medal on the track in the kilometer, a lung-bursting individual race against the clock over 1,000 meters, about two-thirds of a mile. Howard's chances of going to the trials ended abruptly. "I had a bad crash on a training ride in Springfield," he said. "I hit a drainage culvert and went down hard. That fall cost me a lot of skin. It took me a while to recover. I missed going to the Pan Am trials."

He recovered in time for one of the last races of the season, the George Wuchter, Jr., Memorial race, an annual 50 miler in St. Louis that was begun in 1946 as a memorial to Wuchter, who died in an accident three days after capturing the 1945 Missouri title. At the 17th annual Memorial race, the field of more than 50 riders included Dave Chauner of Philadelphia, who had competed in the Winnipeg Pan American Games. He rode in his red-white-and-blue national team jersey, which made him a marked rider, but that didn't bother him because he had speed that nobody else could touch. He showed it by winning.

Howard, in second place, left the race impressed with Chauner's speed and the need to work on his own finishing sprint. Often the final outcome of a race comes down to the final quarter-mile, especially the last 200 yards. Bicycle races are won or lost by inches, but only the winners are remembered.

That autumn, Howard returned to classes at Southwest Missouri with the odds stacked against him, but with time in his favor. He had 11 months to polish his strengths, riding up hills and hammering his pedals relentlessly, and improving his sprinting.

Returning to campus took on added importance for Howard, whose classes qualified him for a draft deferment. In June 1965, President Lyndon Johnson had sent 23,000 U.S. military advisors to Vietnam to "maintain peace." By the end of that year, more than 184,000 American troops were in South Vietnam. And only months later, American troop strength there went up to 525,000. The draft was pulling in single men between the ages of 18 and 26 who were not enrolled full-time in college or otherwise exempt.

Howard trained arduously through the winter of 1967. His spring campaign got off to a slow start as a result of preparing for exams. In a 40-mile race appropriately called the Roller Coaster Race, which Morton promoted that spring from Springfield to Silver Dollar City, Howard was third in a field of 40. After his exams were over, he got serious about preparing for the Olympic trials.

Soon came the 35-mile criterium in Moline, Illinois, across the Mississippi River from Davenport, Iowa. The race drew some of the best talent from the Midwest, including Eddie Doer of St. Louis, Olaf Moetus of Indianapolis, and Siggy Koch (pronounced Coke) of Chicago. In the final miles, Howard broke away with Doer, Moetus, and Koch. They battled it out in a showdown to see who had the fastest speed.

"That was when my sprint was coming on," Howard said. "The practice I had been putting in on my sprint was starting to pay off. I won the sprint to take the race."

It was an important victory. Doer, Moetus, and Koch were proven champions. They were at the top of their game and never gave anything away. Beating them had meaning. The measure of Olympic caliber, however, lies in an athlete's consistency, and Howard was still a long shot.

His next important race was a 50-mile event in Marion, Indiana, around an undulating course on the Veterans Administration grounds. Howard was in the field against Doer, Moetus, and Koch. It was a fast, aggressive race, and Howard uncorked another winning sprint. His time of 1 hour, 56 minutes took two minutes from the national record that Karl Napper of Indianapolis had set seven years earlier.

Howard was becoming recognized as a rising talent, but he had to qualify for the upcoming Olympic trials at the 100-mile Missouri state championship at St. Louis in July. He and Mullikin rode there with Morton driving the Impala. Howard served notice with his victory that he was going to be a contender in the Olympic trials—particularly by the manner in which he won. A shower after the start soaked the roads. Cornering at speed was hazardous as the rain water mixed with the oil residue that had been left from car traffic. Fifty miles into the race, Howard's tires slid on wet pavement. "I went right down," he said. "But I wasn't out of the race. I got back up again on my bike and kept going."

He caught the pack and attacked up the course's only climb. Only three others could respond, including Doer and another St. Louis rider, Dennis Deppe. In the last five miles, Howard bolted away for a solo victory.

His teammate and occasional training partner, Mullikin, 14, won the junior boys' 25-mile state championship. That meant the upstart Springfield Racing Club, whose bicycles could all fit in Morton's car trunk, had usurped top honors from the venerable St. Louis Cycling Club on its home turf. It was the Missouri cycling version of David slaying Goliath.

Going to the Olympic cycling trials (which included the national road racing championship) north of Los Angeles in the demanding Agoura Mountains was an honor, but Harry Howard figured an airline ticket, food, and lodging would cost his son a total of $1,200. In those days before corporate sponsorship, there was considerable in-fighting for what little was available in the ABL's budget. Riders like Howard were left to forage for themselves.

Howard handled himself well and Springfield residents repeatedly saw him out training, which earned him respect in the Show Me state. He was lean as a greyhound—6'2" and 155 pounds—with a swimmer's wide shoulders. His square jaw, blue eyes, and quiet demeanor appealed to Midwesterners.

"Ralph Foster, owner of KWTO Radio, said he would donate money to help cover John's expenses," Mary Howard explained. "He said he could spot a winner when he saw one, and started a fund raiser. The president of the Springfield Chamber of Commerce donated money. So did a bank president, members of the Kiwanis, and others. It was a community effort to get the local boy to the Olympic trials and the nationals."

Harry flew out with his son, who was taking his first flight. The Olympic trials were in mid-August, allowing plenty of time to select and groom the team bound for the Mexico City Olympics, which would be held October 12 to 27. The road trials were on Monday and Wednesday, with the top four finishers in each race earning berths on the Olympic road cycling team. The trials consisted of the 100-kilometer (62.5-mile) four-rider team time trial and the 196-kilometer (121-mile) individual road race. On Friday was the national championship, over the same course.

Near the road trials were the track trials on the Encino

Velodrome—an outdoor cement velodrome. Jack Simes III earned a spot on his third Olympic cycling team, to represent the United States in the matched sprints and the kilometer. Dave Chauner also made the Olympic cycling team in the four-rider 4,000-meter team pursuit.

At the Olympic road trials were more than 100 of the best cyclists from around the country. Because cycling was an underground sport and lacked a timely national racing publication, the Olympic trials were a welcome convening of road talent. Road racing on a national level was still quite new—the national road racing championship had begun only three years earlier.

Howard, making his debut in national-level competition and out of the Midwest for the first time, was an unknown. Other Olympic hopefuls saw him ride—pedaling big gears so that he was pedaling slower than others riding the same speed—and dismissed him as a novice. He was also marked by his Ozark twang. "Riders saw John and said, 'Look at the hillbilly from Missouri pushing those big gears,'" recalled Harry Howard.

Pre-race favorites were 1964 Olympic veterans John Allis and Oliver "Butch" Martin, both army soldiers riding for the Special Services team in California. Other favorites were defending national road champion Bob Parsons, and Dave Brink, Jim Van Boven, Mike Pickens, and Dan Butler—all from California. The prevailing wisdom held that only riders who had been preparing for the trials in California stood a chance to make the Olympic cycling team.

"I didn't know who the others were, and I had never been in a race like the Olympic trials, but I knew I was ready," Howard said.

The road races were 12 laps of a hilly course slightly more than eight miles around for a total distance of 103 miles. The races included a steep, grinding climb a mile and a quarter long in each lap, that proved to be the break point in deciding who would go to the Olympics and who would stay home. That climb also helped determine who the next national champion would be.

The first race went close to pre-race predictions. On the final lap, Parsons, who grew up riding the hills of Southern California, rose out of the saddle on the hard climb and hammered his pedals up the grade for his victory bid. Van Boven and Dave Mulke went with him, leaving the others to watch the trio escape with only two miles left. Parsons, 23, skillfully sluiced at speed through turns down the descent without applying his brakes. He had experience riding for an amateur team in Paris and had won numerous races from California to Massachusetts. He worked with

Van Boven and Mulke for a mile before surging ahead to win alone. His victory confirmed him as America's best road rider. Van Boven nipped Mulke for second. Allis, a Princeton graduate who knew how to read a race, won the pack sprint for fourth to secure a berth on his second Olympic road team.

"I was flushed out and didn't make the team [yet]," Howard said. "But I was fifth on the first day. That made me a contender. The second race was going to be do or die."

As in the first race, the second was decided on the last lap up the hard climb. Howard made an all-out effort up the hill and broke away with Mike Pickens and Dan Butler. "Pickens aced me out in the sprint, but I was second, and Butler third," Howard said. "I made the Olympic team. I was in hog heaven."

"After John made the Olympic team," his father burbled, "riders were saying, 'That hillbilly can sure push those big gears.'"

Among the eight who made the road team, the two coaches would select the four riders to compete in the road race and make up the foursome in the team time trial. That made the national championship to be held two days later important.

Howard, the only one of the eight not based in California, pulled off the surprise of the week. As in the previous two races, a three-rider breakaway escaped on the final climb: Howard, Parsons and Van Boven. They finished that way.

Howard had gone to California as the new Missouri state champion and returned home the national champion. He had overcome major odds and gone to the top of American cycling. That affirmed the faith that the people of his hometown had put in him. Hard work had led to fulfilling the lofty goal he had set. Now he was bound for the Mexico City Olympics, with teammates like Jack Simes III, Dave Chauner, and Bob Parsons.

Chapter 3

"Citius, Altius, Fortius." (Faster, Higher, Stronger.)
—Olympic Motto

Of the American cycling team members, Jack Simes III most embodied the sport's spirit. He was a third-generation racer who had won three open-division national championships and was on his third Olympic cycling team. For much of the century, a Jack Simes was either competing or training a son to race.

Simes's grandfather turned professional in 1904 after winning a 100-mile race in Boston. The Olympics, its revival then in infancy, was of minor importance compared to professional cycling events. (The International Olympic Committee doesn't even recognize medals awarded at the 1904 St. Louis Olympics because few foreign athletes competed.)

Simes's father grew up on cycling. "One of my earliest memories was playing on the boards of the New York Velodrome when I was five years old, in 1919," said Simes II. "When I was in high school, my parents had moved to Harrington Park, New Jersey, and I used to go with my father to watch the six-days in Madison Square Garden. After the 10 two-mile midnight sprints ended, we would drive back home in time to hear the radio broadcast of the 2:30 a.m. sprints."

This second-generation Simes cyclist began competing at age 15. By the time he graduated from high school in 1933, his winnings included an Indian Chief Motorcycle (won in a two-thirds of a mile race on the New York Velodrome) and a red Chevrolet convertible. The car he won in a 1933 revival of the Irvington-Millburn Classic, a 25-mile race in northern New Jersey that dated back to 1889. For 20 years, until trolley tracks in the roads forced its discontinuance, the winner of the race called "Bicycle Derby of America" was awarded a brace of horses and a mahogany carriage. When the event was revived in 1933, the traditional prize was updated to a new Chevrolet—a rich reward for an amateur race during the hard times of the Depression.

In 1936 Simes won the national ABL championship in St. Louis and soon turned professional. Understandably, from an early age his son, Jack Simes III, was inculcated with cycling legends, race tactics, and speed work. That contributed to his winning the junior national championship in 1959 at age 16 in Kenosha, Wisconsin, where he dominated the four events—from the half-mile to five miles. He developed a snappy acceleration that was as effective as a fastball no batter can hit. In 1960, at 17, he followed in his father's wheelmarks by winning the national championship in Flushing Meadows, New York. He was on his way to becoming the first Simes to compete in the Olympics, which were to be held that year in Rome.

Simes returned from the Rome Olympics to dominate American cycling for that decade, which aficionados have come to call "the Simes years." Talented and versatile, he remains unique for setting national records both at 200 meters, the province of pure sprinters, and 50 miles, a distance that road racers consider their turf.

Sports Illustrated introduced the Simes family to the American public in an issue before the 1964 Tokyo Olympics, in a four-page feature that Bob Ottum wrote. The three Jack Simes were shown on the porch of the New Jersey home where they all lived. That may have influenced "ABC's Wide World of Sports" to include Simes in its limited television coverage of the Tokyo Olympics.

"I was glued to the TV coverage in 1964," Howard said. "All that was shown of cycling was a match race that Jack was in on the velodrome—took less than a minute. But watching him on TV crystallized my desire to be in the next Olympics."

Four years and more than 25,000 miles (enough to ride around the globe) later, Howard made the team with Simes. Simes trained for the Olympics while in the army, riding for the Special Services team at Fort MacArthur in San Pedro, California.

ABL officials, led by Al Toefield of New York City, were overhauling their approach to Olympic cycling in a sometimes frantic effort to make better use of American riding talent against the Europeans, who ruled the sport on the tracks and roads. The United States was an undisputed military and industrial superpower, but when it came to cycling it was on a level with third-world countries. One of the new ABL approaches involved expanding the number of rider berths on the Olympic team, from 10 in 1956 to 18 in 1968, to take advantage of a more efficient division of labor in the events. Support staff was boosted from two (a coach and a manager) to five (a manager, a road coach, a track coach, and two mechanics).

After the August Olympic trials, team members scattered to their home bases until mid-September, when the Olympic cyclists reconvened in Los Angeles three weeks before the opening ceremonies in Mexico City.

In Los Angeles, the Olympic cyclists and support staff were together for the first time for inoculations, photos, and their team issue clothing. (Women's cycling wasn't introduced until the 1984 Los Angeles Olympics.)

What was it like for Howard to meet Olympic teammate Simes? "It was a great feeling, " Howard said, "one of fulfilling a long-held inspiration."

This feeling of fulfillment was short-lived as they traveled by plane to Mexico City, which lies at 7,373 feet above sea level. ABL officials sent the Olympic cyclists three weeks early to Mexico City to get adjusted to the thin air. The decision had disastrous effects.

"We went out riding for six to eight hours a day, going out into the mountains, putting in miles and exploring," said Howard. "Mexico City had thick industrial pollution, but once we were out of the city, the area was gorgeous."

When they train, today's national team members are routinely accompanied by a coach, who drives the team car containing bottled water and snack food. But Howard and his teammates were on their own under the hot tropical sun.

"When we had drunk the water from the bottles we had carried from the training village, we bought vending-machine soft drinks," explained Butch Martin. One by one, Martin, Howard, and the other riders were stricken with what travelers have come to know as "Montezuma's revenge." They made regular visits to the Olympic Village dispensary for medication. European cycling teams also arrived early to adjust to the rarefied air, but took care to bring their own bottled water.

Howard and his teammates entered some of the frequent pre-Olympic road races, where they encountered more intense racing than Howard had ever experienced. "I was still such a neophyte that I didn't know what was going on in the races," Howard admitted. "Being with the Europeans was so intimidating, but we learned a lot. One thing I learned was how to jump a curb without slowing down."

Another lesson was in racing downhill. Howard's riding in the Ozark Mountains had helped him develop strength for climbs, but his technique for going down hills at speeds faster than 50 MPH was another matter. "I remember riding with one of the Italians up a long hill during a race. Our road coach, Bob Hansing, was riding in a car next to us and he kept telling me to stay with the Italian, to hang in there, to keep going. It was really hard, but I stayed with him—all the way. But on the descent, the Italian dropped me like a stone. He went downhill and through turns so fast I couldn't handle his speed. It was trial by fire in my first international racing."

On training rides he and other cyclists saw people living in widespread poverty. Children ran around dirty and naked and begged for food. The vast sums the Mexican government had spent on building facilities for the Olympics prompted some 300,000 Mexican university students around the country to protest. The students felt that a country with so much poverty was misguided in spending money on the Olympic Games. With the Olympics drawing international media attention, the students decided to use the Olympic Games as the forum for their protests. On the night of October 2, 10 days before the Olympic Games were to open, a crowd of 10,000 students held a demonstration in the Square of the Three Cultures in Mexico City.

"Mexican police flew over in helicopters, dropped flares, and fired heavy machine guns down on the students," recalled Butch Martin. "We saw the flares and heard the shooting form the Olympic Village, about two miles away."

The deaths that resulted were largely overlooked in the U.S. press, but John Rodda, an English journalist covering the Olympics for the *Guardian*, reported that more than 260 were killed and 1,200 injured from the shooting.

Howard said that the next day he went with Bob Parsons into Mexico City where vendors hawked *El Sol* newspapers that published dramatic photos and graphic accounts of the slayings. "The vendors spotted our blazers and refused to sell us copies of the newspaper," Howard said. But we passed newsstands and saw color photos of dozens of bodies of the students."

Security was bolstered and there was no further civil unrest. Ray Florman, who drove from St. Louis to take a pair of wheels to Howard and watch the Games, recalled that Mexican soldiers were stationed every 50 feet for miles along the roads the riders trained.

The XIX Olympiad opened October 12 as scheduled in a remarkably clean Mexico City that tourists and locals rarely ever see. "The factories were shut down for the Olympics, and the air was clean," Howard said. "We could finally breathe comfortably."

Eighty thousand spectators filled Olympic Stadium to watch 6,082 athletes from 109 countries march in the opening ceremony. The United States had the largest contingent of athletes—387 (292 men and 95 women).

By the end of the Games, U.S. athletes would also have the largest accumulation of medals. None of those, however, were won buy U.S. cyclists. Simes had the best performance, in the kilometer time trial on the velodrome. He rode 1 minute, 5.67 seconds, which was 12th in close competition—less than three seconds behind gold medalist Pierre Trentin of France, whose time was 1:03.91 seconds. Simes's effort was significant; his time became the new U.S. national kilometer record.

Just before the start of the 122-mile road race, Bob Parsons pulled out of the Games. Later he cited the tremendous political unrest. "I saw violent suppression of those demonstrations, brutal murders by the government that were covered up. You never heard about any of it, but we were there and we saw it."

Howard was appalled at the suppression he witnessed, but he was focused on competing in the Olympics. Parson's withdrawal and Howard's decision to ride marked a clear succession from one generation of leading American road cyclists to the next. Yet Howard found that competing on an international level was fraught with difficulties.

"I had such a terrible case of diarrhea that I had to go to the dispensary. I remember being there with Mark Spitz, the swimmer, both of us so sick we had yellow complexions. I asked him what he was there for. 'Same thing you are,' he told me."

Howard recovered enough to ride in the road race, where he was impressed by a higher standard of performance than he had ever seen. "I had never ridden that fast before. The Italian, Dutch, French, Belgian, and Swedish riders were really tough. During the pre-Olympics races I was continuously getting adjusted to the faster pace, but I still had a long way to go on the day of the Olympic road race. It was so hard, and so tactically sophisticated—far superior to what we experienced in the United States."

He rode in the peloton, fit enough to go the distance as filler, but still too raw to be absent from the front where the seasoned warriors battled. Records show he finished 44th, in 4 hours, 32 minutes, 87 seconds. Teammate Dan Butler's place was too far back to be recorded.

The four-rider 100-kilometer team time trial held better prospects for the Americans because it is a race against the clock and tactics have considerably less influence than in the road race. In the team time trial, each team sets off at two-minute intervals. Cyclists ride a close, wheel-to-wheel pace line, with the leader taking a hard pull for about 200 yards before peeling off to the back to draft and recover as the other riders alternate their turn at the front. Team time trials resemble rowing on a crew team— everyone is working in unison and the team is only as strong its weakest member. Each team is allowed to sacrifice one rider, who has the option of pulling longer and harder than the others to keep the speed as high as possible. The third rider across the line determines the team's finish time.

Howard's powerful riding secured him a spot on the team time trial. He was joined by Van Boven and Olympic veterans Martin and John Allis. Any hopes for an impressive ride, however, were shattered in a bizarre incident only minutes before the team was to start their ride. They were standing together, making final checks of their tire pressure and equipment, when a Mexican man committed suicide with a pistol within five feet of the team. Howard and Martin were splattered with blood.

"About 20 soldiers rushed over to the body, which was lying in a pool of blood," Martin said. "An officer took charge and put sheets of newspaper over the body. The soldiers kept the crowd away. I had to get a towel to wipe the blood and brains off my arms and bike. Later, we learned that the guy had committed suicide because he couldn't find a job to support his wife and kids."

Howard said, "Had the gory suicide not occurred, the U.S. press would not have reported the race at all. In fact, the coverage omitted the results, and no other cycling events were even mentioned."

The violent suicide so near the young cyclists ended their innocence and idealism. But they still responded when called to the starting line. The team finished 20th, 17 minutes behind the victorious Dutch squad.

Martin subsequently looked back upon the Mexico City Olympic experience and saw the team as the beginning of a breakthrough in American cycling. "The guys felt they could do something when we went to the Mexico City Olympics," Martin said. "That was a feeling that was lacking on the 1964 team and before. We were coming on as a cycling team."

By the time the Mexico City Olympics concluded on October

27, Howard had missed the autumn semester and risked losing his draft deferment. Vast numbers of college students on campuses across the country were staging protests against the Vietnam war. They were also sporting long hair, wearing tie-dyed T-shirts, and bell-bottom jeans. They listened to the acid-rock guitar of Jimi Hendrix and the mournful blues that Janis Joplin sang.

"I knew all that was happening, but it was a distraction for me," Howard said. "My sister was active in protesting the Vietnam war, but I wasn't. My brother had been second alternate to West Point. For a while, I had been in ROTC [Reserve Officer Training Corps] on campus, but I blew it off. I was training and racing—that was my focus. I had been dedicated to cycling, which got me to the Olympics. Then, suddenly, I was exposed to international competition, where I saw just how fast the riders from Europe really were. That inspired me to be totally dedicated to bike racing, to get better."

When Howard returned home, one of the last cycling competitions in Missouri was the national cyclo-cross championship—a rigorous hybrid of cycling over muddy fields and running with the bicycle over obstacles like logs and tall fences. The national cyclo-cross that year was on a farm outside of St. Louis. Howard managed a respectable second to Leroy "Tyger" Johnson of Madison, Wisconsin, who specialized in cyclo-cross.

Soon came the news that Jack Simes had traveled to the world championships in Montevideo, Uruguay, where he won a silver medal in the kilometer and finally cracked the European domination of world championships. His medal was the first since 1949, when Jack Heid, whom Simes II had coached, won a bronze medal at the world championships in Copenhagen. Heid—a gutsy New Yorker who, as a child had caught cycle fever watching the six-day racers train in Center Park in the 1920s and 1930s—competed in the 1948 London Olympics and stayed in Europe to ride with the best. A pioneer American cyclist in post-war Europe, he remained there until 1951. He then settled in New Jersey, and became a mentor for young Simes.

Howard re-enrolled in classes at Southwest Missouri State University to keep his draft deferment for the winter semester of 1969 and continue taking art classes. Like other students, he spent his March spring break in Florida—but his way, which meant bike racing. He drove the Speedy Banana from Springfield to St. Louis, where he left his car at Ray Florman's home to ride in Florman's van 1,000 miles to West Palm Beach, Florida.

Their destination was the start of the fourth annual Cross-Florida tour, a weekend stage race. It went 120 miles east across the state from West Palm Beach to Fort Meyers on Saturday, then back on Sunday. Motorcycle sheriffs escorted riders from county line to county line. When riders broke away from the front, or fell behind and trailed, a motorcycle with flashing red lights announced their approach.

"It was the big event of the year, and special for being so early in the season," Howard explained. "The Canadian national team members came down to compete there, along with many of the best riders from around the United States, and some of the best South American cyclists. They were always fond of Miami. "

Next up was the Tour of Louisiana, two days of racing a variety of distances. Between the two events and the intervening week of training, riders got in valuable miles with other riders, which contributed to their base fitness, which traditionally requires at least 2,000 miles. More importantly, they were racing into shape. Most of the rest of the country wouldn't have races until late April.

Florman was becoming important in Howard's development.

Florman, then 52, had grown up in St. Louis and had been in cycling since he was 15. "My first race was in 1932. I won a turkey that weighed 26 pounds." Born without a right hand, Florman never let its absence slow him down. "I rode the Olympic trials and was very close to making the team in 1936 and again in 1948. In 1948, at the trials in Milwaukee, I was the only one who finished both 138-mile road races."

When the six-days went to St. Louis and Kansas City in the 1930s, Florman hustled and found work as a runner. He pumped tires, fixed equipment, and ran errands for riders in the two-man teams. "The pros were making $200 to $300 a night racing the six-days, a lot of money back then," he said. "I saw a lot of the really good riders: Jimmy Walthour, Fred Spencer, Jules Audy, Torchy Peden and others. The German team of Gustav Killian and Heinz Vopel competed in the sixes wearing a swastika on their jersey. Killian and Vopel won so many six-days that promoters split them up and put them on different teams to make the racing more competitive. Killian was the national team coach of the West German riders at the Mexico City Olympics."

Florman was a metallurgist who worked for a steel foundry in St. Louis to support his wife and three children. He saved money to open his own bicycle shop—A-1 Bicycle Sales—in 1953. Business flourished. (Today A-1 Bicycle Sales, Inc., has 12,000 square feet of floor space and is managed by son Raymond.) Florman prevailed upon Pat Murphy at the Schwinn Bicycle Company to provide Howard with a new Schwinn Paramount. "Schwinn gave good bikes to good bike riders," Florman said.

Jimmy Walthour liked what he heard about Howard and gave the younger rider his black leather hairnet helmet. Howard wore it until 1985, when the ABL's successor, the U.S. Cycling Federation, began to require racers to wear hard-shell helmets.

After classes were over for the semester, Howard devoted himself full-time to his sport. He developed a routine of commuting to Florman's home late in the week to set out in the van for weekend races around the Midwest—to Chicago, Indianapolis, Milwaukee, Dayton, Detroit, and other cities where bike clubs put on races. He and Ray learned the names of all the highways, and what restaurants served the biggest portions. They also learned the landscape of every city.

"Detroit is flat, flat, flat," Florman observed. "North Chicago's lakefront had a nice course that was flat by the lake and then had a hill that went right up in the air."

The bread and butter of American bicycle racing, particularly in the Midwest, was criteriums. In a criterium, the circuit is small enough that spectators can walk around and watch from different venues as riders lean at speed through the turns. Hay bales are usually set in front of parking meters, street signs, and fire hydrants to protect riders from careening into them. Spectators watch for free as the pack whips past for another lap.

"Howard was a very aggressive rider," recalls Donald Nelsen. "I remember at the Olympic trials, I was riding 25 miles on the rest days between the road races, and Howard was riding 50. The following year, he was awesome. He had such power. He would go from the gun. Sometimes some of us could stay on his rear wheel and eventually wear him down. Otherwise, he would go out and lap everybody in the criteriums."

"Racing then had few attacks," pointed out Eddie Van Guyse, who lived in Chicago when he raced and now lives in Long Beach, California. "The first race I saw Howard in was in 1968 in Marion, Indiana. He broke away early and that was the last we saw of him. That got everybody's attention. He made a name for himself rapidly. Then, at the national championships after the Olympic trials, he was out of the saddle hammering a big gear in the final sprint against Bob Parsons to win the title. We were especially proud of Howard in the Midwest because most of our races were criteriums. The West Coast boys had road races. Howard beat one of their boys on their home turf.

"He and one other rider were key individuals who raised the level of racing in the Midwest. The other was Siggy Koch, who came from West Germany and settled in Chicago. Physically, they were a study in contrasts. Siggy is 5'4" and Howard is a head taller. Both of them pushed big gears and forced the pace. With these two guys, it was either go fast or get dropped."

Koch had a Continental mystique. He had immigrated to the United States about the time Howard came into the sport, and started winning everything he rode. His deep-set eyes and chiseled cheekbones gave him a preoccupied look. He walked with a limp, the result of a collision he had had on his bicycle with a truck. Compound leg fractures had caused a difference in leg lengths, which he overcame with different-sized crank arms. He was rumored to have ridden professionally in Europe. Koch was the former West German national champion in the cyclo-cross.

"Siggy was my main competition," Howard said. "When I got into the sport, he was a model rider. He was also the first European I rode with."

The late 1960s were a time when American racing was strictly amateur. Most top riders worked daytime jobs, trained evenings, and raced weekends, ordinarily in their region. Full-time jobs were a requisite because prizes were mostly trophies, with merchandise that often consisted of bicycle components, with occasionally a new bicycle or a television for a major event. "At the Tour of Kettering, a 50-mile race in Kettering, Ohio, Siggy Koch won first prize, which was a color television set," Howard said. "I was second, and my prize was a spray can of Dog Halt."

At the Missouri state road racing championship, Howard successfully defended his championship. But he was a marked rider at the nationals in Detroit. His head-down, hammering style worked against him as rivals followed every move and took shelter in his draft. "I did too much work at the front," Howard admitted. "I finished 10th."

That excluded him from the small number of riders whose expenses to the world championships in Brno, Czechoslovakia, late that summer would be covered by the ABL. Bicycle racing had doubled its numbers. The ABL now had 3,000 members, but its annual budget was still only about $20,000. Florman felt it was so important that Howard compete in the world championships that he spent $1,000 of his own money to buy Howard the round-trip air fare and cover some expenses.

"I thought John should be representing the USA," Florman explained. "My wife didn't know about that ticket."

The world cycling championships were held over two weeks that included August 20, the first anniversary of the lightning Russian invasion of Czechoslovakia. Russian troops had remained in Czechoslovakia, and their presence precipitated open protests, sometimes violent. The atmosphere was tense. "I had a tough time at the airport in Prague," Howard said. "Russian guards armed with AK-47 assault rifles met me when I got off my flight, and wouldn't let me leave. I told them I was there to travel to Brno for the world cycling championships. My passport, visa, ABL license, and other papers were all in order. The guards had me wait for what seemed like forever in a cubicle, all alone. Finally, I told them, 'Hey! I'm here to travel to Brno and race in the worlds! Czechoslovakia is the host country!' They let me go."

In Brno, he saw a city under military occupation, with Russian tanks parked prominently everywhere and armed soldiers on patrol in the streets. Road pavement had been torn up by steel tank treads. "I saw people throw Molotov cocktails out of the windows at the tanks below," he said.

Howard met with the rest of the U.S. contingent, including Simes and Audrey McElmury of La Jolla, California. McElmury was the women's national sprint champion. She regularly raced against the men in open competition and consistently finished in the top 10. In July on the Encino, California, outdoor velodrome, she had set 16 national records, from two miles to 25 miles—all in one ride. She was a commando athlete who worked full-time as a medical lab technician in genetics at the University of California in San Diego to pay for her equipment and travel expenses. Since 1965 she had competed in the worlds in San Sebastian, Spain; Frankfurt, West Germany; and Imola, Italy, where she finished a remarkable fifth in the women's 1968 road race. In Brno, she was regarded as a serious contender for the women's world championship road race.

"The day before the world championship road race for women and amateur men, Audrey, Jack, John Vande Velde, and a couple of other riders and I went out to a vineyard where we drank wine all afternoon like other American tourists," Howard said.

They returned late in the evening to the 20-story hotel where they were housed. At midnight on this, the anniversary of the Russian invasion, rioting broke out in downtown Brno. A squadron of tanks revved up their diesel engines near the hotel. "It sounded like a train coming into the room," McElmury said. "We all ran out to the balcony and were confronted by the almost unbelievable sight of tanks rumbling down the street."

Rumors flew that the road races would be canceled. They were held anyway, but tanks were parked among the trees bordering the 8.7-mile course. It was a rolling circuit designed for grand-prix car racing, and featured a 2.5-mile hill in the middle. The next morning, McElmury lined up for the five-lap race with three teammates in the field of 43. They represented 16 countries, and included a strong Soviet team.

McElmury won the women's road race by 70 seconds, ahead of Bernadette Swinnerton of England and Nina Trofimova of the Soviet Union. McElmury became the first American—man or woman—to win the world road racing championship. (Greg LeMond was next when he won the world junior road race in 1978 and the world professional road race in 1983.) So many years had passed since a U.S. cyclist had won a world championship that race officials didn't have a record of the "Star Spangled Banner" on hand, and there was no band to strike up the music. McElmury, Swinnerton, and Trofimova were left standing on the awards podium outside in the rain for more than half an hour while officials scurried around Brno to find a recording of the American national anthem for the awards ceremony.

Finally a record was found and whisked to the ceremony. When the phonograph needle found the appropriate groove, a new era in American bicycle racing was heralded. McElmury's performance was the highlight of the U.S. cyclists' efforts at the worlds, but Howard made a good showing and gained valuable experience in the 113-mile road race.

"I felt good and was leading the charge up the hill on some of the laps," he said. "I rode too hard at the front, though, and got dropped by the leaders. On the last few laps, I was struggling up the hill. But the Czechs were so supportive of the United States and there were so many spectators lining the course that people took turns pushing me up the hill. They really tried to help me. Ordinarily, pushes like that would have caused me to be disqualified, but there was a special atmosphere that day in Brno. I was the only U.S. finisher. I finished in the top 40."

After the world championships, Howard went with teammate

Sam Zeitland to Amsterdam, Holland, to race there for a couple of weeks. On one of his first rides in Amsterdam, Howard struck a trolley track the wrong way and fell. "I injured a knee and couldn't ride the bike, so I relaxed and enjoyed myself as a tourist."

His knee had healed by the time he returned to Springfield. In mid-October, he traveled with Florman to Chicago for the national cyclo-cross championship in Palos Park. "I rode cyclo-cross races in the fall because I wanted to be as versatile as possible and master all aspects of cycling. Cyclo-cross riding is a good way to sharpen reflexes. You're sliding in mud, jumping off your bike to run over hurdles, then getting back on and riding. It stresses bike balance and handling."

Chicago was cold and wet when he lined up for the start against 30 other mudders. "I went out as fast as I could go. Really found my rhythm early. I was on that day."

He won the national cyclo-cross championship, ahead of Herman Kron of Chicago and defending national champion Tyger Johnson. In addition to adding another gold medal and national champion's stars and stripes jersey to his growing collection, he was asserting himself as a leader in American cycling.

As the decade closed, 1969 marked a profound turning point for America. Apollo II astronauts, Neil Armstrong and Edwin Aldrin, Jr., walked on the moon and returned home to become national heroes. The New York Mets, which, for the seven years they had been around, had provided comic relief in the National League, rose from the cellar that season to win the National League pennant. *Life* magazine devoted its June 27 issue to publishing in yearbook fashion, portrait photos and names of the 242 U.S. servicemen whom the Pentagon listed as killed in action in Vietnam for the week of May 28 to June 3.

Howard's life changed when he re-enrolled on campus for the winter semester of 1970 and met Kim Kynion, a freshman, in an art-history class.

"He was completely different from anyone I had ever met in college," Kim said. "I think that was what attracted me to him. I knew he had been in the Olympics and rode a bike and had a Jaguar. All that was quite an oddity. That was back when you cruised downtown in your Ford or Chevy and went to the Steak-n-Shake for excitement. But never in my wildest dreams when I met John Howard did I ever think we would get married."

Friends describe the couple as polar opposites. Kim is vivacious, extroverted, and has always made friends easily. John is shy and introverted.

"There's a John Howard that a lot of people don't know exists," she said. "[In college] he enjoyed a good laugh. His head went back, his mouth opened, and he roared with laughter. He had a beautiful mane of kinky blond hair and crystal blue eyes. He wasn't Joe Cool or Joe Campus. He was himself. He wanted to teach art and be an artist."

On a bicycle, Howard was shaping a change in American racing. Shaping the sport requires being stronger than everyone else in it so they follow the lead, and Howard worked hard at improving his fitness. He started the 1970 season by traveling with Florman to West Palm Beach for the Cross Florida Tour, then to the Tour of Louisiana. He returned to campus for another three months with a tan that few others could match.

For Kim, dating Howard meant going to bicycle races when classes were over. Kim discovered that cycling was an open secret in America. "The first big race he took me to was the Old Towne Criterium in Chicago. I thought there would be 10 or 12 racers, but there were 70 or more. Thousands of people lining the course knew him and called his name. That was when I realized what he was doing. He was pretty big. And he won the race."

Traveling with Howard raised eyebrows. "When I was introduced onto the bike scene, people who knew him were surprised that John Howard had a woman in his life. Cycling had been an obsession with him, and suddenly here I was."

"Until then, I didn't have much time in my life for girlfriends," Howard said. "I was focused on my cycling. But Kim was vivacious, outgoing, energetic. I found her very attractive."

Howard continued to make the Midwest racing circuit, dominating races even more than before. He was regularly winning 15 to 20 races a year. Races that he didn't win, he influenced with his aggressive style, which helped up the speed.

But his extensive travel schedule had cost him his draft deferment. He faced the prospect of being drafted into the army.

Al Toefield, president of the ABL, had been working with Pentagon officials to develop the long-standing Special Services program for athletes into the country's first national cycling team. The Armed Forces had a scattered Special Services program that gave athletes limited freedom to train on bases where they were stationed nationwide. Such training freedom varied widely, depending on the commanding officer of each base. Toefield built on this. He persuaded Pentagon officials to organize an official U.S. Army Cycling Team, arguing that there would be a public relations benefit needed during an increasingly unpopular war. He encouraged top riders to enlist, with the army issuing them orders to the same army base so they would be together.

Toefield had raced with minor success in the 1930s in road and velodrome events on the Eastern Seaboard. After World War II, he remained in cycling as part of a small corps of dedicated volunteers who organized races and kept the sport going through its lean years. He had a commanding presence, developed as a beat cop in the New York City Police Department, which he had joined in 1945. On the street, he was Sergeant Toefield, whose dark eyes rarely missed anything. His gravelly voice could soothe frayed nerves or bark commands with authority. On his own time, he was devoted to the ABL and co-owner of the Kisenna Bike Shop in Queens, New York, where hard-to-find racing supplies were available. When the 400-meter Kisenna track nearby needed resurfacing, Toefield paid out of his own pocket—a gesture consistent with the dedication he brought to cycling as he helped pave the way for many riders on the local and national levels.

In the mid-1960s, the Army Cycling Team had started with talented riders like Jack Simes, Butch Martin, John Allis, and others who had been stationed on bases as far away as West Germany. Toefield had them transferred to Fort MacArthur in San Pedro, California. Toefield became president of the ABL in 1967. That year, he managed the cycling team that went to the Pan American Games, where Jack Simes won a silver medal. Toefield also managed the cycling team that went to the Mexico City Olympics.

"The team didn't do that well, but he really felt for us," Simes said. "You always knew that Toefield was in your corner."

Toefield had better luck managing the ABL team in Brno, where McElmury won the women's world championship. "When I got back home, I was invited to be a guest on a couple of television shows in New York," she said. "Al drove me around and parked his car right in front of the network buildings. He was with the police department, and nobody messed with Al."

Right after his final exams in the spring of 1970, Howard's draft board reclassified him 1-A, eligible and ready for the draft. He prevailed upon Toefield to help him continue cycling. "Al told me that if I enlisted in the army, I would go through basic training. Afterward, I would get orders for Special Services to ride for the Army Cycling Team. He was going to get Dave Chauner and other top riders into the army to ride for the team."

Howard, preparing to enter the army at the end of the year, got in as much racing as he could. He won his third consecutive Missouri state road championship. In a break from the past, the national championships—in New York City that year—were held after the world championships in Leicester, England. Because McElmury had won her race the previous year at the worlds, Howard had finished respectably in his, and Simes had earned the silver medal in 1968, the ABL received enough funding from the U.S. Olympic committee to buy them tickets for the flight to England. The ABL was even flush enough to send a men's team in the 100-kilometer four-rider team time trial, an event that Toefield and other officials were expecting to generate a medal-winning performance.

The American squad, however, finished way down in the 100-kilometer time trial, and the 113-mile road race didn't offer much consolation. "The pace was fast and I never really settled into it," Howard admitted. "I had a new Schwinn Paramount, and after the first third of the race I developed derailleur problems." He dropped out of the race.

Back in the United States, the national championship road race around the 5.1-mile course in New York City's Central Park wasn't much better for Howard. "Early in the race, I smashed into a horse cart parked beside the road. The impact twisted my front fork. My bike was unrideable. Another rider lent me his bike, but it was a couple of inches too small. I got on it and chased the field. Catching the field really took a lot out of me. Then Ray Florman came through and repaired my frame right there in the park, so I stopped on the next lap and switched bikes. I had to chase the field again. By then I was shattered. Mike Carnahan had gone off the front in a break. I still managed to finish 10th."

Carnahan, looking woolly with his hairy legs and like a renegade in his trademark black socks, stole the national road-racing championship.

When Howard wasn't out training, traveling to a race, or competing, he occasionally went to a movie with Kim. One was *Joe*, which featured Peter Boyle and Susan Sarandon. Boyle played a construction worker who meets a businessman (actor Dennis Patrick) who has just killed his daughter's drug-addicted lover. The two men become buddies in their hatred of hippies. *Joe* was highly successful as a backlash against the permissiveness that came to represent the 1960s.

"John was crying during the movie," Kim said. "I thought it was wonderful that a man would cry."

Early that December, Howard boarded the bus that would take him to Fort Leonard Wood in the black hills of central Missouri for nine weeks of army basic training. Kim stood outside in the cold with his parents to see him off and wave good luck.

"After basics, I was sent to Fort Polk, in southern Louisiana, for Advanced Infantry Training, and I was starting to get nervous," Howard said. "The army was preparing to send me to Vietnam. I kept calling Al Toefield. He kept telling me that my orders would come through for Special Services. But I was in training for the infantry during all this. I was a private first class training to shoot or be shot. I felt like an idiot for not specializing in something, like becoming a radio operator."

In one of the more unusual developments in the army, his battalion commanding officer, a colonel, announced to the 1,500 soldiers standing out in formation on a hot, humid morning, that the army had a new open-door policy—any soldier who wanted to talk to his commanding officer needed only to step up and speak, completely bypassing the established, complicated chain of command.

"As soon as we were dismissed, I went right up to our colonel. I told him that I was national cycling champion, had competed in the Olympics and two world championships, and that I could better serve the army and the United States if I could train for the Pan American Games later that year and the Olympics in 1972."

His colonel, a graduate of Indiana University in Bloomington, Indiana, was extraordinarily understanding. The Little 500 bicycle race, a spirited four-rider relay team the fraternities put on for 200 laps around a quarter-mile cinder running track, is an annual spring rite at Indiana University. The colonel told Howard he had participated in the Little 500 in all four years he had been at Indiana University.

"My colonel told me to fly back home and drive back with my bike. He said there were good roads to train on, off-base. He gave me a four-day pass. I began wondering if someone was watching out for me."

Howard promptly went back to Springfield, where he bought a new burnt-orange Volkswagen Superbeetle. "I had sold the

Speedy Banana before I left for the army. Didn't get much for it. Back then, the market for Jaguars wasn't much."

He visited Kim and his parents before driving back to Fort Polk. He took back to the base with him the Schwinn Paramount that he had gotten through Pat Murphy, and stored it in the room that the quarter-master locked the weapons in. Howard was required only to stand in for morning formation. After that, he could devote the rest of the day to training 60 and more miles. One morning, Dave Chauner was riding in a troop truck when he saw Howard, wearing the national team jersey, pedal over the brow of a hill. Spotting his Olympic teammate was encouraging because he, too, had been calling Al Toefield to ask when his orders would come through for Special Services.

"In March the orders came in for me to report to Special Services at Fort Wadsworth on Staten Island, New York, where the Army Cycling Team had relocated. Chauner got his orders on the same day." At Fort Wadsworth, Howard joined the other 12 members of the Army Cycling Team, including Chauner, Mike Hiltner, Gary Campbell, and Steve Woznick. The army provided its cycling team with vans, gasoline, room, and board. Their main duty was to ride for the Army Cycling Team, which beat going to Vietnam or picking up cigarette butts from the grass.

"Our commanding officer was a big black man who told us that we had it pretty easy, but we had better win and keep winning, or we would be in Vietnam shouldering a rifle," Howard said. "Fear was a motivator. My parents wrote about a high-school friend of mine who had gone to Vietnam, but didn't come back."

In an era of amateur cyclists who worked jobs and rode when they could, the Army Cycling Team members were the first organized national team—where members lived together, trained together, and went to races together. Led by Howard and Chauner, they regularly stacked the top finishes in every race they entered on the Eastern Seaboard as they prepared for the Pan American trials in June.

For U.S. athletes, the Pan American Games were an important trial run in the year before the Olympics. For U.S. cyclists, the Games were especially important, because they didn't have the opportunity to travel to Europe or compete outside the United States. Few American cyclists ventured across the Atlantic. Simes had devoted several summers to competing in Denmark, France, Belgium, and Italy, and Butch Martin had spent two seasons competing in Italy. But they were exceptions, and both Simes and Martin went as individuals and had to forage on their own.

The VI Pan American Games were to assemble 30 nations from North and South America. That gave important international exposure to the cyclists the ABL was grooming for the upcoming Munich Olympics. A total of 595 medals—194 gold—were up for grabs.

ABL officials were expecting that improved depth among U.S. cyclists would lead to a gold medal in the four-rider 100-kilometer team time trial. The cycling trials to determine who would represent the United States at the Games in Cali, Colombia, were organized in Detroit that June. The trials had an expanded format, opening with a 17-mile individual time trial on a course around Belle Island, a flat spit of land in the Detroit Strait separating the city from Windsor, Ontario.

Howard was the pre-race favorite. Many of his criterium races had turned into time trials as he broke away from the starter's pistol and kept going alone until he lapped the peloton, sometimes even breaking away a second time to gain another lap. Moreover, as a member of the Army Cycling Team, he was expected to make the team or risk going back to the infantry.

But surprises and enterprising individuals keep sports dynamic. Mike Neel of Berkeley, California, arrived in Detroit as a virtual unknown, which freed him of pressure. Neel, nearly as tall as Howard and just as lean, had been in the sport only two years. He was discovered by Pete Rich, who closed his shop—Berkeley VeloSport—for the day when Neel tapped on the door to see about getting the bicycle he used for transportation repaired. Rich, a veteran of more than a decade of racing, had unlocked the door and opened a new friendship. Rich had competed in Italy with a coterie of other northern California riders in the early 1960s, and was a good judge of talent. Under Rich's tutelage, Neel went to Detroit ready to make the team.

"Pete had built me super light wheels—the lightest rims available, with only 28 spokes, when most everybody else had 36," Neel said. The light wheels were critical, as rolling weight, like rims and tires, is what makes the greatest difference on a bicycle. Fewer spokes were also a factor because spokes act as a drag; having fewer spokes reduce wind resistance.

Rich also supplied Neel with a bicycle custom built by Albert Eisentrout. It was equipped with a six-speed derailleur mounted on the bicycle, at a time when five-speed derailleurs were standard. "Everything was state-of-the-art," Neel said.

None of it was wasted on him. One by one, the riders went off at one-minute intervals. When all the riders had finished and their times had been ranked, Neel had scored an upset victory over Howard, who was two seconds behind, with third place nearly a minute back.

"The New York riders were so surprised at what Neel had done that they demanded he take a dope test because he was from California," Howard said. "In those days, riders and officials dealt with issues on a regional basis—guys from the Northeast versus the West Coast, or Midwest. The New Yorkers ganged up on Neel. So the top three finishers submitted urine samples. It was probably the first dope test in American cycling. No traces of any dope were found. Neel and I rode in the two-man team time trial, which was 30 miles long, and we just waxed everybody."

Howard and Neel hit it off at the trials. "I was impressed with John right away," Neel said. "I woke John up when I beat him in the time trial, but he was nice about it. He was an established star and had never heard of me, but we rode around the course together and talked, and he was quite helpful."

A series of four 100-mile road races were scheduled over the next week around the appropriately named Proving Grounds, where General Motors tested cars. Howard and Neel both rode strongly enough to make the road team, as did Rick Ball of Madison, Wisconsin; Frederick Beckwith of Dearborn, Michigan; Dennis Deppe of St. Louis; Jim Huetter of Buffalo, and New Yorkers Martin and Michael Levonas. Howard's Army Cycling Teammates, Chauner and Hiltner, made the team in the 4,000-meter (2.5-mile), four-rider team pursuit on the velodrome. The U.S. cycling contingent was composed of 16 road and track riders and five support staff, including Toefield, who managed the group.

The team selected raised hopes for gold medals. In the 20 years of the Games, U.S. cyclists had won only two golds, both on the velodrome and at the 1959 Pan American Games in Chicago.

Winning any medal in cycling was going to be difficult in Colombia. Cycling has long been the country's most popular sport—even over basketball and soccer. The U.S. team trained together for three weeks at Michigan State University in East Lansing. The team time trial riders trained hard together to get their timing right and learn about their particular styles. They pedaled over landscape that was similar to what they would find when they arrived in Cali in the race for the medals.

"Howard had become a lot smoother rider by then," Martin observed. "When he had made the Olympic team three years earlier, he was rough to ride behind, especially when he was following someone else's rear wheel. But by the time he made the Cali Pan American Games team, he was close to riding smooth as silk."

Cali, then a city of more than 1 million, is high up in the Cordillera Occidental mountains of the Andes in southeastern Colombia. "We flew over big mountains into a country with sharp contrasts," Howard observed. "There was rural poverty, but inner cities with modern high-rise office buildings. When we went for training rides, we would be on wide, smoothly paved highways that would abruptly turn into dirt roads."

Colombia's undisputed sports hero was Martin (Cochise) Rodriguez, who reaped two gold medals in the Cali Games—on the velodrome in the 4,000-meter individual pursuit and as a member of the Colombian team that won the 4,000-meter team pursuit. He was also helping power the four-rider 100-kilometer team time trial to a gold medal until he had a flat tire near the end. The squad managed a silver medal, anyway.

Chauner won a bronze medal in the 4,000-meter team pursuit with Hiltner, John Vande Velde, and David Mulica. Harold Halsey of Shrewsbury, New Jersey, won a bronze for the United States in the kilometer.

Expectations for the 100-kilometer team time trial were high, but they dissipated when the team accelerated to reach race pace and Howard discovered he had nothing in his legs—what the French call *un jour sans*. "I didn't realize how badly I felt until we started the race," Howard said. "My temperature was 100 degrees. Here we had worked so hard and I just had nothing that day. I dropped out. The team finished sixth. Afterward, I had to have time to myself. I think that helped. It allowed me to get my head back together and get mentally ready for the road race."

Two days later, on the final day of the Games, came a magnificent surprise that had been years in preparation. Neel, who had opened the Pan American trials with his surprise victory, played a key role in the 122.5-mile road race. Soon after the peloton of riders representing more than two dozen countries rolled away at the start, Neel attacked off the front and escaped with Augustin Alcantara, a pre-race favorite on the Mexican national team. Neel's move was strategic, designed to force the other teams to chase, while Howard and other U.S. riders sat in the protection of the peloton.

"Basically, our breakaway neutralized the race while we were away," Neel explained. "The Colombians, Cubans, and riders from other countries had to work at the front and bring everybody else up to us. I believed that the best way to race that race was to really go hard and make the other teams work equally hard to stay in the action."

Neel and Alcantara alternated, working smoothly together. Crowds of spectators, two and three deep on both sides, lined the roads yelling, "Ole!" in the excitement of watching the two riders out ahead. Alcantara worked hard to keep their lead secure. He and Neel built a maximum lead of three minutes over two loops of the large circuit up and down the Andes foothills.

The peloton mounted a relentless chase that caught the breakaway half-way through the race, when the course changed to four circuits around downtown Cali. When the breakaway was caught, most of the riders in the peloton started to relax. Then Howard got out of the saddle and sprinted off the front. Only Luis Carlos Florez of Brazil, second in the 1968 world championship road race, went with him.

"The second half was like a long criterium," Howard said. "We never got very far ahead of the pack. But the crowd was fantastic. Florez and I worked together and managed to stay out ahead. We were going 60 MPH down the descents. It was really exciting."

Neel, back in the peloton, was trying to recover from his exertion. In the race, which would take 4 hours, 47 minutes, 34 seconds, a designated feed zone was marked after the mid-point. Riders were handed up musette bags containing 16-ounce plastic drinking bottles and food. When Neel went through the feed zone, he was handed up green bananas. "I couldn't get enough food to keep going," he said. "I had to drop out."

In the feed zone, Martin made sure that Howard was served up a drinking bottle containing a mixture that Martin had learned about while racing in Italy: Espresso, Cognac, and sugar. "I drank it right down and felt great," Howard said.

On the final lap, however, a spoke in his rear wheel popped. "I had a 32-spoke wheel. When the spoke broke, the rim was rubbing against the brake block with every revolution of the wheel. The pack was chasing us down. It was really tense in those last few miles. But the crowd kept Florez and me pedaling for all we were worth."

Florez led out the sprint when he saw the finish line. He put everything he had left to take the speed up as fast as he could go. Howard sat on his rear wheel and drafted snugly.

The entire race—and Howard's career up to then—came down to his move in the last 100 yards. Howard took advantage of the wind protection Florez provided and went around him like a slingshot, winning by four lengths.

The only person yelling louder than Howard was his father, who was by the finish line, jumping up and down.

"As soon as I crossed the line, the leaders of the pack caught me," Howard said. "That's how close they were."

Howard's gold-medal performance generated unprecedented media attention for U.S. cycling. He received the 105th gold medal of the VI Pan American Games, ending the Games on an upbeat for the United States. That gave the U.S. media, until then indifferent to cycling, a news angle they could work with. A woman spectator was so carried away in the excitement of the moment that she attempted to put a rosary over Howard's head, but the beads caught his hair and he pulled the rosary away with his hand. A wire-service reporter filed a story about PFC Howard clutching a rosary in his victory ride. Photographers sent photos of Howard crossing the line, arms upraised in victory, over the wires worldwide.

Chapter 4

"Their separate, diverse flight,
she hers, he his, pursuing."
—from "The Dalliance of
Eagles," by Walt Whitman,
Leaves of Grass

When Harry and Mary Howard left Cali the next day, Friday the 13th, for the flight back to Springfield, they discovered their son's victory was national news in the United States. During a layover in Miami International Airport, the Howards picked up a copy of the *Miami Herald* and read, "Soldier Gives U.S. First Cycling Gold." The Associated Press story by Will Grimsley told readers how Howard, "a 23-year-old U.S. Army G.I., clutching a rosary in one fist, won the grueling 198-kilometer individual road race [after he] fought off weariness and leg cramps and battled Brazil's Luis Florez, ranked No. 2 amateur road cyclist in the world." *The New York Times* ran Grimsley's story on page one of the sports section with a United Press International photo of Howard crossing the line, arms upraised in victory.

Arriving home in Springfield, Harry and Mary Howard read in the local *Leader-Press*, "Howard Becomes First U.S. Cycling Winner." A representative of Springfield Mayor Carl Stillwell's office telephoned to arrange the presentation of a key to the city when their son returned. Ned Reynolds of KYTV television station called to schedule an interview at the station.

Howard's gold medal, and the bronze that his Army Cycling Teammates Chauner and Hiltner had won in the team pursuit, were welcome news to army brass, since anti-Vietnam War protests were at their height. Vietnam was an increasingly unpopular war, and anti-war sentiment was directed at anyone wearing a military uniform. The Army Cycling Team's success was a rare public relations bright spot for the armed forces. Pentagon officials were moved to write letters of commendation for all the Army Cycling Team riders who had competed in the Pan American Games. "We had letters of commendation signed by Army Chief of Staff General Westmoreland placed in our records," Howard said.

Cycling itself was undergoing a transformation. For as long as anyone could remember, children had cycled up to age 16, at which time they traded their bicycles for cars. But the fitness boom was starting. Millions of adults were taking up tennis, running, swimming, and cycling. Adults were buying bicycles faster than they could be made. The Schwinn Bicycle Company in Chicago announced in May of 1971 that it had sold out its entire production of 1,225,000 bicycles for the year. Bicycle sales surged to nearly 9 million in the United States—double what sales had been when Howard had watched Jack Simes compete in the Tokyo Olympics.

Cycling as a recreational activity enjoyed good press. When 16 Seattle youths pedaled 3,617 miles cross-country in 57 days and arrived August 9 in Washington, D.C., President Richard Nixon invited them to the White House for a personal greeting. Chicago Mayor Richard Daley announced at a press conference that he was going to ride to work in the summer on a bicycle, to encourage more commuting by bicycle as a means of cutting air pollution. City officials in Madison, Wisconsin, voted $80,000 to develop a 28.5-mile bike path in the city. Madison was among the first of hundreds of cities to create a network of inner-city bike paths, most of which were bicycle trails paved over former railroad lines.

Howard flew with his teammates back to Fort Wadsworth in Staten Island, New York. They were given a hero's welcome. Soon Howard was issued a pass to take leave to fly home, where he was greeted at the Springfield Airport by several dozen family members, friends, area cyclists, and Mayor Stillwell.

"John put Springfield, Missouri, on the map," Kim said. "The two best-known people in Springfield were John Howard and Mickey Cohen. I met Mickey Cohen at a Christmas party at the hospital. The band, Lavender Hill Mob, was there. Mickey Cohen didn't wear prison garb. He dressed real sharp. Even wore an ascot. He showed me the scrapbook that he kept on John. He told us that, if we went to Los Angeles, we should contact a person whose name he gave us and tell that person that Mickey Cohen had sent us. Then we would have a place to stay and a car to drive while we were there."

Howard arrived in Springfield Airport wearing civilian clothes and his gold medal. "It seemed like all of Springfield went to the airport to greet John," Kim said. "The mayor presented him with the key to the city. It was all quite exciting. People were calling out his name, reaching out to shake his hand. The day he arrived was August 16, his 24th birthday. It was quite a birthday celebration."

For all his shyness, Howard was relaxed before the group, even as the center of attention. "Part of what helped me stand before people and talk was a public-speaking class I had taken in college. It was taught by Kim's mother, Patricia Kynion," Howard explained.

Kim was preparing to start her junior year at Southwest Missouri State University. "I had a 3.8 grade-point average and was going to get a bachelor's degree in sociology," she said. "At the airport when John arrived, he took off his gold medal and put it around my neck. I felt so proud. That night, we decided to get married. We set the date for October 15."

While John and Kim discussed their wedding plans, North American representatives of Raleigh bicycles of England and Pete Rich of Berkeley, California, were making final plans for the Tour of California, one of the most remarkable bicycle races ever held in the United States: an eight-day race in northern California covering 685 miles.

The Tour of California was the first modern stage race in the United States. It went on for eight days straight, rain or shine, with a variety of competition. Final standings were determined by each rider's total elapsed time. Events like the three-week Tour de France, which dates back to 1903, are common in Europe, and stage races had been held in Mexico and Canada for many years. But none had been put together in the United States because nobody had tackled the logistics of organizing one. With sales of bicycles soaring in the United States, Raleigh was looking to raise its visibility and increase its market share. Pete Rich wanted to put on an American stage race. Rich pooled resources with Raleigh to finally put together this first Tour of California.

Rich is an entrepreneur whose role in American cycling is as one of a small number of tugboats pushing a huge ship reluctantly out of port into the open ocean. He began racing in the late 1950s and totally committed himself to the sport. He opened VeloSport Bicycles in Berkeley, and when he wasn't minding the shop, he trained with the goal of making the Olympic cycling team.

The Bay area had a hardy group of racers who competed in four clubs. To help provide information for other Bay-area riders,

Rich published *VeloSport Newsletter*—eight mimeographed pages stapled together. He published it when he felt like it, to pass along local race results and tips on training or racing. When the four Bay-area clubs organized the Northern California Cycling Association to coordinate a racing calendar in early 1962, he gave the association his newsletter. It was renamed the *Northern California Cycling Association Newsletter* and went through numerous format and title changes as cycling expanded domestically. By 1971 it was called *Bicycling Magazine*, and was floundering for lack of advertising revenue.

When Rich spent a season competing in Italy during the early 1960s, he saw major league racing up close. Italians like Ercole Baldini and Gastone Nencini dominated as giants of the road in international competition. Rich watched big stars compete in popular point-to-point races that went from one city to another, in stage races and one-day events. Part of the excitement was the fans, called *tifosi*. They lined both sides of the roads and waited for hours for the racers to spin past. Upon seeing the racers, *tifosi* became scandalously unruly, particularly up long hills where racers toiled against gravity and the peloton strung out. *Tifosi* spilled onto the roads, patted them on the back and shoulders, and yelled encouragement. American sports fans who watch baseball, football, and basketball games never set foot on the playing field and see their heroes up as close as *tifosi* see cyclists. Such contact with the riders has long added to cycling's popularity in Europe.

American racing had nothing comparable. Races were mostly criteriums around downtown circuits of about one mile. Snow fences and other barricades were set up to keep spectators off the streets. What occasionally passed for a stage race was a weekend of racing tailored to meet the limited time that riders had at their disposal and what officials could achieve in gaining permission for restricted use of local roadways.

Rich never made the Olympic team, but the event he was instrumental in creating—the Tour of California—was an achievement of Olympian proportions. He mapped out the entire course and arranged for a challenging variety of daily stages. Most were point-to-point and took racers in a clockwise serpentine across the breadth of northern California, with a few short criteriums in city downtowns to draw spectators, and a 12.6-mile team time trial. He designed the course with rigorous climbs and fast, dangerous descents up and down the Sierra Nevadas that were as demanding as any in European events. Every road required that Rich get permission from state, county, or local government officials. He recruited six-rider teams from around the country, Canada, Mexico, and Germany. Rich made arrangements for restaurant meals and hotel accommodations for riders and their support crews at every venue where the race stopped for the day. He published a 36-page souvenir race program with a glossy cover and oversaw myriad other details that would ordinarily take a staff a year to arrange.

"The budget was $50,000," Rich said. "It took me six or seven years to pay off the debts I accumulated from that race." Yet for American bicycle racing, the money proved to be an investment. Rich's organization and Raleigh's involvement had far-reaching consequences not apparent right away. But some of what was to come was felt across the country.

"I knew that something big was going on when I got a call from Bill Kerns of Raleigh's headquarters in Boston," explained John Allis, Howard's teammate from the Mexico City Olympics. As a Princeton freshman in the spring of 1961, he helped his team win the national intercollegiate championships against Dartmouth, Yale, Williams, and Farleigh Dickenson. His Princeton cycling team represented the United States at the 1963 world championship road race in Ronse, Belgium. He settled in France, studied at the University of Paris, and the following spring competed as a member of the Athletic Club Boulogne-Billancourt, a large squad that acts as a feeder club for the French professional teams. That summer he astounded the French by winning the 120-mile Paris to Cayeux-sur-Mer race. He returned to the United States in time to make the Olympic team bound for Tokyo. Afterward, Allis completed his degree at Princeton and raced domestically for another four years, to make his second Olympic team for the Mexico City Olympics. In 1969 he went back to his French team to see about racing again for them, but was given disillusioning news. The team director asked him his age. When he replied, "Twenty-six," the director said, "Too old." The philosophy was that if Allis hadn't turned professional by then, it was time to get on with his life.

Allis went back home to Cambridge, Massachusetts, and decided to quit racing and work a demanding full-time job as administrator at Massachusetts General and Peter Brent Brigham Hospital (now Affiliated Hospital) in Boston. But in 1971, with the next Olympics approaching, Allis was tempted. He started to train and entered local races—enough to tease his talent, but not enough to compete on a national level. Then came the telephone call that changed everything.

"I just flipped out," Allis said. "Kerns was in charge of product development and ran the show for Raleigh in North America. He invited me to help form a team. At first I was skeptical, because this sort of thing had come up in the past but had always fallen through. I couldn't see flying out to California at my expense when I wasn't in such good shape.

"But Raleigh was solidly behind the Tour of California. Kerns and I met and we filled out a team. Raleigh provided us with new bikes, which was rare at the time in the United States. We had a carte blanche for the team's expenses. We were ecstatic. We were given airline tickets to fly to California. I started training hard again— up at dawn to get in a workout before going off to my job, then later, when I got back home, I got on my bike for another workout."

Howard passed up the national championships in Portland, Oregon, to take leave and be with Kim and his family. Rich's protégé, Mike Neel, went to the nationals and won the 4,000-meter track event. Neel's triumph encouraged him to start thinking seriously about going to France to break into racing there for the next season.

Teams of six riders from around the United States were assembled geographically for the Tour of California. Howard was on the Midwest team, which included Steve Dayton of Indianapolis, who had won the national road racing championship in Portland. Howard, as a member of the Army Cycling Team, was cut orders which authorized him more time for racing. He drove his orange Superbeetle from Springfield to California.

A field of 79 riders embarked on the first stage, which began at 7,000-feet altitude in the Sierra Nevadas of eastern California. The tour started at the Bear Valley Ski Resort, midway between Lake Tahoe and Yosemite National Park. "What a spectacle they made," observed Owen Mulholland of San Anselmo, California, a race staff volunteer. "Riders swishing along between the trees of the high Sierra trailed by a giant cavalcade of cars."

The course serpentined west, dropped to sea level in Stockton, then rose along coastal hills to the San Francisco East Bay in Berkeley. Then the event resumed on the other side of the bay, with riders and the caravan crossing the Golden Gate Bridge. From there, the course went north up rugged Pacific coastal hills, shifted inland to Santa Rosa and continued east across Central

Valley for Sacramento. It concluded with three days of arduous climbs up Sierra Nevada passes so steep they required car drivers to shift down to second gear. Altogether, the tour demanded the best efforts of every rider just to finish.

Riders were out to prove what they could do, and to claim some of the prizes—a mix of merchandise and cash in an era of strict rules governing amateurs. Overall winner of the tour was to take home $1,385, which was regarded as generous. The best team would earn $1,600. Merchandise, with each prize limited to a $100 value under prevailing amateur rules, depended on what Rich himself supplied, or what he had hustled in donations from businesses along the route.

"The prizes were quite good, especially for the time," Allis said. "Flowers were presented to the winner of each stage, like in European races. The top 10 finishers of each stage got something. Some of the prizes were more symbolic than valuable, like the bottle of California champagne that went to the winners of the team time trial. Supposedly, the team split the bottle six ways."

Opening the race was a stage of 96 miles, mostly downhill, to Stockton. Repeated attacks off the front resulted in an eight-rider group forming a successful breakaway midway through the stage. In the group were Howard of the Midwest team, and Neel, who was riding for VeloSport Berkeley. The pace, aided by long descents, was fast but dangerous around hairpins on narrow roads. Breakaway riders sped into Stockton, where they sprinted for the right to wear the yellow jersey that designates the race leader—in this case, the first ever yellow jersey to be worn in U.S. stage racing.

Howard and Neel led the charge to the finish. The two lanky riders gripped the drops of the handlebars and rose out of the saddle to wind up their sprint. Throwing their bicycles back and forth between their knees with each quick pedal stroke, they surged above 40 MPH. At the line, Neel edged Howard. The other six riders sped across the finish line in their draft, followed closely by the rest of the peloton. The tour was off to a competitive start.

Neel recalled the stage 21 years later with an edge of frustration in his voice. "I was penalized five minutes for taking my hands off the handlebars when I crossed the line in a victory salute," he said. "That was the kind of rules the ABL had back then."

Instead of donning the race leader's yellow jersey, Neel was demoted to ninth place. Howard took over the honor of being the first to wear the yellow jersey.

Next came a double-stage day that started with a 4:30 a.m. reveille for breakfast, ahead of the 7 a.m. start of a 74-mile stage into Berkeley. With 30 miles remaining, Emile "Flip" Waldteufel of nearby Mill Valley attacked a hill with his VeloSport teammate Dave Brink and Francisco Huerta of the Mexican national team. Brink, who had retired after the Mexico City Olympics but was inspired by the Tour of California to get back into shape, was determined to win the stage into his hometown of Berkeley. He helped to keep the trio working a pace line together and to stretch their lead to a minute over the peloton. Brink rode with more determination than fitness, but he summoned enough to dash ahead of his partners to win the stage. Waldteufel, in second, crossed the line a minute ahead of Howard. Waldteufel had made the previous day's breakaway with Howard, thus acquiring the yellow jersey as the new race leader.

At 7 p.m. riders assembled for the second stage of the day, a fast 20-mile criterium around downtown Berkeley. To the delight of the thousands of spectators who crowded the course, Huerta took off ahead on his own to try to lap the peloton. He stayed out in front for 15 laps, prompting raucous cheers from the crowd. They were further stirred when the riders sprinted for merchandise "premes," (a popular reference that came from the professional six-day races that offered premiums to keep the racing lively for riders and spectators.) Neel grabbed the last preme sprint. At sunset the peloton had absorbed Neel and Huerta and surged at 40 MPH in a spectacular curb-to-curb pack sprint. Howard nipped local riders Kim Bruseth and Neel. Howard's prize included a time bonus that put him within six seconds of Waldteufel.

But the following day had double stages that would change everything. Stage 4 was a morning race of 84 miles from San Francisco to Santa Rosa. Siggy Koch broke away with two others to gain more than three minutes on the peloton, including Waldteufel and Howard, by the finish. Koch riding for the British Columbia team, became the third rider of the race to don the yellow jersey.

That afternoon came Stage 5, the team time trial of 12.6 miles in Santa Rosa. Rain poured. That not only made roads slick, but also meant that riders drafting close behind the rear wheel in front had a rooster tail of water in their face for the entire distance. Nevertheless, Howard helped power the Midwest squad to victory four seconds ahead of the Mexican national team. Koch and his team lost time, putting Howard only a half-minute away from regaining the yellow jersey.

An accident the next day, on the 83-mile Stage 6 from Santa Rosa to Davis, spoiled Howard's chance for victory and illustrated how vulnerable cyclists are on the road.

"Howard was in a breakaway with Tom Baker of the British Columbia team, Tim Kelly of Berkeley, and me," recalled Don Davis of Nevada City, California. "We were going fast down a short, sharp hill on Trinity Mountain Road, when we went around a blind hairpin turn going about 40 MPH. Suddenly, a van was stopped right in the middle of the road, taking up half the road. Baker was leading Howard, with Kelly and me right behind. I remember seeing and hearing the crash. Baker hit the van straight on—wham! John slammed into the van at an angle and crashed hard. Kelly and I barely missed the van. I thought Baker and Howard were dead."

Baker suffered the worst. "He struck the vehicle head-on and cartwheeled quite a distance," Howard said. "He nearly bled to death and broke a number of bones. He suffered a compound fracture of the femur. He never raced again."

Tour officials in the following car screeched to a stop. They rushed to give Baker first aid and to call for an ambulance.

Howard managed to get back up. "The top tube of my frame was dented and the front derailleur was broken," he said. "That was the yellow Schwinn Paramount I had won the Pan Am road race on. I had numerous cuts and bruises on my legs and arms, and my left wrist was hurting like hell. I think I broke it, but there was no time to go to a hospital for an X-ray to check it out. We tied a bandage around the wrist and I got back on my bike. The pack had caught us and went on past. I had to chase on my own for miles and miles. But I kept hammering alone and just managed to catch the tail end of the field as they crossed the line, so I didn't lose any time."

As the race headed into the mountains, Howard's injured wrist kept him from gripping the handlebars tightly and hampered his climbing. It looked like Koch, with his European racing experience, had the race all to himself.

But stage racing is always full of surprises. In the spectrum of sports, a stage race has no comparison. Competition is daily, and there is no allowance for a single bad day—one rider's loss is always another's gain. Moreover, a good stage race, like the Tour of California, is effectively a triple cycling event. Winning requires that a champion sprint fast in the pack finishes, time trial well, and ride up mountains with the leaders.

The Mexican national team waited to show their talents until the three hardest stages—up and down the Sierra Nevadas—when the miles took their toll and the roads climbed up to touch the sky.

Augustin Alcantara was in seventh place, 7 minutes and 25 seconds behind Koch, when the racers embarked on Stage 7, a 91-mile stretch from Sacramento to Grass Valley. Alcantara was a wily competitor. In 1969 he had gone to France, where he had won a stage in the prestigious Tour de l'Avenir, the amateur version of the Tour de France. Then he had won the 1970 Tour of Mexico. On the road to Grass Valley, the climbs toward the end grew increasingly stiff and he played them to his advantage. Alcantara, two teammates, and eight others escaped off the front in a break that left Koch, Howard, and Waldteufel in the peloton. Alcantara won the stage with such a lead over the peloton that he rose in overall standings to become the new race leader.

On the penultimate day, during the stage that went 101 miles from Lake Tahoe over three major climbs to Bear Valley Ski Resort, Sabas Cervantes upstaged his teammate, Alcantara. It was early September, and the temperature at the start was 28 degrees. Riders rode in a tight peloton to reduce wind chill.

Cervantes, at 37 one of the oldest in the peloton, was so far down in overall standings that he had to make a do-or-die effort to do well. Right after the start, he decided to forgo the comfort of the peloton and rode away solo. The peloton broke up on the first climb, up Luther Pass, and Alcantara went in pursuit of his teammate. Then Ebbetts Pass, and finally Pacific Grade hammered the riders. Cervantes stayed ahead to win solo. Alcantara followed him in for second. Yet Koch rallied to limit the damage. Alcantara had taken 13 minutes out of Koch over the last three days to build a margin of six minutes. But Koch held on to second place. Cervantes' victory in the penultimate stage catapulted him to third place, one minute behind Koch.

Concluding the race was a final 27-mile criterium around the Bear Valley Ski Resort, on a flat circuit in the parking lot and service roads. Alcantara showed he had the best legs in the peloton by breaking away again for a solo victory, to cap his overall tour triumph.

Koch preserved his second place, holding Cervantes at bay in third. Top U.S. finisher was Allis, in fourth. Despite limited preparation, he rode strongly. Following Allis was Brink, then Howard in sixth. "It was my first real stage race and I learned a lot," Howard said. "Stage racing requires real experience."

Waldteufel was eighth, Neel ninth, and Davis 10th. Mexican

riders led by Alcantara and Cervantes took top team honors.

The Tour of California was a *success d'estime*. It earned Pete Rich immense respect from the riders and support crews involved. But as a sports event, it was ahead of its time and suffered from a complete lack of media coverage.

"It was such a great race, but if you weren't there, you wouldn't know anything about it," noted Mulholland. "I wrote up an account of the race for friends. There was nothing to publish it in here in the United States. I gave a copy of my account to Pete Rich, who was contacted by *International Cycle Sport*, a magazine published in England. Pete gave the editor my article, which was published in four pages."

The finances of the stage race so overwhelmed Rich that he never mounted another tour. But it was a gallant effort. It introduced U.S. cyclists to European-style racing, and they performed admirably. It also received international attention with Mulholland's article.

Howard drove back to Springfield and made arrangements with Kim and their respective families for their marriage on October 15. "It was a quiet ceremony in my parents' home, in southeast Springfield," he said. "Just our immediate families attended."

Reverend Curtis March, a Presbyterian minister, performed the nuptial services.

"Two days after our marriage," Kim said, "we drove to California, which took three days. John was going to ride in the Tour of Mexico. John's Volkswagen didn't have a radio. We talked and talked. I read Carlos Castenadas books out loud. At night, in bed, we read poetry from Walt Whitman's *Leaves of Grass*."

The newlyweds drove to northern California to visit Mike Neel in Berkeley. Howard and Neel were to fly from San Francisco to Mexico City to compete in the Tour of Mexico, an international stage race that went 1,250 miles in 15 days, from October 29 to November 14, with one rest day.

When Howard and Neel caught their flight to Mexico City, Kim stayed with the George Farriers in their sprawling ranch house. "John and I hadn't been married a week when he took off to Mexico," Kim said. "Mike Neel went on my honeymoon."

Howard and Neel joined Allis, Waldteufel, and two others on the U.S. national team to compete in the Tour of Mexico, officially called the 18th Vuelta Cycliste de la Juventid. It drew 138 starters, with European squads from Italy, Holland, and Belgium, and Latin American teams from Mexico and Cuba. The race began in Mexico City, went north and then counter-clockwise to finish back in Mexico City.

"Neel broke away on the first day," Allis said. "Later, down the road, we found him lying in the gutter. He had crashed. That was kind of the way the race went for our team. Accommodations were bad. The sun was awfully hot and we had to take water from spectators on the course. That is always risky."

Howard realized on the second day of the race, in the 31-mile individual time trial, that he was struggling. "I had a stomach virus and couldn't keep food down. The individual time trial was on an open road and I remember cars passing me as I rode. I felt horrible. Out there under the Mexican sun, it was just brutal."

Howard, Neel, and Waldteufel lasted less than a week in the Tour of Mexico, but they stayed on to watch and lend support to Allis, who gamely kept in the race. Strong but lacking the quickness for a sharp sprint, Allis finished in 16th place overall, behind winner Mario Conti of Italy and Feder den Hertog of Holland. Only 55 of the 138 starters finished.

Returning to the United States, the Army Cycling Team at Fort Wadsworth continued their training. While the overwhelming majority of those serving in the army had a regimented life in uniform, Howard and his teammates enjoyed unusual freedom to train and race.

"The army essentially didn't know what to do with us," Chauner said. "They stuck us together on the top floor of a barracks at Fort Wadsworth, where we were left pretty much alone. Of course, it helped that John won the gold medal at the Pan Am Games road race, and some of us won the bronze in the team pursuit. We had letters of commendation signed by General Westmoreland in our files. That made life easier for us."

The army provided vans and gasoline, important for commuting to better training venues on Long Island, away from the urban density of metropolitan New York City. The major drawback to life at Fort Wadsworth was that Howard and other married riders had to leave their wives at home.

"There was nowhere on the base for John and me to live together," Kim said. "I stayed with John's parents in Springfield. He called me and wrote to me there."

The barracks had ample room for the bunk beds where the

riders slept, and enough space to make a flat indoor track, 38 laps to the mile, for the riders to pedal inside when the weather was foul. Its cement floor was never cleaned, and accumulated assorted skid marks and pedal gouges from crashes. "We had ruined the floor," Howard admitted. "We never cleaned it, never washed the windows, either. They were streaked with dirt."

On every military base, there is the time-honored Inspection General—the dreaded IG—when the base's commanding officer and top brass inspect the installation in minute detail. They are major events, announced in advance for troops to clean and polish everything. Leaving even lint behind after polishing a window can be interpreted as recklessness. Troops are mustered to stand at rigid attention in front of their bunks and footlockers to await scrutiny—from the closeness of their morning shave, the sharpness of the crease in their trousers, and the stiffness of the starch in their uniform, to the cleanliness of the barracks, which is subject to an officer sweeping a white-gloved finger over areas to check for dirt. For unexplained reasons, everyone at Fort Wadsworth had prepared for the IG except the Army Cycling Team.

"I was the only one awake in the barracks and was cleaning my bicycle when the general, colonel, and our commanding officer, a captain, came walking in," Howard said. "The CO looked around and made a bad face. He looked upon us like we were lesser humans. I was hunched over, working on my bike, when they came in. The CO couldn't seem to find anything to say for a moment, so I kept working. Finally, he asked me to explain what I was doing. I said, 'Well, sir, I am cleaning my chain.'

"The CO got a pained expression on his face. He said, 'No, no, no. What are you doing at Fort Wadsworth?' I stood up, grabbed a rag to wipe the grease off my hands, and explained that we were on the Army Special Services cycling team, that our job was to win bicycle races for the army. I told him we had competed in the Pan American Games and we were preparing for the Munich Olympics the next summer.

"The general intervened and told us not to worry about it. He looked around and shook his head a little. Some of the guys were snoring. The general said he would send a clean-up crew to take care of things. He waved a hand to indicate that he and the CO and the captain were leaving. Before they went out the door, the general stopped and turned around and said, 'You might as well splash some water on the windows. Get some more light in here.' "

In January 1972, the team was transferred across country to Fort MacArthur in San Pedro, California. Fort MacArthur, located in the southern sprawl of Los Angeles by the Pacific Ocean, offered better weather for winter training. Kim moved out to join Howard and they lived in an apartment off the base.

"Life in California was different and fun," Kim said. "There were a lot of things to do outdoors. John would ride his bike home for lunch so we could eat together. We finally had the chance to be together more often."

Friends like Don Davis felt that Kim helped Howard drastically improve his diet. Like many athletes, Howard's approach to eating involved shortcuts that fed him as quickly as possible. "I couldn't believe how bad his diet was," Davis said. "I saw him eating cans of ravioli and junk food."

The Pentagon had stationed the Air Force Cycling Team at Fort MacArthur with the Army Cycling Team, mixing not just military branches but also enlisted men like PFC Howard with officers like Air Force Captain Jim Montgomery. "The Air Force guys had really good jobs, but what they really wanted to do was race their bicycles," Howard said.

The combined team was called the Armed Forces Cycling Team. Members had ample time to train through the winter and take advantage of the mild Southern California climate. Howard was fit when he, Montgomery, and other team members followed the sport's March migratory flow east to southern Florida, where Olympic development races inaugurated the season. Al Toefield and other ABL officials had established a series of Olympic development races designed to raise the level of competition. Promoters counted on top riders in their events, and riders sought races in the series for improving their fitness and skills.

"There used to be a set pattern of races," Montgomery explained. "They started deep in the South and then moved north during the spring. It was early summer before there were a lot of races around the country. That made the early-season races in Florida and Louisiana really important."

Montgomery, a native of Seattle, had taken up cycling a few years earlier after he had burned out on championship chess. While playing chess may lack anaerobic conditioning, it does require concentration and promotes tactical prowess. Montgomery raced his bicycle as if he still played chess, with strategic feints and calculated intimidation augmented by a naturally explosive sprint. He was emerging as a national-class cyclist that season.

"He had a good sprint," Howard acknowledged. "I never wanted to see Jim Montgomery around at the end of a race."

Howard and Kim drove their Superbeetle across the country for the season's first event, the seventh annual Cross-Florida Tour, which Howard knew well by then. "Making a drive that far in a car without a radio really lets a couple get to know one another," Kim said. "John and I talked a lot, and I continued to read Carlos Castanadas novels out loud while he drove."

South Florida's balmy breezes and sunshine were a welcome relief for riders coming from the Northeast and Midwest. While the Sunshine State's landscape is utterly flat in the south, riders were subjected to windy riding in their 240-mile race over the weekend. The route was from West Palm Beach on the Atlantic Coast west to Fort Myers on the Gulf of Mexico, then back to West Palm Beach.

"John was at the top of his game," Montgomery said. "A big thing then was to honor the top rider with the competitive number one. That was John's in the races. He was quite well-known and recognized everywhere he went."

Riders and American *tifosi* were familiar with Howard's deep-set blue eyes and jutting jaw. He sat on the bicycle with his back arched slightly at the shoulder blades and exuded determination as he rode.

Howard and Montgomery, riding for the Armed Forces Cycling Team, pedaled at the front of the peloton to stoke the pace and keep the speed high. Riders were racing into shape. Their shared destination, ultimately, was upstate New York, where the Olympic road racing trials were to be held in June.

Howard turned in the best overall performance, scoring the cycling season's first victory. Then everyone packed up to commute to the northwest panhandle for the Tour of Tallahassee.

"The Tour of Tallahassee was a big race then," said Ed Pavelka, who lived in Tallahassee. "It was a stage race back when there weren't many in the United States. In 1972 the race had an all-star cast with Howard, Mike Neel, Jim Montgomery, and others. Howard was king of the roads, the way Elvis Presley was the king of rock 'n' roll."

The stages over the weekend tour were a mixture of an individual time trial and a criterium around the Florida State University football stadium on Saturday, and a road race that radiated out of the city over rolling north Florida hills on Sunday. The race covered nearly 200 miles.

"The time trial course was one that the local racing club, Tallahassee VeloSport, used. About 10 miles," Pavelka said. "Howard's time trialing ability gave him such an advantage that he [in effect] won the whole race in the time trial. His margin of victory meant that all he had to do was keep anyone from breaking away in the other stages, and nobody could break away from him."

Always pushing his limits, Howard equipped his bicycle with a front chain ring of 53 teeth, at a time when the conventional wisdom was to use 52 teeth. "We all considered it amazing that he could punch a 53," Pavelka said. "In an interview, Howard said, 'Fifty-two-tooth chainrings just don't cut it.' That became a famous quote. We had it printed up and mounted on a wall of the bike shop where I worked."

Howard won the Tour of Tallahassee, keeping his momentum going on his road to the Olympic trials. Next, riders migrated to New Orleans for the weekend Tour of Louisiana, which Howard also won.

"Howard was just about unbeatable in a stage race that had an individual time trial," Montgomery said. "Time trials were usually 10 kilometers or shorter, and he would get 30 seconds to a minute over everyone. That just about closed the race for the rest of us. We were left to fight for second place."

After the Southeast sweep, Howard and Kim drove back to Fort MacArthur. They stopped in St. Louis, where Howard visited Ray Florman at A-1 Bicycle Sales Company. Florman took the cycling merchandise Howard had won to sell it for him in his shop.

"Fencing the cycling equipment we won was one of the few ways we had to make any money," Howard said. "It wasn't much. But it helped to pay the gas and other expenses so we could come out nearly even, maybe a little ahead, if we had a good racing trip."

Back in California, Howard scored another victory in a one-day race in Palos Verdes. He stayed on track and qualified for the Olympic road trials from June 11 to 17 in Lake Luzerne, New York.

"I was sure I could win a medal in the Olympics," Howard said. "But first I had to do well in the trials and make the Olympic cycling team."

Cycling nationwide was enjoying a popular cultural wave. *The New York Times* devoted an editorial to the explosion in recreation cycling, with an estimated 80 million people, mostly adults, riding bicycles. Sales of bicycles rose to 13.9 million—surpassing the number of cars sold that year. John Deere & Company officials in

Moline, Illinois, announced that the company would return, after an absence of more than 80 years, to manufacturing bicycles. Chicago Mayor Richard Daley formally opened a new North Side bicycle route. In the nation's capital, Senator Ted Stevens, a Republican from Alaska, noted that about 100 Senate employees pedaled bicycles to work. He called for more places to park bicycles on Capitol Hill. Congress approved a resolution appropriating $16.6 billion in federal road building funds, authorizing the construction of bicycle paths through public parks.

Interest in racing also increased dramatically. Five thousand racers were registered with the ABL—a fourfold increase since Howard had taken out his first racing license. Information on what was going on in American racing, however, was still difficult to come by. Two cyclists in Brattleboro, Vermont, decided to come up with their own publication. Barbara George, a school teacher, and her husband, Robert, a photographer, founded *Northeast Bicycle News* in their home. On March 13, Volume No. 1, Issue No. 1, was introduced as a tabloid, an important development for the sport's growth.

To qualify for the Olympic cycling road trials in April and May, riders went through a series of 80–100 mile qualifier races to earn points. Only 60 cyclists would qualify for the road trials— the top 20 scorers each from the East, Midwest, and West. Those 60 spots were fiercely competed for. All of the Armed Forces Team, except Jim Montgomery, qualified.

The Olympic cycling trials were held on opposite sides of the country. Track events were in San Jose; road events in the town of Lake Luzerne, in northwestern upstate New York, near Glens Falls. For Howard and Kim, it was another cross-country drive in the Superbeetle. They left San Pedro early enough for Howard to tune up for the trials with one last road race of 100 miles in Buffalo, in eastern upstate New York.

"That was a killer race," remembered Wayne Stetina, then an 18-year-old *Wunderkind* from Indianapolis. Stetina, a second-generation cyclist, had grown up in the sport and had been watching Howard race for several years. When Howard made his move to break away in the closing miles of the Buffalo race, Stetina realized nobody could catch Howard, and that for everyone else the race was for second. Stetina won the peloton sprint. His second place made him a serious contender for the Olympic team.

When Howard, Stetina, and the other qualifiers made their way to the road trials on the other side of the Empire State, ABL officials were trying to shuffle their resources to come up with a winning hand for the Olympics. Ernest Seubert, a successful road racer of the 1950s, was in his second year as ABL president and took over as head road coach of the Olympic cycling team. He worked with fellow New Yorker Al Toefield, team manager, to devise ways to better use the talent at their disposal.

The road trials favored selecting time trialers. The first day opened June 11 with two time trials: an individual of 25 kilometers (15.6 miles) in the morning and a two-man time trial of 50 kilometers (31.5 miles) in the afternoon. Then followed three successive days of progressively longer road races: 100 kilometers, 100 miles, and 120 miles. A dozen riders would be selected for the long team, which later would be reduced to a short team of eight, based on results at races that would end in the 120-mile national road racing championship in Milwaukee seven weeks later. "I'll never forget those Olympic trials because that was when John was talked into shaving the hair off his arms," Kim said. "John already shaved his legs, like the other riders, but Rick Ball had talked him into shaving his arms, to cut down on wind resistance."

Rick Ball, 28, was completing his course work for a Ph.D. in math at the University of Wisconsin in Madison, and approached cycling scientifically. "He was a pure time trialer," Howard said. "Rick Ball had no sprint, but he was a real spark plug. He was way ahead of his time. We wore leather hairnet helmets then, and he wanted to put points on the helmets to cut wind resistance. (This actually came about years later with hard-shell helmets designed aerodynamically with teardrop shapes.) Rick was also the king of interval workouts. He would do morning rides with us, then in the afternoon do workouts of 15 to 20 one-minute intervals. He really blasted in those intervals, too. He got me doing them. Before I met Rick Ball, I used to mostly just go out and ride."

When Ball turned in the fastest time trial in the opening time trial, he really made an impression on Howard, who was 30 seconds behind for second, with Stetina in third.

The next day was the first road race—100 kilometers over a course noted for its hilliness, including one monster climb every lap that didn't allow time for recovery. "I was just pounding," Howard said. He kept pushing the pace and won decisively over Californians Tim Kelly, Ron Skarin, Waldteufel, and Ken Fuller. Allis, trying for his third Olympics, finished eighth, one place ahead of Ball.

Only a dozen finished. With the emphasis on making one of the top five spots to earn a shot at making the long team—which would determine who was bound for the Munich Olympics—riders went all out. If they felt it wasn't their day, they would quit to save something for the next race, a 100-mile event. One rider who abandoned in the first road race was Bob Schneider, who pulled out with 15 miles remaining. Schneider, 29, was a doctoral candidate in Agri-Economics at the University of Wisconsin where he had met Ball and discovered bicycle racing. That had been in 1970, when Schneider returned to campus after Peace Corps duty in West Africa. He bought a used Atala racing bicycle from a student and entered five events in 1971, achieving modest results. Classes curtailed his training time until the following April, when he completed exams and entered a few Olympic development races. Finishing second to Ball in a tortuous road race in Wisconsin earned him an invitation to the Olympic trials.

Riders teased Schneider, saying that his hairy legs made King Kong look like a queen. Ball's discourses on the advantage of slicing through the air faster without body hair went right past Schneider, who also wore a full beard. He said his goal was simply to ride well enough to avoid embarrassing himself. When he saw others pulling out during the first road race, he realized they were hurting as much as he was. His self-confidence rose. He approached the next day's race ready to ride onto the Olympic team.

Howard forced the pace and led up most of the hills. Schneider hung in with Howard and the leaders over every hill and persevered over the distance. As a newcomer to the sport, Schneider was uncomfortable in a crowded peloton, riding elbow to elbow and wheel to wheel at speed. He also lacked the fluid pedal stroke that comes with experience, but he made up for it with strength. He held his own up the climbs that were taking their toll on others, including Stetina, who faltered and fell back through the peloton until he dropped off the back. Until the Olympic trials, most of Schneider's limited racing—fewer than a dozen events—had been in criteriums. These favor a classy rider like Stetina, who pedaled with a quick spin of 90 or more RPM to facilitate a frequent changing of speed around sharp corners—breaking into turns and sprinting out of them. Road racing, with its sustained effort and climbs and descents, suited Schneider.

When the crowd of ABL officials and relatives of the riders, including Kim, came into sight by the finish, Schneider boldly charged to the front of the peloton. That put him at a tactical disadvantage. But he didn't mind that everyone was strung out behind in his draft. Schneider knew that everyone was suffering as much as he was and he wasn't going to let that bother him.

Howard must have realized that Schneider was on his way to becoming the phenomenon that he himself had been in the previous Olympic trials, so he deftly maneuvered to Schneider's rear wheel to take advantage of the sweet spot as they wound up for the finish.

"I sat in behind Schneider and came around to win the race," Howard said. That gave him three straight victories at the trials for an automatic berth on his second Olympic team. Schneider was right behind for second. That got him a spot on the long team. Other Midwest riders mobbed him at the finish. Schneider burbled, "I just can't believe it's happening to me."

Howard, with the pressure off, moved out of the motel where he had been with the cyclists, to spend the night with his wife.

"I stayed across town in a pine cabin on the freeway," Kim said. "We seldom got to spend time together at big races like the Olympic trials. It was an oddity for road riders to be married then, mainly because there was no money in racing. Riders were amateurs and couldn't accept a gift valued at more than $100, otherwise they would lose their amateur standing. And there was no professional racing then, at least not in this country."

Seubert announced that the long team of 12 riders were Howard, Ball, Allis, Stetina, Waldteufel, Tim Kelly, Schneider, Ron Skarin, Mowen, Fuller, Deppe, and Jim Huetter. Final selection of the eight for the Olympic team depended on results of races over the next seven weeks, leading to the national road racing championship August 6 in Milwaukee. "For most of us," Allis said, "that meant we had to fight tooth and nail every day to make the final cut."

If Allis could make his third Olympic cycling team, he would join a small elite of American cyclists. In cycling, competing in three Olympics is a post-World-War-II phenomenon. From the time the Olympic Games were revived in Athens in 1896, through the 1930s, the best home-grown talent turned professional to take advantage of better cycling opportunities. Many riders, like Jimmy Walthour, who won national road and track championships in 1927 and was a likely prospect for the 1928 Olympic team, skipped the Olympics to turn professional. But the Depression and then World War II effectively knocked American cycling flat.

What remained was amateur racing, for which the Olympics were the ultimate competition.

Allis was still working as a hospital administrator in Boston when he went to the Olympic trials. "I quit the job to devote myself full-time to training and racing to make the Olympic cycling team," he said. "I was expecting to go to graduate school at the Harvard Business School in the fall anyway."

Free of his job, Allis joined Howard and other Olympic hopefuls in eastern Canada for the Tour de l'Estre. It was a five-day stage race that started in Quebec and serpentined over 440 miles to finish in Montreal. Canadian races were far more liberal about rewarding riders, who received cash in envelopes awarded discreetly by race officials. Against the top riders of North America, U.S. riders made a sweep. Howard won, with Allis second and Tim Kelly third.

"The Tour de l'Estre was a really good race for us," Allis said. "We worked well as a team, and team riding was a new concept for American riders. We rode to help Howard win by chasing down breakaway attempts from other teams and otherwise making sure that Howard had protection from the wind. It was our first real team race, as opposed to being a bunch of riders in the same-colored jerseys who rode independently."

Afterward, the long team went to a three-week training camp in South Branch, New Jersey. "We were going to do nothing but eat, sleep, ride our bicycles twice a day, and take in weekend races," Allis said. "Four of the guys were going to be cut from the team. It may have sounded good on paper, but what the training camp effectively did was beat it out of us."

Kim drove back to Springfield to stay with Harry and Mary Howard. The cyclists checked into the South Branch Hotel, a Civil War mansion ordinarily used as a Hebrew language camp.

Most of the riders complained privately of the pressure they were under. Waldteufel had been selected as an alternate on the previous Olympic team but stayed home in Mill Valley, California. He wanted to make sure he made the traveling squad this time. "Whittling the team down from 12 to eight introduced a real needle," he said. Howard, however, felt relaxed. "I used the camp to unwind," he said. "I had no doubt that I was on the team. Allis was under pressure, though. He had made two Olympic teams already and was real close to making this one. But he never was a sprinter and the races were decided in a sprint. He was really working hard to make the team again."

The riders traveled to weekend races, which they dominated

to impress Seubert. "Almost every race we rode," Waldteufel said, "the 12 of us just took off."

Their itinerary included the Gotham Cup, a 50-mile race in Allentown, Pennsylvania, which Howard won. Another race was the 50-mile Tour of Nutley, a criterium in northern New Jersey, where Howard's competitive spirit overcame him and taught Stetina a lesson in racing mentality.

"At the training camp, I spent a lot of time truing wheels for the riders," Stetina recalled. Making wheels true is a routine task that involves using a spoke wrench to adjust the tension of the spokes for each wheel, so it rolls straight and round. Spokes lose their proper tension when the wheel strikes a hole or strains under torque from hard turns at speed. "John had asked what I should pay him for truing his wheels and I told him not to pass me in Nutley.

"In the Tour of Nutley, I was in a long sprint against Ron Skarin at the front of the peloton. We had our heads down, really going for it. We blocked out everybody else. It was like we were in a two-up race. Near the line, I started to pull ahead. I thought I had it. Then, wham! John whipped past the two of us to win. After we coasted past the finish, I asked him about his promise to let me win Nutley. He laughed and said he didn't realize it was me."

A pecking order naturally evolved among the riders in the training camp. Seubert tentatively selected three of the four team time trial riders: Howard, Ball, and Skarin, which left one berth open. Allis and Kelly were tentative picks for the individual road race of 200 kilometers (125 miles). Two berths remained open on that team.

Schneider, the revelation of the Lake Luzerne Olympic trials, had slipped in the ranking. Seubert told him he likely would be cut after the final selection race, the 120-mile national road racing championship in Milwaukee on August 6. Results there would determine the final team. Schneider made up his mind to ride the race of his life. But so did everyone else.

The race was 30 laps of a four-mile course through Milwaukee neighborhoods. "The pack was rolling fast all day," Stetina said. "It was really unusual for a field of more than 50 riders to take turns pulling at the front before going to the back to rest. But it was the final selection race to see who was going to make it to the Olympics."

In the second half of the race, down the swift descent to the lakefront, a tired rider misjudged a turn and about a dozen riders crashed. "It happened suddenly," Stetina said. "It was like a drunken driver just plowed into us. All these guys went down left and right. I barely squeaked through and escaped. But Tim Kelly crashed badly. We were going faster than 40 MPH. He slid a long way on the pavement and lost a lot of flesh. It was the worst luck. That crash cost him a chance at riding in the Olympics."

With two laps to go, Howard attacked up the hill and opened a dangerous gap. "It was a good move," Stetina observed. "Dennis Deppe, Allis, and I tried to bridge up to him, but we couldn't. John was gone. But we worked together and caught him at the end of the lap, just as officials were ringing the bell for the last lap. He was spent from riding solo. We thought we were going to drop him. He was just hanging on. Sometimes I really thought John was a bad tactician. And then he would do something that would make me look like an idiot. Later, I learned that it is difficult to be clever when everyone is keying off you."

Stetina, who prided himself on the endless practice he had devoted to his sprint, felt confident that he would win the national championship that day. "I took off with about 350 yards left and opened a good lead," Stetina said. They had been racing for four and half hours. Stetina could smell victory.

"I was standing up out of the saddle and was pulling away when my legs turned to molasses. It was like I was coasting all of a sudden. I was stunned that I got so tired so fast. It was like someone disconnected my legs. I had never raced that far before. This was a new experience."

Howard, close behind, rallied. He lifted off his saddle and stood on the pedals as he came off Stetina's rear wheel and drew even on the right, close to spectators lining the edge of the road. Schneider moved up and caught Stetina's rear wheel. Stetina spun in the saddle as best he could. In the last yards, Howard surged ahead to win by six inches. Stetina was second, Schneider third, Deppe fourth, Allis fifth, and Ball sixth.

Afterward, Seubert reconsidered Schneider's performances and took in the events of the past two months. Finally he announced that Stetina would join Howard, Ball, and Skarin in the team time trial. Allis was selected for the individual road race to make his third Olympic team. Others picked for the road team were Waldteufel, Mowen, and Schneider.

"We had a very good time trial team," Howard said. "Rick Ball and I felt certain our team was ready to win a medal."

Chapter 5

"We have only the strength of a great ideal."
—Avery Brundage, President,
International Olympic
Committee

The route to the Munich Olympics next went south along Lake Michigan to Chicago, where the Schwinn Bicycle Company presented new Paramounts to the Olympic cycling road and track team members. In addition to the eight road team riders, 10 others had been selected at the track trials in San Jose. The 4,000-meter (2.5-mile) pursuit team included veterans Dave Chauner and John Vande Velde. "All the bikes were lined up in a presentation ceremony," Howard said. "The frames were sky blue. Each bike had our name painted on the top tube."

"We couldn't afford for me to fly to the Olympics," Kim said. "I had to stay home and watch them on television. There wasn't much cycling shown then, either. We had to get as many people as we could to sign a petition that we sent to ABC Television, asking for them to show the cycling track and road events on TV."

For making the Olympic team, Howard was issued orders from Fort MacArthur authorizing him to travel with others on the team to Munich. He and his 17 cycling teammates and five support staff soon flew to Washington, D.C. They joined the rest of the 342 men and 89 women athletes making up the largest team the United States had ever sent to the Olympics. In Washington they underwent perfunctory physical exams, posed for portrait photos, and received their official Olympic clothing, which they would wear in the opening ceremony before 80,000 spectators in Olympic Stadium at the XX Olympiad, August 26 to September 11.

The Munich Olympics would change the Olympic Games forever. When Baron Pierre de Coubertain, the French educator, had worked to revive the Olympics in Athens in 1896, he hoped that the Olympic Games would foster better international understanding, especially among youth. Unfortunately, Coubertain witnessed the extravagant abuse of his intentions with the German militarism that permeated the 1936 Berlin Olympics. He died the following year at age 74. Then World War II doused the Olympic flame for 12 years. When the Olympics resumed in 1948, Germany was divided in two. The 1972 Munich Olympics in West Germany were a $650 million stage to host the biggest Olympics ever and to erase the memories of a painful past.

Howard and the other U.S. cyclists roomed on the third floor of a coliseum-sized condominium that faced a courtyard. "We used to shoulder our bikes and run up and down the steps because that was faster than waiting for the elevator," he said. "Out on rides, we pedaled through the Olympic Village and went through the city of Munich pretty quickly, then rode on roads up the Bavarian Alps. We passed the water course that was built for the kayak events. The views up in the Alps were stunning."

Schneider grew to know Howard over the summer. They traveled to many of the same races and competed as rivals. "Most of the time John was laid back, easygoing," Schneider observed. "But he became really intense around race time. Sometimes after we left the hotel for a race, he suddenly would start tearing through his bag, worried that he had left behind a wrench to adjust his seat height, or his helmet, or because he thought he had left water bottles back in the hotel. And once we got going in the race, he was very aggressive, always forcing the pace."

Off the bike, Schneider saw that Howard was relaxed. "John was interesting because he was an art major. I had the feeling that there was another side of him, but it was undeveloped. Cycling requires such a big commitment in order to succeed. But I could see that John was quite creative. Some of that shows in his racing."

One by one, in the five cycling track events that preceded the road races, U.S. riders finished way out of the medals. John Vande Velde's experiences were characteristic of the way events were unfolding for the team. He had expected a top-five place in the 4,000-meter individual pursuit, only to finish 12th. Three days later in the team pursuit, Vande Velde's squad, with Chauner, was 17th.

Howard trained with the road team, spending considerable time with Stetina, Ball, and Skarin to get their pace line working in smooth harmony. Skarin, 20 years old, was more suited to road racing, with a fast sprint that would win many criteriums in his career. But he was versatile and worked well in a precision pace line to help keep the speed rolling fast.

Soon after they arrived in Munich, Howard and the other road riders entered a 50-mile criterium in a Munich suburb, around a circuit that included a stretch of cobblestones every lap. "I finished seventh," Howard said. "That showed I was ready. I was confident."

Stetina, however, was feeling the strain of a long, hard season. "With all the training and racing and traveling we did to make the team, I felt like I was burned toast in Munich," he said. "I was so overtrained that I needed a long warm-up to race."

Allis felt the same. "When you take into consideration the racing we had to do to qualify for the Olympic trials, then the Olympic trials races, followed by the post-trials races, the three-week training camp—which was a contest to see who survived the cuts—and the national championship road race, riders on the team were starting to burn out. I know it really got to me by the time we arrived in Munich. I left my best rides back on the East Coast."

At 4:30 a.m. on September 5, the 11th day of the Games and the day the team time trial was scheduled, Howard awoke abruptly. "I heard gunshots across the courtyard," he said. "At first, people were saying, 'Stay down! Terrorists have broken in!' There was confusion all morning. Helicopters were going back and forth. Every five minutes, there was another new rumor."

Eight Palestinian terrorists had broken into the Olympic Village and made their way to the dormitory of the Israeli wrestlers. Two Israelis were shot fatally in their room. Nine others were taken prisoner. Terrorists who said they were from the Black September group brandished automatic rifles and dropped papers to the street below demanding the release of more than 200 Palestinian prisoners held in Israel. The terrorists also demanded safe conduct by helicopters to Munich airport, with their hostages, and planes to take them to three destinations in the Arab world.

While negotiations went on fitfully that day, television cameras showed an armed terrorist, a ski mask over his head, guarding the cement balcony of the captured Israeli dormitory. That image became the haunting symbol of the Munich Olympics.

Around midnight, terrorists and hostages were flown by helicopter 20 miles away to Fürstenfeldbruk Air Base where a jet airliner was ready. West German sharpshooters killed three terrorists and a firefight broke out. Hand grenades exploded, killing all nine Israeli hostages as well as two more terrorists and a Munich police officer. Three surviving Palestinians were captured.

For 36 hours, the Olympic Games were suspended—for the first time in modern history. The next morning, September 6, a

Wednesday, the cycling team joined 80,000 athletes, support staff, and others who packed into the Olympic Stadium for a mass memorial service on the track infield. Surviving Israeli athletes wore *yarmulkes* bearing the Olympic symbol of five interlocking rings. The band that had been playing the national anthem of the gold medalists in the preceding days played the Funeral March from Beethoven's "Eroica." Requests to halt the Games poured into the International Olympic Committee office from all parts of the globe. "People everywhere in the Olympic Village were arguing about whether we should continue," Schneider said.

After the memorial service concluded, Avery Brundage, the autocratic IOC president and the most powerful figure in the history of international sports, stepped up to the microphone to address the audience. He was 84 years old and in his last days at the helm of IOC. "The Games must go on," he said to thunderous applause. "We cannot allow a handful of terrorists to destroy this nucleus of international cooperation and good will we have in the Olympic movement." He ordered that the Olympic flag and all the 126 participating nations' flags fly at half-mast, and that the Games extend for one day longer than scheduled. "We have only the strength of a great ideal," he said.

Later that same day, the Israelis put their dead on board an El Al jet that took them home on the eve of Rosh Hashanah, the Jewish New Year.

Howard, Ball, Skarin, and Stetina lined up as one of the 35 teams that went off at two-minute intervals in the 100-kilometer team time trial. The Games went on.

"It was really weird," Howard said. "You devote all this time— months and years—and energy concentrating on the Olympics, to make the team and then be ready for that one day. What the terrorists did was absolutely awful. When something like that happens, it just blows your mind. But the Games continued. We were there to do our best. I wanted very badly to win a medal."

On a humid afternoon under a glaring sun, the four-rider team mounted their road bikes and dashed away after the starter's command. Stetina soon found their speed to be nearly overwhelming. "I started hurting early. It was a course with long, rolling grades. Up every one I was having a tough time."

Howard felt strong, and the performances of Ball and Skarin encouraged him to make their ride count. "We had worked out a drill in which we each would take a turn at the front, pulling the others for about 200 meters, about 10 to 12 seconds, then swing out and drop neatly to the back," Howard said. "I was taking double and triple pulls. I was so hot that I was on fire. I was so intensely ready for the Olympics."

Stetina tried to recover so he could make a contribution later. "I sat at the back until the last quarter, when I started to pull hard," he said. "I got so tired and was hurting so bad that I couldn't take my left hand off the handlebar to reach the downtube to shift my front derailleur. I was ready to quit cycling altogether. That team time trial was one of the worst experiences I have had on a bicycle. If I had dropped off the back then, I would have just quit the sport. It was a very hard two hours."

They finished in 2:17:24.5 for 15th place, six minutes down from the Soviet team that won the gold medal.

"After the race, officials who followed our team in a car pulled me aside and ordered me to report to the dope control with the riders of the top three teams," Howard said. "I was the only one on our team who had to take the dope test. I thought, 'Why me?' By the time we finished the time trial, I felt wrecked."

Howard passed his urinalysis. But one of the Dutch riders, Aad van den Hoek, on the third-place team, tested positive, which disqualified the Dutch team.

Although the U.S. team finished out of the medals, Howard, Ball, Stetina, and Skarin were consoled by a new national 100-kilometer team time trial record. They shattered the existing national record by six and a half minutes.

Ordinarily there would have been a day of rest between the team time trial and the 182-kilometer (114-mile) road race, but the schedule of events was jumbled and the road race took place the next day. Coaches picked Howard to take the place of Keith Mowen. "John was clearly our most competitive road racer," Schneider said. "Mowen had sinus trouble and felt that Howard could ride better than he could." Howard joined Schneider, Allis, and Waldteufel in the road race. "It was a dispirited race," Howard said. "I felt kind of empty after what had gone on at that point. The Olympics weren't as intriguing to me any more."

Schneider held a similar view. "I thought it was silly to continue. What allows you to be competitive in the first place is a lousy perspective on life. To be a world-class competitor, you convince yourself that this is the most important thing to do in life. The massacre of the Israelis abruptly brought into perspective that these were the Olympic Games, and games sometimes are silly."

Nevertheless, Schneider and Howard were among the 163 riders from 48 countries who lined up for the road race. "It was a very demanding course," Schneider said. "We went around the course six times. It dropped to a river basin, then we had a long hill to ride up. The hill was really hard, especially at the speed we went. On the first lap, Waldteufel crashed in front of me and I crashed right over him. By the time we got up, I had to chase alone. It took me a whole lap to catch the peloton, but I detached off the back at the top from all the effort I had spent chasing on my own. That ended my race."

Howard and Allis rode much of the race at the front. They watched one of the pre-race favorites, Freddy Maertens of Belgium, being shadowed by Dutchman Cees Priem. Because the Dutch had forfeited their medal in the team time trial, they were riding defensively to win a medal in the road race. The team worked to protect their best rider, Hennie Kuiper. Every time Maertens made a move to dash off the front and get a breakaway going, Priem was snugly drafting on his rear wheel and refused to come around and take a turn pulling Maertens. After a couple of hours of this, Maertens grew so frustrated that he tried to punch Priem in the face. Priem later explained, "We worked for Hennie because he is one of the nicest blokes around."

In the closing 25 miles, Howard and Allis, who lacked the team support that the Dutch were exhibiting, were near the front of the peloton when the decisive attack took place. "I saw a French rider go, then several others, and Hennie Kuiper made his move," Howard said. "I saw it as an important opportunity, but I just wasn't in the race mentally anymore. The breakaway group went up the road and they were gone. I blew it."

Kuiper was on the Dutch team time trial squad that was disqualified, but he made up for the team's disappointment in the road race. He fled from the breakaway and finished solo to win the gold medal in 4 hours, 14 minutes, 37 seconds. Howard finished 61st, with Allis right behind, in the peloton, two minutes later.

After the Olympic Games concluded, Vande Velde elected to remain in Europe. He took out a professional license and bought a car which he and his wife, Joan, drove to Rotterdam, Holland. He joined Jack Simes to ride in criterium races and prepare for indoor track six-day events they would ride in as a team.

Howard flew home to Springfield to unwind and spend time with his wife and parents. He still had open temporary orders from the army, without anything assigned.

Howard then received a telephone call inviting him and Kim

to northern California to compete in the four-day Italian Swiss Colony 100, named for an ambitious series of 100 assaults on national time trial records. Heublein, Inc., had put up $20,000 to fund four days of competition—a cheap date in sports promotions. ABL officials authorized a prize list of $6,200 in gift certificates, which was regarded as attractive. George Draper, who covered the event for *Sports Illustrated*, wrote, "U.S. amateur bicycle racing, a sport with the financial brakes on despite the bike boom, finally started freewheeling."

The race Heublein sponsored provided a stimulating format for a few dozen of the top riders who were invited to compete against the best. John and Kim Howard flew to San Francisco and made their way west to Asti, 85 miles north, in Alexander Valley, where lush vineyards shared the rolling hills with plum orchards.

Riders converged on Asti for the first comprehensive time trials ever held in the United States. Some of the records on the ABL books, like that for the mile—established in 1914—even pre-dated the ABL, which was founded in 1921. With Heublein's financial blessing, top riders, including Howard and three other Olympians, were invited to challenge the records and rewrite the ABL record books. The main event of the competition series was the individual 25-mile time trial, a three-way duel between Howard, Rick Ball, and Mike Neel. The existing record was 58 minutes and 8 seconds, which Bill Kund of Riverside, California, had set in 1965. Over the preceding two seasons, Ball and Neel had been the only riders to beat Howard racing against the clock. A race involving these three riders was a likely prescription for a new national mark at a popular time trial distance.

Neel was back from a season of racing in France. Four years younger than Howard, Neel was a risk-taker. It had cost him a likely berth on the Olympic team. "I wish I had concentrated on the Munich Olympics like John did," Neel recalled and paused in reflection. "But we're different people. I went to France with $100, learned to speak French there, and stayed for half a year."

The itinerant life of a bicycle racer appealed to Neel's free spirit. He passed up high school to work racehorses at Golden Gate Fields Track. "I started as a walker of horses, walking them after workouts. I cleaned stalls, put in fresh hay. After a while I worked my way up to become a groom, and then later I started training horses. Eventually I was training 12 horses. Sometimes I left the track to travel. I've hitchhiked from Berkeley down to Mexico, all the way to the end, to the Guatemala border, then back."

His introduction to cycling was accidental. A new Raleigh racing bicycle caught his eye at Pete Rich's store. Neel made a partial payment and rode the bike out of the shop. He stopped 100 miles later, in Mendicino. "I spent the night sleeping under a tree, and pedaled back the next day. I liked riding. My first race was a criterium in Sacramento. I won $200 in prizes and thought that racing a bicycle was easier than training horses. Going to races was like hitchhiking with a bicycle."

When Howard competed in spring Olympic trials qualifier racers, Neel went to Grenoble, France, to join Bay-area cyclists Owen Mulholland and Joe Harvin, who were struggling to break into French racing. Grenoble, at the base of the Alps in southeastern France, had a rigorous and busy racing calendar.

"Joe and I lived in a house we shared with another couple," Mulholland said. "There was barely enough hot water for one person to bathe daily. We weren't living a life of luxury. The racing was real hard—French riders went faster than we were accustomed to, and the courses were hilly and tough. Joe and I rode for Association Sportif Grenoble, a local club. Neel arrived in the spring, a couple of months after we had been there, and with his sharp sprint he won his first race, a criterium in Grenoble. He also finished in the top three in his next few races. Those results were very important. They earned him an invitation to join a sponsored club, Pont de Claix. They provided him with a racing bike, a Peugeot, an apartment, and a small allowance."

One-day races were important, but moving up in the sport meant performing well in stage races. An attractive international stage race that would give a promising rider like Neel important visibility was the Tour of Britain Milk Race, which covered 1,100 miles in 12 days. No U.S. rider had ever been in it, but Neel managed to talk his way onto a squad of promising hopefuls from English provinces, and Scotland, Canada, and France. They were hardy individuals, whose aspirations in some cases exceeded their abilities. The rest of the peloton were national teams from England, Poland, Belgium, Italy, and Sweden.

Neel's Tour of Britain started disastrously. On the first day, only a few miles after the start in the south seacoast town of Brighton, he was knocked down in a crash that involved about 50 of the 69 starters. (Ten teams of seven riders each, with the Polish team one rider short in a chivalrous tribute to a teammate who had been killed in a race accident in the previous Tour of Britain.)

Neel's front tire burst in the crash, so he took a wheel change from a support vehicle and chased gamely along. The fall, however, had cracked the frame near the headtube where the handlebars fit. Neel kept an eye on the crack as he pedaled and succeeded in catching other riders. Approaching a set of railroad tracks that crossed the road, the group spread out to take the tracks individually and get back into their pace line on the other side. When Neel touched his brakes to slow for the tracks, his cracked frame snapped apart and catapulted him over the handlebars. He landed hard on the cement. The other riders sped away without a glance back.

He got back up and discovered his frame was broken and his front tire had blown out. An ambulance crew hurried over to swab his cuts and scrapes and cover them with bandages. Still game, Neel took a replacement bike from a support vehicle. The bike was a bad fit. His right shoe wouldn't slide properly into the steel toe clip, which hampered his pedaling and deprived him of some power. But he kept on. Miles later, he overtook another small group and joined their pace line. One of the riders, too tired to realize what he was doing, finished a turn at the front and, as he dropped back, chopped across the path of Neel's front wheel. Neel was knocked over for his third crash, and third front-tire blowout, in 30 miles.

After another wheel change, Neel was left to struggle alone— for 70 miles. He fell so far behind the peloton that race officials opened the roads to traffic, which further slowed him. He finished the race exhausted, his arms and legs cut and scraped and bruised, an hour and a minute behind the winner. He was dead last.

Nor did his luck improve. By the fifth day, he was so ill with a murderous cold that he finally quit. Riders and officials who saw Neel lagging behind were left wondering if cyclists from the United States were victims of a soft life that kept them from performing well in international stage races.

Neel dragged back to Grenoble. Despite hardships, he recovered and won another race, in nearby Chambery. Over the season, he improved significantly, a result of racing against Frenchmen with thighs as hard as wine casks. "Mike heard about the Heublein races that were going to be held in Asti," Mulholland said. "Joe Harvin and I certainly didn't get an invitation, but Mike did. He left France in time for the races in Asti."

One of the few invited riders who didn't make the trip was Wayne Stetina, enrolled as a freshman at Indiana University. Neel took his place in the four-rider 100-kilometer team time trial with

Howard, Ball, and Skarin. The foursome finished in a drizzle around a rectangular course that was almost six miles a lap. Their pace line work was a smooth rotation appreciated by those who watched from the sidelines. The foursome's time was 2:18:43, short of the 2:17:24 that the team with Stetina had ridden in Munich. But ABL officials, sensitive to the importance of good press and with *Sports Illustrated* represented, declared the time to be the new national record. They hailed it as a quantum improvement over the 2:24:00 that U.S. riders had ridden in the 1960 Rome Olympics, in which the American squad finished 11th.

Howard, Neel, Ball, and Skarin finished the time trial with mud splattered on their faces, legs, and arms. Their wool jerseys and black wool shorts were muddy and dripping wet. But that didn't dampen their spirits.

Nearly every rider seemed to get credit for a new national record over the four days, especially with so many distances and combinations of single riders, two-man teams, four-man teams, and tandems. The mile record of 2 minutes, 8 seconds, set in 1914 by Berthold Baker in Grant City, New York, was improved by Harry (Skip) Cutting of Riverside, California. Cutting, a barrel-chested sprinter and veteran of the Tokyo and Mexico City Olympics, lowered the mark to 2:02.6.

Over the four days, the main event was the 25-mile individual time trial against Howard, Neel, and Ball. A 25-mile time trial on a bicycle is comparable to the mile for track runners—both events combine hard speed and brute stamina. The cyclists, still in the era of pedaling road bicycles in time trials, rode with their backs flattened over the top tube and handlebars to cut wind resistance.

One by one, the three went off at one-minute intervals. Ball, who joked to friends that he sprinted like a turtle and climbed up hills like a snail, made time trials his specialty. He was the eldest of the three and the most focused on this race. In a *Northeast Cycle News* interview, he said he alternated between being a mild-mannered Clark Kent who worked as a math teaching assistant at the University of Wisconsin during the week, and Super-Racer at the weekends. As Super-Racer, he rode like a demon, jazzed up on adrenaline and endorphins.

The disparate lives inspired him to consider writing a comic strip. "The thing that bicycle racing has to recommend itself to comics is lots of villains," he said. "Can you see it? Snively Wheelsuck, Cannibal Crashalot, Badguy Bentspoke, Freewheelin' Freddie, Gerry Gear, and our hero, Neil Neverflat."

In the 25-mile time trial, Rick Ball was riding like a time that put him even with Howard halfway through the race. Trailing slightly, Neel remained within striking distance.

The race on closed roads that wound through Alexander Valley's lush countryside was remarkable for being a national sports event so quiet that none of the action kept spectators from listening to the chirping of birds. In this remote setting, the only people there were relatives of the racers. Fewer than 100 witnessed the epic duel. As Howard approached the end of his fourth lap, with some two miles remaining, his eyes staring fiercely at the pavement ahead, Kim broke the silence to yell, "You're 50 seconds ahead!"

But Howard misunderstood. He thought he was 50 seconds behind. He dug deeper and hammered the pedals harder to the finish. To his surprise, he crossed the line and learned he had toppled Kund's record by nearly three minutes to win in 55:16.

Ball finished in 56:43.1. He kept going to make it one full hour for a new ABL record of 26.52 miles.

Neel was 11 seconds short of Kund's 58:08.

Howard thus set two national records in September.

The photo of Howard taken during his national 25-mile record ride was published in *Sports Illustrated*. He was also written up in a feature for school children nationwide in *Read* magazine, which made him the cover story.

"John Howard is a champion athlete, but you've never heard about him," *Read* said. "Why? He's a bicycle racer. Americans pay about as much attention to bike racing as to the annual Tiddlywinks Tournament."

But when his photo was published in a three-page *Sports Illustrated* account, army brass suddenly paid a lot of attention to PFC Howard. He hadn't been in his army uniform since he had left Fort MacArthur in early July for the Olympic trials. He was also unaccounted for.

"I was at home when I received a telephone call from Colonel Montgomery at the Pentagon, telling me I was AWOL," Howard said, acknowledging the seriousness of the charge. "Colonel Montgomery reamed me out every which way over the telephone and told me I had exactly 24 hours to report to Fort Polk, Louisiana. He ordered me there by sundown the next day. I thought that maybe he was going to try to get me court-martialed."

Howard put on his army uniform, packed his bicycle and extra clothes, and drove to Fort Polk. He expected the worst. By then the Vietnam War was winding down and the Pentagon had begun bringing whole units back to the United States. Troops who returned from Vietnam with a year or less remaining in their active duty were eligible for release back to civilian life. Howard's two-year enlistment was nearing its end. Discipline for being AWOL would not mean being issued orders for Vietnam, but Howard was anxious about having to account for where he had been in the month since the Munich Olympics concluded.

"When I arrived at Fort Polk, I thought I would be greeted by the Military Police. Instead, everybody treated me like I was a hero. The Sergeant Major on duty said he was glad to meet somebody who had competed in the Munich Olympics. When I checked in with the base CO, I realized that he hadn't been briefed by Colonel Montgomery. I showed the CO my letter from General Westmoreland and he said he was glad to see me. The CO asked what I would like to do next.

"I sort of scratched my chin and said, 'Well, there is a bike race in New Orleans this weekend.' So I was given a pass to go to New Orleans for the weekend to race."

Howard drove to New Orleans for La Boucherie Grand Prix, a popular 35-mile criterium on narrow streets around the French Quarter. "The race was fast, and there were six premes, all for dinner for two in fancy restaurants," Howard said. "I had broken away and won all the premes. But in the closing laps, I was caught. When we sprinted for the finish, Montgomery beat me to win. Afterward, I gave all my premes away to friends."

PFC Howard reported for duty on Monday morning. His uncanny good fortune in the army still had some play left. "They still didn't know what to do with me at Fort Polk. I pointed out to my CO that I hadn't used any of my annual vacation time. We checked my records and they showed I still had 30 days of annual leave. So the CO gave me the whole month of October off."

Howard drove back to Springfield. After making telephone calls, he was on another informal U.S. team to return to the Tour of Mexico. Unlike other countries, particularly in Europe, the United States still lacked a designated national cycling team selected by the governing body's officials to represent the United States in international stage races. But the top U.S. riders knew one another and went ahead making their own arrangements. As Howard and Kim had done the previous year, they drove west for three days to Carmel, where Kim stayed as a guest of the Farrier family in their home overlooking Monterrey Bay. Howard and

Neel flew with Waldteufel to Mexico City, where they joined Allis and two others to compete in the Tour of Mexico.

"At the beginning, I rode well," Howard said. "But, just like the year before, I wound up getting sick and had to drop out by the end of the first week. So did everybody else, except Allis. He was the only one to finish the race."

Afterward, it was back to northern California for another long drive back to Springfield. He and Kim finished his 30 days of leave there. Howard reported back to Fort Polk for the first of November. By then he was such a short-timer that he could, as the army expression went, sit on a dime and his feet wouldn't touch the ground. "I had only a month to complete my enlistment, so I was given an early-out," he said. "By the first week in November, I was a civilian again."

Yet, like others who long to get out of the military and finally see that day arrive, Howard was then confronted with a decision about what to do next. He was eligible for the G.I. Bill of Rights, which entitled him to college expenses, but campus life was tepid compared to heading off to a far-flung venue to race and push his physical limits. Cycling remained his passion, and he felt he still hadn't reached his potential.

Ray Florman recalled that on numerous cross-country trips in Florman's van, Howard used to proclaim his goal was to avoid a 9 to 5 job that would reduce him to being a weekend-warrior athlete. But there still was no way a cyclist could support himself by racing in the United States. When it looked as if Howard was stymied, he received a telephone call that set him up with the opportunity to stay active in American cycling and to keep pushing his limits.

"I had no idea what I wanted to do," Howard admitted. "Shortly after I went back to Springfield, my brother called. He had a job in Austin, Texas, restoring cars. David said there was a big bicycle race called the Octoberfest coming up in New Braunfels, just outside of Austin, in the Texas hill country. David said the promoter wanted me to come out and ride the race. I said, 'Yeah!'

"When Kim and I drove out to Austin and met the promoter, he said he wanted me to ride a new Swedish bicycle called the Monarch Crescent. He gave me one. It had a bright orange frame that matched our VW Superbeetle. The race was three stages over a weekend. I won two of the stages and finished well up in the third to win the overall race."

Although the United States lagged behind countries on the

other side of the Atlantic in Olympic and professional bicycle racing, the burgeoning market for lightweight and racing bicycles made America a highly attractive country to foreign bicycle manufacturers. One importer, Mel Pinto, a Moroccan expatriate who had settled in Washington, D.C., had a thriving dealership of Gitane bicycles, made in France. "I was selling bikes when they were still on the high seas on their way to my warehouse," he said.

Another French manufacturer selling out of inventory was Peugeot. England's Raleigh Bicycles was topping 500,000 bicycles sold that year to their former colony. Italian bicycle makers such as Atala and Cinelli were growing rich selling to America. The management of Sweden's Monarch Crescent Bicycles wanted to get in on the action. Their distributorship in Houston, Peden Equipment Company, was looking for a sales representative who knew the sport and was recognized in it. Howard was in the right place at the right time.

In the early 1970s, the company opened five distributorships in North America (one in Vancouver, British Columbia, and the other four in the United States), under the name Monarch Crescent Bicycles. In Sweden the company was called Monarch, with the name on the frame downtube. The company advertised that the four Pettersson Brothers had ridden to a silver medal in the Mexico City Olympics team time trial on Monarchs. But the name used in North American distribution became Crescent.

"After I won the Octoberfest, I was offered a job to represent Monarch Crescent Bicycles as a sales rep and work the retail outlet in Houston," Howard said. "They wanted me to keep training and racing. I was to be paid a salary, plus a commission on sales. It was a great opportunity."

An added benefit was Houston's mild winter, which would allow more time for training. Howard still had limits to push.

Chapter 6

"Things are in the saddle,
And ride mankind."
—Ralph Waldo Emerson,
Ode to W.H. Channing.

When John and Kim Howard moved to Houston, the biggest city in the South and Southwest, its 1.2 million population was growing daily. Howard and his wife moved into an apartment near downtown Houston, on Marshall Street. "We lived in the Montrose area, Houston's artsy community, where writers and artists lived," he said. "Of course, living near downtown Houston made it difficult to get out to train conveniently. But Memorial Park and Herman Brown Park were nearby. When I didn't have time for a long ride, I rode over to one of the parks to do some fast laps and work on my speed."

Months after the Howards relocated to Texas, Middle Eastern countries embargoed oil exports to the United States, forcing the price of oil to quadruple in 90 days. The price of gasoline in America shot up to over a dollar a gallon. Shortages developed nationwide and cars lined up around the block to get to local service stations. That heightened the importance of Texas oil, which led to a gush of wealth for Houston.

The quadrupled price of oil added emphasis to alternative energy sources. Cycling's popularity gushed like Texas oil. Bicycle sales soared to 15.2 million in 1973, the all-time industry high in the United States (considerably greater than the 10.2 million sold annually from 1988 to 1992). The number of racers registered with the ABL rose 70 percent over the previous year to top 8,600.

For American cycling, 1973 was a banner year. Barbara and Robert George, recognizing the national importance of their tabloid, changed its name from *Northeast Bicycle News* to *Cyclenews*. The ABL sent copies to licensed riders to spread information and help American cycling progress from its provincial limitations to national scope. Two other publications were introduced. One was

Bike World, a monthly magazine founded as a companion publication for *Runner's World*, a monthly magazine that was riding high on the wave of running's popularity. The other new publication was *Competitive Cycling*, a tabloid. Publisher Jim McFadden lived in Santa Monica, California, and set *Competitive Cycling's* frequently irreverent tone by telling his readers that his office was in Crazy Woman Lodge. He was Louisiana's state road champion and a veteran of the 1972 Olympic trials. His cycling contacts helped him assemble a network of correspondents to submit race reports, personality profiles, and photos.

In April, ABL officials announced the first-ever national road and track cycling teams. The seven road riders who were picked were familiar names: Howard, John Allis, Rick Ball, Mike Neel, Ron Skarin, and Flip Waldteufel. The seven track riders included Dave Chauner. With the ABL's annual budget of $38,500, however, being named to the national team still meant paying for much of the 30,000 miles a year they traveled to races.

It was still essential for riders to have outside sources of income. Howard's job with Monarch Crescent bicycles gave him a steady paycheck, with fringe benefits like health care, and the job allowed flexibility to train and commute to races.

"My job was basically working public relations," he explained. "I traveled around the Midwest in a white company van. It gave me the opportunity to visit friends in the industry. Other foreign bike companies already had a good foothold in the country—Raleigh, Gitane, Peugeot, and Atala. Monarch Crescent was trying to get in, too.

"We offered five models, and the racing model was excellent, as good as any of the best available. But the Swedes painted every bike an ugly orange. They made good, solid, workhorse bikes. But the pretty, artsy bikes were coming into the United States. They were all made beautifully and caught the eye. We had trouble selling Monarch Crescents when those other bicycles were available."

Part of being in retail cycling involved attending the annual New York bicycle show, the industry's major event, held in February to introduce the next year's product line of bicycles, components, clothing, and other related goods. At the bike show, Howard renewed his acquaintance with Fred Kuhn. Kuhn was the proprietor of a shop—located down an alley near downtown Princeton, New Jersey, and operating under the name of a long-gone founder—that was, in the early 1970s, the unlikely headquarters of one of the country's best teams.

ABL officials took pride in announcing their official national cycling team, but Kuhn quietly went about assembling his own "dream team." It included some of the ABL selections, which he likely took as confirmation of his own taste. He was a stubborn man, full of contradictions. "Fred would go to great lengths to avoid selling equipment, like Campagnolo derailleurs or racing tires that were in short supply, so he could give them to his riders," Howard said. Kuhn, highly protective of riders on his team, never stopped smoking cigarettes when talking to them. "You put up with Fred," Howard said. "If he didn't like you, he would let you know."

Kuhn never lavished praise on anyone, but he shopped around for riders with the guts and talent he admired, and got what he wanted. Kuhn's team was the Century Road Club of America, designated by the acronym CRC of A.

Raleigh Industries opened a warehouse in Secaucus, not far from Princeton, to take shipments of bicycles from the United Kingdom to be sold in North America. The warehouse was where Raleigh's manager of product design for North America, Karl Barton, had his office. Barton was a former British national sprint champion with a rider's predisposition for spotting talent, which Raleigh encouraged in light of Barton's selling everything they could ship to Secaucus. Barton and Bill Kerns (of Raleigh's office in Boston) worked with Kuhn, a Raleigh dealer, in getting the Raleigh sponsorship for Fred's team.

"It was the first major sponsorship in this county," Allis said. "It was a $10,000 sponsorship package—not much by today's standards, but at the time it was groundbreaking. Whenever you are breaking new ground, there is always a lot of hassling, and the ABL officials could do a lot of hassling."

Allis spoke from experience. ABL officials had suspended him for three months after the Tour of California for wearing a CRC of A jersey with "Raleigh" on the front and back. Such advertising, common in Europe then, was unprecedented in America in 1972, and ABL officials sought to squelch it. The suspension, however, was a moot point as it took place over the winter when the racing season was over. Officials were begrudgingly recognizing that commercialism was inevitable.

Howard first met Kuhn during the Olympic training camp in South Branch. "Fred's shop was one of the few on the East Coast that carried racing equipment," Howard said. "His shop was a good ride, about 30 miles one way. [It] was just a little hole-in-the-wall place, but he did enough business to support his wife and three kids, who were grown up by then."

At the New York bicycle show, Kuhn saw Howard and lit up a new cigarette. "He told me, 'Kid, you're good and you ought to ride for us,' " Howard recalled. "Like that. Not a lot of compliments or promises. He had Allis on his team, Chauner, Bobby Phillips of Baltimore, and other good riders. Fred knew I was from Texas and places west, but that didn't bother him. He knew we all went to the national-level races. Fred looked highly unlikely to be a team director, but that is what he was, all right. His CRC of A team was the team to be on at that time. So I became a member."

Howard's move to Houston had coincided with a sharp rise in cycling across the Lone Star State. The number of ABL riders spiked up from 25 in 1972 to 250 in 1973. While the state lacked any cycling clubs in 1972, eight were formed in 1973. Clubs held monthly meetings, published newsletters, and put on a weekly series of training races. Texas also went from having few ABL-sanctioned races in 1972 to having 20 in 1973.

"Talent was moving to Texas, and local talent was improving," Howard said. "Races were going from the pack just rolling along until the sprint at the end, to attacks off the front and breakaways. Texas was becoming a 'happening' place."

A national-class rider who moved to Texas from southern California was John Potoschnik, an all-round rider whose work had taken him to Dallas. A member of the early Army Cycling Team, he had represented the United States at the 1970 world championships in Leicester, England, and placed a respectable 21st in the Tour of California. Potoschnik had only recently settled in Dallas when he finished second to Howard in the November Wurstfest in New Braunfels.

Englishman Peter Green moved from Toronto to Austin, bringing with him Continental racing experience. Dallas also had rising talent with David Klenk and state sprint champion Del Blundel.

As national champion, Howard was privileged to wear the Stars and Stripes jersey, but it offered no protection from deconditioning, as Howard discovered in the opening race of the 1973 season, the Texas Primavera. It was two loops of a 33.5-mile course in Texas hill country, near Austin.

"Before the Primavera I had done a big Midwest tour for Monarch Crescent," Howard said. "We drove 2,000 miles in 10 days, visiting shops and setting up accounts. It was good for business, but bad for conditioning."

Howard and Potoschnick broke clear with 13 miles remaining in the 67-mile race. They worked together in a pace line while the other 30 riders in the peloton rolled briskly. The breakaway stretched their lead to a minute and a half. With nine miles left, the road went up a long, straight hill. Potoschnick, two years older than Howard, wisely decided to take a reading of his partner's road rust and attacked.

"He dropped me," Howard said. "I struggled up the hill and watched the gap grow longer and longer. I felt worse and worse all the way up. Out alone, that far from the finish, I was going to have all I could do to keep the pack from catching me. They were definitely reeling me in toward the end. I barely held them off for second place."

Winning races was the powerful incentive that compelled Howard to train exhaustively, travel far, and race all-out. Watching Potoschnik drop him up the hill as he gasped for air made Howard determined to get back to a regular training routine.

"John's shyness and work ethic sometimes were counter-productive," Kim observed. "I overheard him say to other riders that he wasn't in very good shape because he wasn't putting in the miles. I took John aside and told him to quit talking like that. They had no way of knowing what he was doing, or not doing, unless he told them. I told John to say that he had been putting in tons of miles—500 or more a week."

The next weekend they drove to Forest, Mississippi, for the March of Dimes Criterium. "It took a whole day to drive there, but races were hard to come by then, so we drove lots," Howard said. Wayne Stetina made the commute with Mark Dayton and Gary Rybar from Bloomington, Indiana. Jim Montgomery arrived from Montgomery, Alabama. The event was 50 laps around a course of seven-tenths of a mile. Considerable handling skill was required for riders to negotiate eight turns every lap at speed, over 50 laps. Only 16 riders lined up, but many were the best from the Midwest and South, eager to battle one another for wall plaques and cycling merchandise prizes. When they arrived in town, they stayed overnight in the homes of friends, or friends of friends, to race the next morning around the downtown grid of streets.

Experienced riders like Howard, Stetina, and Montgomery forced the pace right away to avoid the demolition derby that was inevitable on such a tight course. Dayton, the younger brother of 1971 national road champion Steve Dayton, and Rybar pedaled like demons to keep up. Their speed and the uncompromising demands of the corners soon left the five riders alone.

Spectators who lined the sidewalk around the course were treated to a display of a precision pace line followed by a gap of lesser cyclists who overlapped wheels and crashed or careened into curb corners and flipped over. The race was ballet at the front and carnage in the rear.

Around the last turn, Stetina strategically led the other four up the final straight of 150 yards for the finish in front of the brick Goodyear Tire Company store. He was at top speed by the time the others swept through the turn. Not even Montgomery could summon the speed to overcome Stetina. Howard was third, followed by Dayton and then Rybar.

"When you get your ass kicked," Howard said, "you work hard so that it doesn't happen again." He and Kim drove back to Houston, and the following week he strove to regain his championship form. At the next weekend's April Fool's Criterium of 45 miles around Memorial Park, he was on his training ground and his form was coming back. In the second half of the race, he charged away from the peloton. He stayed away for a solo victory, a minute and a half clear.

While his fitness came back, Howard was further inspired by new developments across the Atlantic. Victor Kimmel of the Peden Equipment Company, which issued Howard's paychecks, was talking with company officials in Varberg, Sweden, about inviting Howard and his wife overseas for a month.

"It was a timely gesture with cycling taking off in the United States," Howard said. "The Monarch Crescent people in Sweden knew who I was and wanted to meet me. Kim wanted to make the trip to see Sweden. I wanted to go, see the country, and gain experience competing internationally. It would also be a chance to meet the famous Pettersson brothers."

Meantime, Raleigh Industries of England was marketing its line of bicycles aggressively. Raleigh introduced a major-league professional team of 20 riders who competed in the big races of Europe. Raleigh was selling 500,000 bicycles a year to the United States at that time, so they could afford to give Bill Kerns of Raleigh North America a good promotions budget to keep their name prominent. For a modest expenditure, Kerns and Karl Barton made Raleigh the title sponsor of the Tour of Louisiana in April. Sponsorship made the Raleigh Tour of Louisiana the biggest race in the South, offering $2,000 in merchandise prizes.

Raleigh also signed on as a title sponsor of the Tour of Ireland in mid-August. Company officials on both sides of the Atlantic were looking into sending the Raleigh-CRC of A team to compete in the eight-day Tour of Ireland. It would be the first time an American squad would compete in a stage race overseas—although only the eager Americans were optimistic about any real showing against riders of the United Kingdom and other countries.

Howard's victory in the April Fool's Criterium helped bolster his confidence for what lay ahead. Two weeks later, he and Kim loaded up their Superbeetle and drove to New Orleans for the Raleigh Tour of Louisiana, where 70 Category A riders, from Texas to New Jersey, converged for the weekend event. Louisiana's muggy heat was a welcome relief for those from the Northeast and Midwest, who wore shorts and short-sleeved jerseys for the first time in months. Rumors that Howard was out of shape circulated on Friday evening. As riders arrived and picked up their competition numbers and race packets, stories made the rounds that Howard was being dropped and had lost his road sprint. Howard was issued No. 1 as the defending champion, but he wasn't expected to uphold it.

Early Saturday morning the riders assembled on a road near the shore of Lake Pontchartrain for the individual 4.5-mile time trial. Howard was the first rider off, with the rest following at one-minute intervals around the flat course following the shoreline. When he sped across the finish line in 9:12, Howard served notice that he was better than ever—he had trimmed his previous winning ride on the same course by 25 seconds.

Howard's riding in all three stages squelched the pre-race rumors. He seemed to have the race locked up as the Sunday criterium of 38 miles—60 laps around a grid of downtown streets—started. Several thousand spectators turned out to line the course and watch.

Potoschnik attacked from the starter's gun, hoping to take advantage of any hesitation in the peloton to lap the field. But Howard and Dan Bir of Dayton had a lot at stake and went right after him. They linked up on the second lap, with the peloton strung out behind in a long pace line. As on the day before, the three riders out in front made a winning combination. Close behind, Montgomery led the chase. But on the fifth lap, Montgomery and another rider misjudged a turn at speed and fell, throwing more than 60 other riders into disarray. Meanwhile, the breakaway trio neatly alternated leading around the turns and caught the peloton in 15 miles. The breakaway rode through the peloton and kept going to lap them again in the final miles.

On the bell lap, spectators yelled excitedly when Howard led through the last turn, making a straight line to the finish banner. Potoschnik drafted on his rear wheel, with Bir right behind. Out of the turn, Potoschnik accelerated off Howard's rear wheel as if fired from a slingshot. Soon after came the peloton, with Montgomery beating the others to the line for fourth.

Howard had successfully defended his Tour of Louisiana championship, nearly two minutes in overall time ahead of second-place Potoschnik.

Afterward, most of the other riders prepared to follow cycling's migratory route south to Palm Beach for the eighth annual Cross-Florida Tour. John and Kim Howard drove back to Houston to prepare for their flight to Sweden.

"When we arrived in Sweden," recalled Kim, "the people who met us at the airport in Varberg suggested that they take us right away to a hotel so we could go to bed. It was the middle of the day and the sun was shining brightly. It seemed like the wrong time to talk about going to bed. But they were doing us a favor when they took us straight to the hotel. Between the time we spent flying and the eight time zones we crossed, we had a case of jet lag that I didn't realize, and it did hit us. "

After the couple rested, one of their first excursions was to visit the Monarch Crescent bicycle factory in the town of Varberg, located on Sweden's southwest coast, on the Kattegat Strait that separates Sweden and Denmark.

"Monarch Crescent's factory was incredible," Howard said. "Besides bicycles, they made motorcycles and medium-sized boats. The company president wined and dined us. After dinner, he took us on a walking tour of the town. Varberg is ancient, with old stone Viking forts on the coast. It is also a busy industrial town. Not a single person was standing around idle; everyone seemed busy, walking, riding a bicycle, or driving a car someplace."

At the factory, Howard was fitted with a new Monarch racing bicycle. Company officials introduced him to the Pettersson brothers, national heroes for having won the world championships in the 100-kilometer team time trial in 1968 and 1969. An inch taller than Howard, they were a formidable combination in team time trials. Their world titles had helped launch their professional careers on the Continent. Gösta, the spark plug of the family team, became renowned for winning the 1971 Tour of Italy.

"Erik was the brother I trained with the most when I was in Varberg," Howard said. "Tomas and Stür had recently downgraded from pro to amateur, and I rode a lot with them as well. They were very fit, as you would expect from world champions. Gösta joined us sometimes. He was an ice-cold Swede who pushed bigger gears than I ever saw anybody use before. What impressed me the most about the Pettersson brothers was the big gears they rode. Every time we hit the road, we were hammering. It was the hardest training I ever did, and it helped me later in the season."

Tomas Pettersson made a comfortable living as an amateur with Monarch sponsorship. He drove a new Mercedes equipped with a roof rack for carrying bicycles and spare wheels. He befriended Howard and Kim, and accompanied them to weekend races around southern Sweden.

"We had a good time," Howard said. "The weather was cold, really chilly, and the road conditions most often were wet, which is a combination that I hate, but we were well taken care of by the Monarch people. That smoothed things along. We raced a lot of criteriums and road races up to 80 miles on weekends. The races were a couple of miles an hour faster than in the States, and never had any lulls. The roads were never flat, either. In the middle of the week, there were usually time trials, up to 10 miles. Racing over there was definitely helping my conditioning."

Races were strenuous, and they were more tactical than in the United States. Riders competed as teams and protected their best sprinter by chasing down breakaway attempts to keep the peloton intact. Each team's designated sprinter was spared the effort of going to the front during a chase. When the finish approached, team riders alternated increasing the pace until nearly everyone was at full speed. With 200 yards left, the sprinters burst away.

"The Swedes loved John, with his curly blond hair and his blue eyes. They called him Juan Haverd. They liked Juan Haverd, but they wouldn't let him win," Kim said.

"I learned about tactics," Howard said. "The best I could do there was a string of seconds and thirds. It was obvious that I couldn't win without a team, but I consistently made top-five places. Training and racing in Sweden got me pushing bigger gears than ever. I was really flying by the time we went home. I knew I was going to win the national road championship again."

By the time the Howards returned to Houston, Fred Kuhn and John Allis had worked out arrangements with officials of Raleigh

Industries in Dublin, Ireland, to enter the Raleigh-CRC of A team in the eight-day Tour of Ireland. Ireland's national tour was one notch in prestige below the Tour of Britain. U.S. teams had tried to enter it before, but Englishman Bill Squance, the Tour of Britain race controller, felt that no American had a right to compete against Europe's elite in a stage race and dismissed ABL requests out of hand. He had only to point to Mike Neel's performance on the international composite team to justify this.

But Raleigh was a title sponsor of the Tour of Ireland, and this provided an invaluable connection for an American squad to enter the Irish national tour. The event's 10 stages covered 740 miles that would test the Americans. Riders from around the United Kingdom would work the Americans over. Race officials and the press would watch the Americans every day.

The silver lining, though, was that the tour effectively became an eight-day audition for a long-shot opportunity to earn an invitation to compete in the next year's Tour of Britain.

Howard prepared by sharpening his speed in criteriums. One of bicycle racing's unique aspects is that long-distance riders like Howard compete against basic sprinters—the equivalent of marathon runners going against quarter-milers. Such a combination is unheard of in track and field, yet it is standard practice in cycling, especially in criteriums. With the dynamic of drafting for wind protection playing a major role, criteriums of 25 to 50 miles make for an exciting mix of speed and stamina.

In the last weekend in June, Howard ventured east for some of the year's most competitive criteriums. The Travelers Insurance Company sponsored a 25-mile criterium in downtown Hartford that featured unprecedented television coverage and a generous prize list. Howard joined Neel, Allis, Dave Chauner, and more than a hundred other riders from all over the country.

The peloton even included four Frenchmen, who rode for the Gitane amateur racing team. The French bicycle manufacturer appreciated the sales of their importer Mel Pinto of Washington, D.C., so much it sent a contingent to the United States to compete in the criterium he sponsored. Gitane's riders would stay over for a few weeks to take in the big East Coast races.

The Saturday morning race was clockwise around a downtown park, with three right-angled turns and a rounded corner leading to a slight uphill final straight on each of the 37 laps. Several thousand spectators stood under the shelter of the park's tall oak trees and lined the sidewalks to watch.

Right from the starter's pistol the race was highly animated, benefiting the film crew and a national television audience, most of whom were seeing bicycle racing for the first time. Chauner and Allis attacked with Jim Ochowicz of Milwaukee and two others. They opened a dangerous lead of 400 yards as the peloton pursued. By 10 miles they had gained half a lap on the peloton, but it was too much effort too soon. Allis couldn't hold the pace and fell off the back of the breakaway. Then Chauner lost contact and the others were losing their pace-line rhythm.

Howard saw Allis come back, then watched Chauner stop pedaling, and made his own move off the front of the peloton. Gitane's Favre Remy sized up what was going on and sprinted after Howard's rear wheel. Howard and Remy teamed together in a pace line to catch the leaders in two laps and fly by. Only Ochowicz, a track racer who had recently taken to criteriums and road races, rallied to stay in the hunt. He linked with the new pair to make it a three-rider breakaway.

"The French guy wouldn't work and take a turn at the front," said Ochowicz. "John and I were doing all the pulling, and we were really riding fast, going awfully hard. We were on national-record pace. At that speed, it makes a big difference if you can get out of the wind and recover behind someone. [Remy] was getting a free ride at our expense."

Ochowicz, 21, a sturdy sprinter who had competed in the previous Pan American and Olympic Games, resented what Remy was doing and became furious as the laps went by. He loved racing and particularly relished the final 200 yards, which gave him the chance to win. In the Hartford criterium, he gave everything he had to keeping the breakaway going to make it a three-rider race for first rather than taking his chances in a mass pack sprint. But when he finished his turn towing the breakaway for 200 yards and then swung out for Howard to take over, Remy drifted back a bicycle length. Ochowicz had to take his place on Howard's rear wheel to recover for another turn at the front in the next 10 seconds. Finally, with a few laps left, he unleashed his anger at Remy.

"I started yelling at [Remy] to take a turn and pull," Ochowicz said. "The pack behind us was trying like hell to catch us. Yelling at [him] didn't work, so on the last lap I grabbed his jersey at the shoulder and told him to start working. He took a swing at me, so I took a swing at him. While we were doing this, a gap formed between us and John. I yelled at John to take off."

"Jim wanted anyone but the Frenchman to win," Howard

said. "We were down the back stretch when the fight broke out. I got out of there fast. The last turn swept around to a slight uphill finishing stretch. I had just enough time to sprint up the hill and throw my hands in the air when I crossed the finish line."

Howard's time was 56 minutes flat—a new national criterium record for 25 miles. Ochowicz easily outsprinted Remy for second. Moments later came the peloton, battling for fourth place, which Gary Campbell of Los Angeles took from Roger Young of Detroit.

The next day was the 50-mile Art Longsjo Memorial Criterium in Fitchburg, Massachusetts, a two-hour car drive away. More than 10,000 spectators turned out to watch. Some 200 riders started the race around the one-mile downtown circuit, but the fast pace reduced the contenders to 16. They sped down the slight descent leading to the finish in front of the red-brick city hall. Steve Woznick, another Pan American and Olympic Games track sprinter, won. Howard was a close fourth.

With the national road racing championship and the Tour of Ireland approaching, Howard had to get in long races for stamina. Some promoters in California were putting on road races of around 100 miles, but nothing approached what the Canadian Cycling Association offered in the third week of July. In eastern Canada, the 172-mile road race from Quebec to Montreal—the longest one-day bicycle race for amateur cyclists in the world—was to be held.

The 40th annual Quebec-to-Montreal race was regarded as a classic, a rare distinction in North America, where races came and went like flowers. This race was known even in Europe. Many Europeans flew over to compete in it because of its challenge and its luxurious prize list. Winner of the 1973 edition would drive away in a new Ford Pinto. A color television set and $6,000 in cash were to be distributed to the rest of the top finishers.

"Canadian officials were quite sophisticated about racing," Howard said. "They handed white business envelopes containing cash to the winning riders after a race. ABL officials didn't dare go up there. They left us alone when we were in Canada."

When Howard and Kim made preparations for the three-day drive to Montreal, they decided they needed to replace their VW. "The odometer had more than 85,000 miles," Howard said. "And we needed more space." They traded it in for a Datsun 610 station wagon they drove from the showroom floor to Montreal.

Once in Montreal, Howard met Allis and the other riders on the Raleigh-CRC of A team: Stanley Swaim of East Burke, Vermont, Jim Heutter of Buffalo, and Bob Fischer of New York City.

Defending champion Vicenzo Meco, an Italian who rode for Atala, arrived with a few teammates from Italy. Montreal had a large Italian population and Atala sent sponsored riders because they were exporting so many bicycles to North America. Meco had won twice in a row and was hoping to score a hat trick. He and most of the other 37 starters were still tightening their toe straps after the start when Allis accelerated away, drawing Horst Stuewe of Germany with him. Howard, Heutter, and other Raleigh-CRC of A riders went to the front of the peloton to control the chase. "We blocked for Allis," Howard said. "We slowed the pace, chased down breakaways and sat on them with the whole peloton behind us—anything to keep Allis out there, with his partner, building up a lead. I really wanted to be up there, because long one-day races were my strength, but Allis made the move, so we were doing our part as a team to help him pull it off."

Meco and his teammates didn't seem to mind the breakaway until enough miles wore on to galvanize them into chasing. But every time Meco made a move to take off, the Raleigh-CRC of A riders were on him. Meco realized he was a marked man and went back into the peloton to discuss strategy with his teammates.

By 100 miles, the church spires of Berthierville poked through the tree tops. Four hours had gone by and all that remained of the breakaway was Allis, Heutter, and Olaf Moetus of Indianapolis, with a 9-minute lead. The rest cracked under the unrelenting effort and dropped back to continue with the peloton.

After 130 miles, Allis and Heutter had the race virtually to themselves. Moetus, an excellent criterium rider, was out of his range in a race this long. Howard was free to make his move and cut loose to salvage what he could. He sprinted away, taking with him longtime rival Siggy Koch and Italian Lorenzo DiPalma as the peloton watched Meco to see what he would do.

As the race closed on Montreal, Moetus finally fizzled. He dropped off the breakaway and was caught by Howard, who went right past and dropped DiPalma and then Koch.

Allis and Heutter rode together into the Galeries d'Anjou Shopping Center for the final circuit—five laps of a one-mile course with thousands of spectators lining the route, all yelling at the top of their voices. Allis, who had more strength than speed, pulled away from Heutter on the final circuit to win by two and a half minutes. Allis was so spent from nearly seven hours bent over his handlebars that his back flared in pain. After crossing the finish, he had to be lifted from his bicycle.

Howard finished third, nine minutes behind, to make a sweep for the Raleigh-CRC of A team. Fourth at nearly 11 minutes behind Allis was Koch, followed by Moetus. DiPalma was 10th, Stuewe 11th, and Meco 12th. Humphreys, Swaim, and Fischer rode in 14th to 16th places. Another dozen finished alone or in pairs over the next half-hour.

The race was a morale booster for the Raleigh-CRC of A squad. They had gone the distance against seasoned riders and triumphed. They felt they were ready to hold their own in the Tour of Ireland. They cheered when Allis was given the keys to the yellow Ford Pinto.

The team's spirits were soaring as they looked forward to leaving for the trip to Ireland and competing in the event, which would run from August 12 to 19. Selected for the team were Howard, Allis, Humphreys, and Swaim. Fred Kuhn, the bike-shop proprietor in Princeton, had organized the first American team to cross the Atlantic and compete in a stage race, and his riders were prepared. One race remained before they left for Ireland—the 120-mile national road racing championship in Milwaukee. Kim had spent enough time in Milwaukee to feel as if it were her second home. "When the races were on, that part of the city just shut down, and everyone in the neighborhoods involved was good about it. And Milwaukee has a lot of Italian restaurants, great for loading up on carbohydrates before the race."

City officials donated $1,000 to the ABL, which persuaded them to hold the national road championships on the shore of Lake Michigan. (Track nationals were held in Northbrook, Illinois.) For the Milwaukee Chamber of Commerce, the donation was a worthwhile investment. More than 600 racers, plus their families and other support, arrived for a weekend of five events for men and women. The money they spent more than replaced the city's donation.

The men's open 120-mile road race on Sunday morning, July 29, drew 150 of the best riders from every state. Jim Ochowicz was the hometown favorite. Wayne Stetina, Mike Neel, Bob Schneider, Rick Ball, and Jim Montgomery were among a dozen likely contenders for the right to wear the national champion's Stars-and-Stripes jersey for the next year.

Milwaukee's rolling four-mile course started on the lakefront and, after a short distance, turned right up a hill that reared 580 feet high, and took about 30 seconds of effort. It is the sort of hill that fresh legs welcome as a chance to get out of the saddle and use different muscles. Later in the 30-lap race, however, the hill seems to grow longer and steeper and eventually "breaks" legs and the will to tough it out. Afterward, the undulating backstretch leads to a serpentine descent over pavement that grows bumpier until it levels out on the lakefront. A mile of gently curving flat road leads to the finish. It is not a course that favors breakaways.

But Allis, recovered from his Canadian victory, broke away anyway. Some riders complained that he had only one speed, which he used all the time. When he took off on the first lap, Bill Guazzo saw Allis's move as one of opportunity and went with him. By the end of the third lap they led by 30 seconds. Guazzo, however, lasted only one more lap after which he couldn't stay on Allis's rear wheel up the hill for the fourth time.

Allis continued as the rabbit. Chases erupted from the peloton over the next three laps. First a group of nine, then five more went after Allis like metal filings after a magnet. On the 10th lap, Howard shot out of the peloton at the base of the hill to join the chasers. Neel missed the various jumps and tried to make up for it by stringing the peloton out behind him in a long line that grew ragged at the end, where frazzled riders dropped off.

A lead group of 14 formed, including Allis, Howard, Guazzo, Schneider, Ball, and Ochowicz. They left Neel, Stetina, Ron Skarin, and other contenders behind in the peloton to make heroic efforts that caused racers to quit.

"Road races like the nationals had really hard riding in the second half, to shut out the pack sprinters like Montgomery or Bobby Phillips or Roger Young," explained Schneider. "Riders like me or Allis didn't have much of a sprint, so we did everything we could to eliminate the pack sprinters."

As the laps wore on under the summer sun, Howard surveyed his breakaway companions, who were working a pace line. The only sprinter was Ochowicz. "I was feeling strong and stormed the hills," Howard said. Eventually the storming wore Ochowicz down. He slipped off the back of the breakaway with eight laps remaining and lost ground until he pulled out at the end of the lap.

With four laps to go, the breakaway had only six left: Howard, Allis, Schneider, Ball, Greg Meeker of Madison, Wisconsin, and Rich Hammen of San Francisco, California, who suffered leg cramps in the 90-degree heat. The pace slowed as the leaders eyed one another to see who would make a move. On the final lap they were rolling at 10 MPH. On the back stretch, with two miles left, Hammen jumped with all he had and took off at 35 MPH. Howard and the others rode up to him and take advantage of drafting until Hammen realized he had played his last move unsuccessfully.

"Rick Ball had no sprint, so he tried to go on his own with a mile to go," Schneider said. "I caught his rear wheel and drafted until about the last quarter-mile, when I went past him. I was out there in front, and I thought I had it."

Ball rode tightly against the right cement curb, which was lined five deep on both sides with excited spectators. In the final 200 hundred yards, grandstands on both sides of the road were filled with several thousand more people yelling for their favorites. At that point, the most brilliant moment in cycling national championships occurred.

"Schneider didn't have the timing just right," Howard said. "I was on his rear wheel and went past him in the last 100 yards."

Howard went wide on left, up the middle of the road, to win by a wheel—the college dropout foiling the best-laid plans of the University of Wisconsin doctors.

Meeker rushed in for fourth. Allis beat Hammen, whose cramps took him out of the contest.

Howard may have started the season with a dose of road rust, but he had clearly polished his form. He was America's undisputed king of the roads. The result of successfully defending his road title, and Allis's great performance, earned them both selection in the world championships in Barcelona, Spain, on September 2. They would fly there after the Tour of Ireland.

"Raleigh was obviously taking a chance with us," Allis said of the company sponsoring the American team in the Tour of Ireland. The team was among 20 four-rider teams that made up a field of 80 riders from seven nations. "We were regarded as very questionable. Raleigh didn't have a lot to gain from our presence, and if we did badly we risked looking even worse for bringing us over. But Raleigh wanted us in it. Our being there was a charity issue."

Raleigh provided a team station wagon, with a roof rack loaded with extra bicycles and wheels, and two valuable personnel—a veteran team director and an experienced mechanic.

Raleigh co-sponsored the race with Dunlop, a tire company with a long affiliation with Raleigh. Officially, the 1973 Irish national tour was christened the Eighth Annual Raleigh-Dunlop Tour of Ireland. It had an ambitious route that started in downtown Dublin, on Ireland's east coast. It went northwest into uppermost Ireland and then back south to Dublin where it finished in Phoenix Park.

Howard, Allis, Humphreys, and Swaim met their team director and mechanic upon arriving in Dublin. Howard, the only married rider among the four, had left Kim at home.

"We arrived during a heat wave," Allis recalled. "The hot weather was a source of discomfort to the Irish and English riders, but we thought it was okay. Big crowds turned out for every stage, especially the noon start, in front of the General Post Office."

The first stage, 97 miles from Dublin northwest to Carrick-on-Shannon, was faster and involved more physical contact in the peloton than the American riders had encountered before. The Irish and English riders were mostly blue-collar workers and farmers for whom bicycle racing was both a passion and an opportunity to move up to the professional ranks and perhaps achieve a middle-class life. They played for keeps when they raced. When a small opening developed between two riders in the peloton, they went right through even when it meant physical contact. This was their national tour, a big step from the weekend local races and a chance to earn recognition that could advance their career.

"When the breaks went off the front and the pack chased, our speed was faster by a couple of miles an hour than our chases back home," Allis explained. "We also experienced rougher riding, with more pushing with elbows and shoulders. The Irish and English were better prepared than we were. This was our first time, and they had done it before and knew the roads and the rugged hills better. Ireland has a lot of steep, devilish climbs, which the race directors sought out to run the course over."

Yet the Americans were ready and game. They adjusted to the pace and the roads. Early in the first stage, a breakaway of 10 riders went up the road and by 60 miles had gained a three-minute advantage. Howard and Allis saw another group sprint away from the front and flanks, and went with them to join another 10-rider group. They formed a pace-line course through the pastoral countryside and closed to within 1 minute and 20 seconds of the first group. It was tough going, but worth it.

"Allis and I shared 11th place overall with six other riders," Howard said.

The next day's Stage 2 went from Donegal straight north over the Blue Stack Mountains to the finish in Buncrana, in uppermost Ireland. The stage proved decisive for the race and the Americans. Howard was ready to respond to a break that went with Englishman Doug Dailey, teammate John Clewarth, and seven others. They worked well together, hands down on the drops, backs low, legs churning as they lengthened their lead to two minutes. At the top of a hill, however, Howard had mechanical trouble and had to stop to take a spare bicycle from the Raleigh team car. Dailey and Clewarth immediately attacked to take advantage. Howard got back on the spare bicycle and chased alone. His training with the Pettersson brothers helped as he caught the breakaway and sat in with them to recover.

Dailey and Clewarth, both from Liverpool, England, remained away, but after Howard rode with the breakaway he decided to try his luck up a short hill. With 20 miles left, he attacked and rode the rest of the way alone for third in the stage. Allis crossed the line 25 seconds later. Here was respectability for the Yanks. Howard moved into third overall, behind Dailey and Clewarth, and Allis was fifth overall. No longer were the Americans seen as "no-hopers."

In the midst of the Tour, Howard's 26th birthday arrived. He had scored the Pan American Games gold medal in time to celebrate his 24th birthday. This time he felt the luck of the Irish.

In Bundoran, in northwest Ireland, the temperature and rain were both falling. Tours are held daily, rain or shine, so riders lined up in the morning for Stage 6, 95 miles south over the Iron Mountains to Athlone on the Shannon River, near the center of the country.

"We were all soaked and shivering in the cold downpour as we waited for the start," Howard said. "I was awfully uncomfortable, but that's bike racing. After we rode inland, the rain stopped. At the King of the Hill premium 44 miles out, a break went off up the hill and I went with it. The hill was steep and down the other side we reached 60 MPH in a matter of seconds. The road was so narrow that it would only allow a single compact car. The road was clear of traffic, but sheep stood on both sides. Tears were streaming from my eyes, and I was really anxious about sheep wandering into the road. They stayed. I lived."

Howard was out ahead with three others. They worked well together all the way into Athlone. Their break never got far ahead, and the nearer they got to the finish, the closer the peloton came. Spectators wearing sweaters and jackets crowded the road behind steel barricades and watched with added interest to see if the breakaway could hold the peloton off.

"The last miles were a long flat stretch to the finish," Howard said. "All I can say is that everything just worked right. Sometimes, once in a great while, bike racing is like that. When the finish line was in sight, I looked over my shoulder and saw the pack gaining on us. But we had enough of a gap that we were going to have a four-way sprint for the stage. I picked the right wheel and timed my sprint right—and won."

A photo of the finish shows that Howard won by a bike length, with the peloton spread out curb to curb another half-dozen lengths behind. For capturing the stage, Howard was awarded a bonus of 30 seconds deducted from his overall time. He also earned respect from officials.

"Winning the stage was a very big deal," observed Phil Liggett, an Englishman who was working the Tour of Ireland as chief international commissaire. "John was a real novelty to us. He was a slow-talking Texan. We weren't used to slow-talking Texans in the United Kingdom. But he and the other riders on his team were putting on a good show."

As the tour continued for another three days, riding remained aggressive, but anyone higher than 10th place overall found it difficult to get included in the breaks. "This gave a few local club riders a chance to pick up stage wins," Howard said.

Bill Humphreys underscored the American presence when he placed third in the 97-mile Stage 8 from Carrick-on-Sur to Arklow on the east coast below Dublin. "That was a real morale booster for the team" Allis said. "We were definitely in the race."

The Tour of Ireland concluded with a 30-mile criterium in Dublin's Phoenix Park, where Howard suffered an anxious moment. Rain had washed in from the Irish Sea and made the roads slick. Howard crashed on a turn and slid on the pavement, which caused cuts and abrasions. "But I managed to get back up and catch the field all right to stay in the action," he said.

Doug Dailey prevailed to win over his Liverpool teammate Clewarth. Howard finished third. Allis was fifth. Swaim was 46th and Humphreys 47th. The Americans finished a respectable sixth in the team competition, based on the total time of the first three riders on each team.

Bicycle racing is arduous and requires a complete commitment at the international level. Howard, Allis, Swaim, and Humphreys had traveled thousands of miles from home with little more than two sets of jerseys and shorts (one set they washed in the sink the evening after the race and the other set they wore the next day), a warm-up suit, a spoke wrench, and pocket change.

The four Americans had come through with commendable performances, which earned respect. After the race was over,

Liggett—the new organizer for the Tour of Britain—met with them.

"I told them that what I saw of their riding in the Tour of Ireland indicated to me that they wouldn't disgrace themselves in the Tour of Britain," Liggett said. "I told them to bring their best six riders and that we would pay their expenses."

For American cycling, it was a big moment—one that made the entire season worth the sweat and sore muscles. Before the Tour of Britain in May, Howard and Allis packed their bags to fly to Barcelona with airline tickets bought for them by the ABL to get to the world championships.

Chapter 7

"We were very tired, we were very merry."
—Edna St. Vincent Millay,
"Recuerdo."

The world championships in Spain turned out to be a low point for the American team. In the 100-kilometer team time trial on August 29, the ABL's squad of Jim Ochowicz, Mike Neel, Ron Skarin, and Ralph Therrio of Torrance, California, finished 21st of 22 finishers, 18 minutes (about eight miles) behind the victorious Polish team. Three days later, in the amateur road race of 101 miles, Howard and Allis started with high expectations in the peloton of 161 riders. But American cyclists were inconsistent internationally; any high was followed by a succession of lows for an overall record that looked like jagged saw teeth.

The road course, nearly nine miles around, was described as one of the hardest in recent world championships—a roller coaster with a severe climb up Barcelona's Montjuich Hill.

"Right after the descent, the road bottomed out on a long flat stretch," Howard said. "The pace slowed, and everyone sat up. Amateur racing at the worlds had hard chases to catch breakaways, and when the breaks were caught the pace would slow until some new break went up the road. It made the pack ride like a huge accordion—stretching out in the chases and then bunching up when the breakaways were caught. After screaming down the descent on the Barcelona course, we hit the flat stretch. Everyone slowed down and sat up. That's when we had a major crash. At least a couple dozen riders went down, including Allis and me."

Howard scrambled back up and pulled his bicycle out of the pileup of bodies and bicycles, but discovered his right shoe was missing. He couldn't ride without it. He searched frantically until someone who had accidentally been lying on the shoe got up and Howard finally found it. He shoved his foot back in the shoe, jumped back on his bike, and chased—only to discover a worse problem.

"Someone had ridden over my left calf. A perfect print of the tire tread on my skin was so vivid that you could see it was a Clemente. My calf was stiff and very sore. And I was bleeding from cuts and scrapes up and down my left leg and arm. It just wasn't my day."

Across Spain on the Atlantic coast, in San Sebastian, Sheila Young of Detroit, a second-generation racer and speed skater, beat Iva Zajickova of Czechoslovakia to win the women's world championship matched sprints on the track. Young's victory was the first world track championship for Americans since 1912.

The sport's governing body, Union Cycliste Internationale, awarded the next world championships to Montreal. Road and track racers would compete on the same venues as the upcoming 1976 Olympics, in Montreal. That meant road riders like Howard could test themselves in the 1974 world championship course in advance of the big race for an Olympic medal.

With the Tour of Britain coming up in May, the world championships late in the summer, and the prospect of competing in another Pan American Games in 1975 and the Olympics on the horizon, Howard was looking at a growing menu of international challenges. But now he had practical, immediate considerations to face. "I had to get back to Houston and go to work," he said.

American cycling in 1974 shifted gears that would make the United States an international power in the sport. To help foster rider development and make the bigger races safer in the Northeast, where promoters tended to lump all men's open riders together, regardless of abilities, the ABL raised the age of senior men's open racing from 17 to 18. The ABL also issued licenses that divided men into three categories: Category I was for national-caliber riders such as Howard, Category II was for those who made top 10 places in regional events, and Category III was for everybody else. Lower categories were especially important for nurturing bike-handling skills and rider confidence.

Importantly, the ABL now condoned Raleigh and other sponsored teams because the ABL leadership realized they could charge a commission for such sponsorships. As a result, French manufacturers like Gitane, Peugeot, and Follis supplied bicycles and team jerseys and shorts to riders who sported clothing emblazoned with brand names—in races and out on the roads while training. Component manufacturers, like Shimano of Japan, and bike shops, like the Turin Bicycle Co-Op, Ltd., of metropolitan

Chicago, sponsored teams whose riders became their billboards. A majority of the sponsorships came from foreign companies. Domestic manufacturers and distributors had not seen the surge for bicycles coming and when it did, they were slow to meet the demand.

Another important development was the ABL's announcement early in the season that it had hired retired racer Butch Martin as men's coach to prepare the men's team for the Montreal world championships. ABL officials recognized Martin as a veteran of two Olympics, one Pan American Games, and two years of racing in Italy. He had a reputation for being a rider's rider. "Butch never rode any harder than he needed to win races," Howard observed.

Texas cycling was also expanding. The number of ABL racers there had nearly doubled from 400 to 700 over the year. Mike Neel moved to Austin to train through the winter. Neel wanted to return to the Continent to race, and he knew that training with Howard and racing against him would enhance his chances of making the team for the Tour of Britain in late May.

All of these developments stoked Howard's motivation for cycling. Over the winter, he considered moving back to his hometown at the end of the summer to resume classes at Southwest Missouri and complete his degree. He weighed the prospects of staying in cycling against the benefits of college.

"If I had gone back and got my degree, all that was available was a teaching job, and that wasn't what I wanted to do. If I had wanted to make a lot of money, I would have finished my college degree, gone on to get an advanced degree, and joined the work force. But making money wasn't what really motivated me. I felt that I had found something I really liked doing, like I was born to ride a bike. I enjoyed the drama of being a player in American cycling and winning races. I was overdosing on a good time. I was also expecting that American cycling was like a sleeping giant, that the sport would wake up and start taking long strides. So I said *hasta la vista* to college so I could stay with cycling."

An advantage that he and Kim had in living in Houston was closeness to his brother, H. D., who lived with his wife, Vikki, and their children in Austin. "H. D. and Vikki had a home on Lake Travis. Kim and I would drive to Austin to visit for the weekend. Austin was a great place to train because it's in Texas hill country. H. D. actually had better oxygen uptake than me, and he was quicker in the sprint. But he preferred family life."

On visits to Austin during the winter, Howard joined Neel for training rides. Both cyclists were determined to make the team bound for England. They took their determination to the starting line of the Texas Primavera on March 10, the season's opening race. Defending champion John Potoschnick had cut back his racing and didn't return. Howard and Neel dominated the race, shortened to 52 miles on a new hilly course west of Austin, with a breakaway in the second half that shattered the peloton. The two riders traded the lead in a pace line until 16 miles to go when Howard charged up a two-mile hill and dropped Neel. Howard rode solo and finished three minutes up on Neel, and five minutes ahead of Del Blundel of Dallas, in third.

It was an auspicious start. Howard showed he was on schedule to make the team going to Britain. *CycleNews* published an interview with Howard as he prepared for the upcoming challenges. He explained that he had altered his training to work on bursts of sustained speed to help him bridge gaps from the peloton to breakaways. "I have a lot of faith in racing in the States," he told *CycleNews*. "It's becoming more dynamic. I enjoy the riders. I enjoy competing over here. It thrills me to see the standards of competition continually going up."

He cited stage racing as "where the essence of bike racing is. It's racing personified. Day after day you're engaging in a sort of battle, in a sense. It's all based on general classification." America's standard fare of 50-mile criteriums limit development, he cautioned. That led to his observing, "I think I haven't reached my full potential yet."

ABL officials encouraged promoters to put on more races as a step toward mastering the logistics of stage races and transforming the domestic racing diet. The ABL designated weekend-long races as part of the Olympic development series. An early one was the March 23-24 event in central Mississippi's bayou, in the town of Sebastopol. Howard and Kim loaded up their Datsun and drove east. "When we hit the road," Kim said, "we always sang Willie Nelson's song, 'On the Road Again.' That was our theme song."

Mississippi's race was a showcase of how well Howard and Neel were riding ahead of the rest of the competition. The weekend concluded with a road race of 96 miles, which Howard won by five seconds over Neel for overall honors.

Afterward, racers took their bikes apart and packed cars to drive northeast to Rocky Mount, North Carolina, for the next weekend's three-stage event totaling 137 miles. Howard won over Stetina, with John Allis third.

Next weekend was the Raleigh Tour of Louisiana, which seemed all but won by Howard as he and Kim pulled into New Orleans. He was riding a hot streak and had already won the two previous editions. But the race had doubled to 150 entries, all of whom were looking to upset Howard. One was newcomer Tom Officer, who, as a sophomore, had dropped out of Dartmouth College in New Hampshire the previous November to train and race full-time.

"I was really excited about bike racing and just could not stay in classes," Officer said. "I had the address of a bike shop down in Tallahassee, Florida, a place called Ten Speed Imports. About four weeks into the fall term, I packed my red Volkswagen bug and drove to Tallahassee. Within an hour of walking into the bike shop, I had a job and a place to stay."

On his bedroom door, Officer taped a photo of Howard cut from *CycleNews*. "Howie was the guy to beat," Officer said. "I drew bull's-eye rings around his face. He didn't know who I was, and he had no reason to know. But all that winter I trained my ass off. I went to weekend time trials of 25 miles that were held in different cities around Florida. I also wrote letters to John Allis and called him on the telephone to ask him about training. He was always very helpful, generous with advice and encouragement. I had tremendous respect for Allis. He definitely helped me become a better bike racer. I showed it at the Tour of Louisiana."

Howard and Kim rate New Orleans as one of their favorite cities. "The food, the people, the French and Cajun atmosphere there were just great," Kim said.

Howard opened the race with another winning performance in the prologue 4.2-mile time trial over Lakefront Drive. He managed to finish in 9 minutes, 17 seconds, five seconds slower than his previous year's course record. One by one the other riders went off at one-minute intervals. Two and a half hours later, Neel was the last rider around the course. He came the closest to Howard's time, but settled for second place with 9:25. Del Blundel of Dallas was third in 9:27.

That afternoon was the 80-mile road race outside of town, in pastoral Covington, where riders rode four laps over an undulating 20-mile course. Ambitious riders launched numerous breakaways, but nothing consequential developed until the middle of the race when six riders crashed and threw the peloton into confusion.

Officer was part of a group forced off the road and into the adjacent grass to avoid hitting fallen riders. "I wound up with Mike Neel off the back trying to chase back to the field," Officer said. "Neel didn't have a clue who I was, but he said afterward he had a hard time holding on to my rear wheel as I towed him to the pack."

Officer recovered and worked his way forward through the peloton. On the last lap, with 20 miles left, Officer and Florida training partner Ed Schaeffer of St. Petersburg dashed off the front. They were not seen as a threat to Howard, whose every move was monitored closely by Neel and Jim Ochowicz. Yet Florida riders who knew Officer and Schaeffer saw what was happening and went to the front to slow the pace and block. The Florida riders, who had adopted Officer as one of their own, were tired of carpetbaggers taking their winter events. They conspired to let the pair pull off an upset.

Several other breakaways in the remaining miles heightened the action and effectively distracted Howard and others in the peloton, which reeled in all breakaways except for Officer and Schaeffer, who finished two minutes clear in that order.

Neel won the pack sprint, a wheel ahead of Howard. They were shocked to discover they were third and fourth.

"They should have known what was happening," Officer pointed out. "The official pace car was ahead of us the whole time." Officer usurped the yellow jersey.

The next morning was the 37-mile criterium in Hammond, around a tricky course seven-tenths of a mile with eight turns per lap. Howard, Neel, Blundel, and Ochowicz exploded from the starter's gun. They tore away to take time from Officer and Schaeffer. But Officer was prepared. He worked with others in the peloton at chasing to limit the damage, although Schaeffer cracked under the speed and lost two minutes. Ochowicz gave all he had, but he fell back to the peloton. Howard, Neel, and Blundel persevered and managed to lap the peloton with five laps to go.

"The three of us really hammered," Howard said. "We worked the peloton over and took time out of Officer." Blundel won the sprint for first, with Howard edging Neel by a tire's width for second. When officials tabulated times, they declared Officer the overall winner. Howard was awarded second, 45 seconds down. Blundel was third, 49 seconds behind, and Neel, fourth, 58 seconds down. Schaeffer hung in for eighth place.

Officer scored an upset victory, knocking Howard out of the winner's circle and making himself a candidate for the six-rider team Allis was organizing. Officer shot out of obscurity and joined the migratory flow south down to Fort Myers for the ninth annual Cross-Florida Tour.

"Racing across Florida was boring," Officer said. "It was just as flat as could be." Officer, 5'8" tall, was best on hills and lacked a fast sprint, which put him at a disadvantage in south Florida. But he gave Howard his biggest challenge as they made the 240-mile event a duel. Howard won, with Officer right behind in second.

They carried their duel to northern Florida for the three-day Tour of Apalachicola, April 19 to 21, in the Apalachicola National Forest south of Tallahassee. The race covered 235 miles in five stages that included northern Florida's hilliest terrain. This area favored Officer, who had trained thousands of miles over these roads and knew the landscape intimately.

The opening 10-mile time trial set the tone for the Tour of Apalachicola. Howard clocked 22 minutes and 34 seconds, his best time for 10 miles. Officer was next. He crossed the finish line so spent that he lost control of his bicycle and fell. He was two seconds behind Howard. "I admired the way he pushed himself," Howard said.

When the rest of the riders finished and times were ranked, Howard's teammate Bill Humphreys was third, one minute behind.

Howard won the next morning's 95-mile road race, then a pack sprint in the afternoon criterium of 31 miles. Officer remained in striking distance, nine seconds behind in second place.

On the third and final day, 51 racers lined up for a road race of 75 miles that made a northern loop into the hills of South Georgia. Within the first mile, Howard and Officer powered away in their own two-man race. They found the scenic hills, with roads that cut through the forest of tall pine trees, to their liking. By the turn-around at 37.5 miles, they led by two minutes. Their lead expanded to seven minutes with four miles left when they approached a three-tiered hill that loomed as a strategic obstacle.

"I picked a place to attack and try to drop John," Officer said.

Remarkably, the place Officer picked was similar to what Howard had spotted during an early-morning car ride over the course. They were like Michelangelo and Da Vinci competing for the same marble stone for their next sculpture.

Officer led up the base of the hill and was about to attack when Howard rushed past on the left in the middle of the road, gaining four lengths. Officer rallied and matched him pedal stroke for pedal stroke up the hill. At the summit, he caught Howard's rear wheel to neutralize their race. They swooped downhill together and rode in tandem to the finishing straight. Howard outsprinted Officer for the stage victory.

Stage 5, a 30-mile road race over a hilly 2.3-mile circuit, was a late-afternoon race that concluded the event. The staged wended around a golf course and featured a half-mile climb up Magnolia Hill, along with a series of short shoots and sweeping turns. Only 23 riders, less than half the original starters, lined up.

Officer was still just nine seconds behind overall. On the third lap, he jumped away to take time out of Howard, who preferred to ride in the peloton and see if Officer would wear down. But Officer appeared to be away for good, and when his lead stretched to 10 seconds, he became the new race leader on the road. Howard saw it was time to react. He sprang from the peloton at the base of Magnolia Hill and caught Officer by the top.

They rode together for a lap. The next time up Magnolia Hill, Howard made his move. For three weekends, Officer had been pushing them both to the physical edge. Howard felt like pushing some more. He sprinted up Magnolia Hill. For the first time in 220 miles of the Tour of Apalachicola and the two previous weekend tours, Howard broke free of Officer. Every pedal stroke put more distance between them. Over the next 15 miles to the finish, Howard gained two and a half minutes to clinch the event.

As the spring Olympic development races in the Southeast concluded and the migratory route went north, Howard planned to cash in on his successful campaign and negotiate for a new job in Houston. He knew of one that would grant him even greater freedom as he prepared to move to Dorset, Vermont, to sharpen his skills for the Tour of Britain and, afterward, to spend the summer training for the national road racing championship in Pontiac, Michigan, and the worlds in Montreal.

Campagnolo, the Italian company whose derailleurs, wheel hubs, brakes, and other components were highly prized for their quality, was identified with championship cycling in Europe. The name carried a certain cachet. Campagnolo was broadening its North American market and had recently opened a large warehouse in downtown Houston, whose gleaming inventory was every cyclist's El Dorado.

"It was the first time that Campagnolo would be imported on a big scale," Howard explained. "Luciano Giomeccelli was the president for Campagnolo USA. He hired me to meet the public at bike shows and answer questions from dealers. In April I left the Peden Equipment Company and Monarch Crescent bicycles to work for Campagnolo USA. My new job title was public relations liaison. It was a much better deal. I nearly doubled my salary, to $18,000, which was a good income in 1974."

His new job gave him freedom to move in early May to Vermont to participate in a new cycling training camp. "It was important to leave Houston for the summer," Howard said. "It was just too hot to train there."

The training camp was the innovation of Wendall and Annie Cram. They modeled the format after the ski camps popular in New England. Wendall had made the 1940 Olympic ski team but the International Olympic Committee canceled the entire Olympics for eight years. Wendall took up cycling as a summer activity to stay in shape for skiing. But he found bicycle racing was a difficult sport to learn.

"We had to learn it from the guys who had been racing," he explained. "There weren't many riders when I got into the sport in the 1940s, and about the only time you saw them was at a race. You can't go up to a guy before the start and ask him what you should do, and afterward the guy doesn't want to talk to a stranger about what he did because he's too tired. When cycling started to take off in the early 1970s, we thought there was room for a cycling camp."

The Crams discussed the idea with Stan Swaim, who agreed to head the camp, but pointed out they needed instructors with established names to help attract attendees. At the New York Bicycle Show in early 1973, the Crams approached Howard about the training camp. "We told him about our idea and asked if we could use his name," said Annie. "We needed a headliner. John supported our idea of the training camp. He became our publicity."

Wendall and Annie traveled to the 1973 national road racing championship in Milwaukee to discuss details of the camp with Howard, Swaim, Allis, and other Raleigh-CRC of A riders. "It was pretty fantastic," Wendall said. "These guys wanted a place to train together, and they could divide the teaching at the training camp."

The Crams advertised their summer training camp in *CycleNews*. Dorset is an idyllic village located in southern Vermont's Otter Creek Valley, surrounded by green mountains renowned for winter skiing. Under the Crams' inspiration, Dorset became a national cycling center. They held evening classes in the basement of the old stone Congregational Church on Main Street. The annex building next to the Dorset Inn accommodated up to 18 campers for each 10-day session, which cost $28 a day. Riders ate breakfast and lunch on long, wooden tables in the annex. Dinners were served in the Cram home, a white two-story split level.

Allis used the Dorset training camp to organize the team he selected for the Tour of Britain, May 26 to June 8. Their arrival in early May was the culmination of considerable planning with ABL officials, national-class riders, and Raleigh USA.

"American cycling was still a bunch of very independent characters, pretty much undisciplined, out doing their own thing," Allis said. "I was calling guys up on the telephone during the fall and winter to keep them informed of my talks with Phil Liggett in England and what our guys were doing. That gave riders on the long team a focus in their training, which helped a lot."

Not everyone Allis invited was interested in going over for the 1,200 mile Tour of Britain. Jim Ochowicz said he wasn't ready and declined. Stan Swaim had performed well in the Tour of Ireland, but was blunt about his prospects from the English tour: "I felt there were other riders who were better." Swaim, 37, felt his resources were better used in applying his teaching experience to develop the training camp. He took over as head coach.

Allis, who had recently completed his Harvard MBA, worked public relations for Raleigh USA. "We needed John Howard because Howie was Howie. Flip Waldteufel was a good team rider, and he had spent the previous summer competing on a French team, so we wanted him. Mike Neel had European experience. I had a lot of confidence in Tom Officer. Rich Hammen had been riding consistently for several years and had a good early season in Southern California and Mexico, so I felt he was ready. And myself, because I had experience racing in France and was running the Tour of Britain team."

The team arrived in the south English coastal city of Brighton a week before the May 26 start of the Tour of Britain. "We arrived early to recover from jet lag, get used to riding on the left side of the road, and to the cold, wet weather," Howard said.

Among 11 national teams of six riders each were some of the best cycling talent of their generation. Ryszard Szurkowski, reigning world amateur road racing champion, led a strong Polish team. Roy Schüten and Jan Raas, both future world professional champions, were on the Dutch team. Bernt Johansson, destined to win a world championship and an Olympic gold medal, was on the Swedish team with Tord Filipsson, another future world champion. Teams from Czechoslovakia, West Germany, England, Ireland, and Norway also sent seasoned talent.

Liggett had put together a high-level international race, and he dutifully assigned the American team an experienced English manager, a soigneur (masseur and coach), a mechanic, and a driver for the team car, also supplied. "All the other teams had their own support crew, but we didn't have appropriate managers to bring with us," explained Allis. "We needed support personnel who knew the race and the course. Phil Liggett gave us them."

After the two-mile prologue time trial in Brighton, on the shore of the English Channel, it was apparent the race would be fiercely competitive. "The Poles, Dutch, and Swedes didn't seem to mind the cold and wet weather," Waldteufel said. "They were right at home, but we weren't at all comfortable."

The Americans faced a long, hard race. It wended 1,200 miles northwest across the country to Blackpool, north of Liverpool, on the coast of the Irish Sea, where the Tour ended June 8.

"We were not taken seriously," Allis said. "We went from being big fish in a small pond to suddenly being little fish in a huge ocean. A lot of the English press picked us not to finish."

On the first road stage, the odds of the American team finishing looked bleak. Allis's rear tire punctured only a few pedal strokes after the chief commissaire waved the black-and-white checkered flag for the rolling start. "It was the first flat of the whole tour, and I got a very slow wheel change," Allis said.

Hammen and Waldteufel dropped back to work with him in a pace line to return together to the peloton. But when they rejoined, they made a grievous error. Instead of moving forward to get the maximum benefit from the envelope of air protection in the peloton as they recovered from the exertion of their pursuit, they stayed at the back. Soon the course went up a long climb. Allis had the requisite training miles in his legs, but few racing miles, and he needed the first couple of days in the tour to adjust to the brisk racing pace. Hammen found the international riders were quicker than he was accustomed to and also needed time to adjust. Allis and Hammen dropped off the back up the climb. Allis struggled for the remaining 60 miles alone and finished 25 minutes behind the peloton; Hammen came in last, 30 minutes down.

"The press leaped on this," Allis said. "Our manager, Johnny Morris, an ex-pro, tried to rationalize it as a matter of our adjusting to the cold, wet weather. Frank Westell, our soigneur, tried to keep our spirits up. Just staying in the race for us became a matter of pride."

The next day, Howard swept around a corner in the peloton and went down with a dozen others. "I fell hard and suffered cuts on my knees, arms, elbows," he said. "I worked with a couple of other riders to finish the stage, but I hated losing that much time so early in the race." He lost more than six minutes.

Officer said, "After the first two days, it became a brutal race. On the third day, the course was really hilly. Near the finish, I got out of the saddle to sprint and stripped a gear. Fell right over the handlebars. But in a stage race, you have to complete every stage and be on the starting line for the next one. I got back on the bike and finished."

Howard and Officer fought one another in the spring campaign for victory, but against national teams from Europe and the Eastern bloc, they were just two riders in the peloton. Continental racing was considerably faster and more tactical. In a crosswind, the peloton broke apart to form echelons, in which riders fanned diagonally across the road, one echelon behind the next so they moved up the road like the pattern of feathers on an arrow. At other times, the peloton strung out in a linear file on a fast pace line as the Dutch and Polish teams kept the speed high for hours, to keep any breakaway from going up the road.

Howard adapted and settled in. By the fourth day he felt ready for a piece of the action. He broke clear with three miles left and gained 400 yards as they passed a sign for a mile to go. But the peloton was alert and swiftly charged in a mass to sweep him up on the closing yards. He finished in the middle of the pack.

The next day, Howard was knocked down again while cruising in the peloton. His front wheel was mangled. Suffering more cuts and abrasions, he lost 20 minutes waiting for a support vehicle to arrive and give him a wheel change. "It wasn't a great race for me," Howard admitted.

"We suffered a lot," Waldteufel agreed. "It rained a lot. We all crashed. I was surprised to see world champion Szurkowski fall down. Here was the world champion, wearing his white jersey with the world champion's band of rainbow colors around his chest and back, going right down on his side and sliding on the pavement. I didn't think world champions ever did that. But he stood back up, got on his bike, and quickly caught the peloton."

The English press sportingly published betting odds of the

American team finishing. But day after day, the Americans endured crashes, were treated for cuts and abrasions, and managed to survive. Occasionally they showed flashes of promise. Allis found his racing legs and rode with panache. He made several attacks that earned him respect and he moved up on general classification daily. Waldteufel got in a breakaway on the eighth day as the peloton approached the base of a precipitous climb called Rosedale Abbey and won the sprint to the summit.

"It was a God-awful steep hill," Waldteufel recalled. "I was breathing so hard and my heart was pounding so that I could almost taste blood. There had been an attack at the base of the hill and I was in a good position to go with it. There were four Swedes and two Dutch riders and I went with them. We opened up 20 seconds by the top. But a few miles later we were caught. Maybe if we had a Pole with us in the breakaway the other Poles wouldn't have chased us down. Those other teams really worked well together."

Waldteufel and Howard both finished in the top 20 that day— a respectable showing. On the final day into Blackpool, Neel sped to seventh place, the best individual performance of the team. Neel had earned redemption for his 1972 Tour of Britain debacle.

The 1,200-mile Tour of Britain concluded with Schüten the winner, seven seconds (about 100 yards) ahead of Szurkowski, and 18 seconds ahead of Sweden's Filipsson. Howard was the best-placed American, in 31st. Allis was 43rd, Neel 49th, Waldteufel 50th, Officer 57th, and Hammen last at 59th, 2 hours and 20 minutes (more than 50 miles) behind Schüten.

"We were fortunate that Hammen gutted it out and finished," Allis said. "He was awarded the red lantern for bringing up the rear. But it was a point of honor not to drop out. We finished with our whole team. We got some good press. The tabloids gave us credit. They said the future of cycling was being re-born with the Yanks. There was the feeling that if the United States ever got into cycling at the international level, our country's wealth would provide a better future for the sport."

Importantly, Phil Liggett extended an invitation for the Americans to return the next year.

Back in the serenity of the Dorset training camp, Howard's cuts and abrasions healed, and his war stories had a ready audience. He worked with Swaim to teach camp participants techniques for cornering and sprinting. He had time for training in the local mountains.

Howard was in Dorset when Butch Martin invited him to head the six-rider ABL team for the Tour of Newfoundland, a 560-mile stage race, June 24 to 29. The Province of Newfoundland was celebrating the 25th anniversary of its union with Canada. To garner attention for its silver anniversary, the Province held an eight-stage bicycle race to crisscross the Island. The Canadian Cycling Federation stacked the race with six teams of its best riders, and England entered a squad. ABL President Ernie Seubert assigned road coach Martin to pick a team that would show the United States was a cycling power.

For the ABL hierarchy, the Tour of Newfoundland was a point of pride. Canadian riders had a reputation for being tougher and better than U.S. riders. Ron Hayman of Vancouver was a veteran of racing in Holland. Canada had been awarded the world championships, which showed its stature in international cycling towered over that of the United States. Martin flew from his home in New York City to join his team: Howard, Wayne Stetina, Dave Chauner, John Gromeck, Bill Humphreys, and newcomer Dave Ware of Tallahassee.

Martin issued them new white team jerseys with a red band across the chest, emblazoned with USA in red, white, and blue lettering. "The ABL was behind the race and picked up the whole tab," Howard said. "That was a first."

Before the opening six-mile time trial in the rugged port town of Port aux Basques on Newfoundland's, windswept southwest corner, Howard said his legs were still weary from the Tour of Britain. But he didn't show any sign of weariness when his turn came to ride. He whipped through in the fastest time, 16 seconds ahead of Richard Foster of England in second place, and 22 seconds ahead of Stetina, third. Howard donned the race leader's yellow jersey. That put pressure on him and his teammates to defend the jersey.

The next day's stage of 55 miles northeast across the island to Cornerbrook was a test of teams and strategy. Riders from the English team alternated attacking off the front. Their attacks were like striking flint over kindling wood—one of them was likely to start a fire. Martin drove the team car and directed his riders to take turns going with every breakaway attempt—if one of the breaks went clear, at least one of his riders would be a contender.

"Butch did a superb job of making sure that there was one of us in every break, " Howard said. "This represented a departure from all of us racing individually. We were racing as a team."

None of the breaks ever got far before the peloton reeled them in. The stage ended in a spectacular mass pack sprint. Stetina galloped home to win. Howard, in fifth, retained his yellow jersey.

Hugh Walton of Toronto, a member of the Province of Ontario team, observed that the ABL team was riding smarter than expected. "Stetina, Chauner, and Howard knew exactly what they were doing in tactics," Walton said.

Even though it was summer, riders saw tall icebergs floating in Notre Dame Bay off Newfoundland's north coast. Stage 4 was the coldest, with the temperature in the low 40s and rain all day. Everyone suffered, but Dave Ware had it the worst. He was clipped by a car on the road and knocked to the pavement. An ambulance took him to a hospital for treatment of a concussion.

Howard and Stetina seemed to have a lock on the race as Foster faded. Canada's Hayman pulled off a pair of impressive stage victories to stay in the hunt.

On the penultimate race day, 92 miles to Clarenville, Howard and Stetina scored a coup. For the first 50 miles, a series of breaks off the front precipitated hard chases. The peloton regrouped near the top of a long hill. As riders relaxed upon regrouping, Howard and Stetina sprinted over the summit. Chauner, Gromek and other teammates promptly moved to the front to block.

For Howard and Stetina, the rest of the stage was a two-man team time trial. They picked up five minutes on the peloton. Howard took the stage, with Stetina on his wheel, to clinch the top two spots. Chauner finished the stage in fifth place to move up to third overall for a potential team sweep.

All that remained was the final day, 117 miles to St. John's, which was the tour's longest and hilliest stage. In contrast to the cold rain two days earlier, the sun burned through a cloudless sky and sent the temperature soaring into the 90s. "The fast change in weather was really weird," Walton said.

Heat and glaring sun convinced many riders to approach the day's ride with caution to avoid dehydration or muscle cramps. Around 50 miles, Chauner audaciously slipped away with Walton, another Canadian, and three Englishmen. By the feed zone at 60 miles, their lead stretched to four minutes.

Another 25 miles later, Chauner's breakaway partners had dwindled to Walton and Englishman Nigel Hall. Chauner paid the price for his efforts, however, and was suffering from the heat and glaring sun. "The only time I ever got sunstroke from racing was that afternoon," he said. "The route followed the ocean. We could see clear, white icebergs floating majestically offshore, and I was suffering chills and fever from exposure to the hot sun."

Howard was the subject of surveillance. Riders anticipated that he would take off. His overall lead of five minutes was in jeopardy if the breakaway gained more time. A race official sitting on the back of a motorcycle wrote the breakaway's lead margin in white chalk on a black slate for the riders to read. When Howard finally got out of the saddle to sprint away, a coterie of others fled with him like commuters hurrying to catch a train.

Chauner's breakaway was greeted boisterously by crowds lining the streets of St. John's, Newfoundland's capital. He forgot his physical discomforts in the excitement as they made the final turn and faced the uphill finish. Chauner led the sprint until Hall surged past to win, with Walton third.

Howard came in fourth, his overall victory preserved, and soon came Stetina. Howard, Stetina, and Chauner led a U.S. sweep for the Tour of Newfoundland. English riders took the next three places. Walton, seventh, was the top Canadian.

The Tour of Newfoundland was a career highlight for Howard and Chauner.

Howard and Chauner next turned their attention to preparing for the upcoming nationals and then the worlds. The Dorset training camp was a lively distraction as new classes formed every two weeks and top riders arrived for short stints to train. "We had a lot of 'hot dogs,' like Tom Officer or Flip Waldteufel," Swaim said. "They would come in, ride with us, teach a class."

On one early Saturday morning training ride, Howard and Swaim pedaled into Manchester Center, where they discovered an unsanctioned 30-mile race. It drew 20 riders, including national cross-country ski champion Mike Gallagher. ABL riders like Howard and Swaim risked losing their racing licenses for competing in an unsanctioned event, but the prospect of testing themselves against a national champion from another sport proved too tempting.

"We entered under aliases," Swaim said. "Two big streams in the area are the Metowee and the Battenkill. I signed up as Fred Metowee and John was John Battenkill. When the race got off, we saw that Gallagher was very strong. Obviously he was used to wearing everybody down. But he wouldn't ride close behind and draft because he was uncomfortable riding near anyone. John and I were doing our thing, working the pace line, and we quickly rode away from everybody with Gallagher. He stayed off to the side of us. His face turned three shades of blue by the turn-around at 15 miles. With three miles to go, Gallagher looked like an eggplant. After that, he specialized in time trials."

The national road racing championships didn't return to Milwaukee, but the city hosted Super Week, a week of racing July 13 to 21, as a prelude to the national road races the next weekend in Pontiac, Michigan.

Howard and Kim lived for the week in a dorm room at the University of Wisconsin where other riders also had accommodations. "I used to get up as early as 3:30 a.m. to cook whole-wheat banana pancakes on a two-burner Coleman stove," Kim said. "We got up that early because when John's races started at seven he had to eat in time to let his food digest."

Butch Martin went to Milwaukee to gauge performances, talk to riders, and pick the world championship road teams that would go to Montreal. (Track coach Jack Disney of Pasadena, California, was at the track nationals in Northbrook, Illinois.)

Super Week featured a variety of races, ranging from two 120-mile road races to a time trial series. Events were held around the city—in Humbolt Park, downtown, and by the lakefront—to help increase interest for spectators and riders. Race organizer Otto Wenz, Jr., who owned a local grocery store, limited the men's open races to 70 ABL Category I riders and a dozen top Canadians.

Hometown rider Jim Ochowicz was the local hero in the 100-kilometer Summerfest Grand Prix around a flat downtown criterium. More than 10,000 spectators lined the streets to cheer. When he won the pack sprint, they went wild in jubilation.

Another crowd favorite was Stetina, who won three races. His second place to Howard in the Tour of Newfoundland showed he was versatile beyond the criteriums he was popular for winning.

Martin went over the roster of riders to select three-man teams for the team trial of 42 miles. He and other ABL officials had long been in quest of the perfect team for the 100-kilometer team time trial in international competition—the ABL's Holy Grail. The team time trial during Super Week—seven laps over rolling terrain in Ozaukee County, just north of Milwaukee—was an important practice run. Martin put Ochowicz, Stetina, and Howard together.

They rode swiftly and smoothly—each rider taking a turn pulling at the front and dropping to the rear in neat rotation. The trio finished nearly two minutes ahead of the next team, which included Chauner and Neel. The winning team impressed Martin

John Howard wears the gold medal after winning the 1971 Pan American Games road race in Cali, Colombia. He remains the only U.S. rider to win the road race at the Pan American Games. *Credit: Howard Collection*

Inset: Howard winning the Hartford Travelers Cup 25-mile race and setting the national record. *Credit: Robert F. George*

Kim and John Howard at the 1972 Olympic road trials in Lake Luzerne, New York. *Credit: Robert F. George*

John Howard, as a member of the U.S. Army Cycling Team, the first American national cycling team, in 1972. *Inset:* When Howard strapped on his leather helmet, he went to the starting line prepared to win. *Credit: Robert F. George*

John and Kim in happier days.
Credit: Robert F. George

A determined John Howard aggressively forced the pace of American bicycle racing in the 1970s. *Credit: Robert F. George*

John Howard won the 1972 Tour de L'Estre in eastern Canada with teammates. From the left, Emile (Flip) Waldteufel, Tim Kelly, Howard, Bill Guazzo, John Allis, and John Gray. *Credit: Robert F. George*

On the winners' podium after the 1972 national road race championship in Milwaukee. Left to right: Wayne Stetina, 2nd place; Howard, winner; Dr. Bob Schneider, 3rd place. *Credit: Robert F. George*

Near the finish of Howard's winning stage in the 1973 Tour of Ireland, a breakthrough victory for U.S. riders abroad. As a member of the CRC of A–Raleigh team, he finished third overall, which opened doors for U.S. riders in international events. *Credit: Howard Collection*

At the 1974 Amateur Road Race in Montreal, Canada, Ryszard Szurkowski of Poland leads John Howard, #351. *Credit: Robert F. George*

After John Allis, shown here, won the 1974 national road racing championship, John Howard and other teammates celebrated by painting Allis's van to match his new stars and stripes champion's jersey. *Credit: Robert F. George*

After a successful performance in the 1973 Tour of Ireland, Howard helped the team earn an invitation to ride in a 1974 Tour of Britain. Shown here is the USA team bound for the Tour of Britain. From left: Mike Neel, Howard, Tom Officer, Dr. Rich (Captain America) Hammen, Flip Waldteufel, and John Allis. *Credit: Robert F. George*

When Tom Officer, right, reached down to fetch his water bottle near the finish of the 1975 national road race, Howard sprinted away for victory. *Credit: Robert F. George*

After Howard dueled against Dale Stetina, left, in 1975, Howard formed a new team for 1976 that included Stetina and brother Wayne. *Credit: Robert F. George*

Forcing the pace in the 1975 national road race championship in Milwaukee, from left, are Dave Boll, Mike Neel, Howard, and Jim Ochowicz. *Credit: Robert F. George*

Howard, middle, won his fourth national road title with breakaway companions Marc Thompson, left, third, and Tom Officer, second. *Credit: Robert F. George*

John Howard savored his triumph in the 1975 national road race championship in Milwaukee. *Credit: Robert F. George*

John Howard shows
determination in the
1976 national time
trial championship
near Louisville.
Credit: Robert F. George

Howard dons his 6th
national champion's jersey
after winning the 1976
national time trial
championship. He set the
new 40-kilometer (25 miles)
national record of 55:36.6.
Credit: Robert F. George

A smiling John Howard at the 1976 Montreal Olympics. Although U.S. cyclists did not win a metal, George Mount showed the U.S. team's improvement when he came in 6th in the road race. *Credit: Robert F. George*

Howard tries out his muscle bicycle designed by Roy "Skip" Hijsak. *Credit: Bruce Martin; Howard Collection*

Howard drafts behind the Pepsi Challenger that Rick Vesco drove, in Baja, Mexico. *Credit: Bruce Martin; Howard Collection*

John Howard nips an opponent in the Japan triathlon series in 1986 in Hondo, Japan. *Credit: Howard Collection*

John Howard and Fast Freddy Markham stand beside their tandem enclosed in an aerodynamic cover. At the national human-powered vehicle championships in 1989, they set a world record of 60.5 mph for the kilometer and 58.6 mph for the mile. *Credit: Howard Collection*

John Howard's riding experience, power, and handling skills help him succeed in a new cycling love—mountain biking. He competes in the pro-expert class.
Credit: Howard Collection

John Howard, splattered with mud from racing in the rain in Asti, California, radiates the determination that marked his career.
Credit: Robert F. George/Kim Howard Collection

as the riders he wanted for the team time trial in Montreal. One more rider remained for selection to make up the four-man team, and Martin had another week to decide at the national road race in Pontiac.

Howard rode consistently well in Super Week, and went to Pontiac feeling ready for his third consecutive national road championship. He was the only repeat winner since the road championship had been introduced in 1965. The 11.5-mile course through Pontiac and adjacent Bloomfield Hills (suburbs north of Detroit) was gently rolling, which put a premium on aggressiveness. The men's open race was 10 laps, a distance that would give Howard opportunity to show his speed and strength. But the past doesn't reliably indicate the future. As in the Tour of Louisiana, Tom Officer would play a key role as spoiler.

In the preliminary events, David Mayer-Oakes, an 18-year-old from Lubbock, Texas, and an occasional training partner of Howard, broke away in the 46-mile junior national boys' road race for an impressive triumph. His fitness and bold riding with a long solo showed that Texas raised champion cyclists.

The men's open race drew more than 220 starters, which made for an unwieldy peloton. Allis attempted to steal the show with his trademark early break, but the others were wise to him and chased. Some two dozen riders went down in a crash over a double set of railroad tracks. Race officials had packed the rails with dirt to round the rough edges and then laid rugs over the rails and dirt, but wheels still crumbled like paper and caused spills. Stetina and Ron Skarin were among the casualties.

Allis was caught, but others went off the front, prompting more chases. One breakaway after another, often composed of one to three riders little known outside their region, kept going up the road. None lasted long or gained enough to ride out of sight but they kept the action relentless. By 90 miles, Alan Kingsbury of Dayton forged a lead of one minute. Neel, Chauner, Officer, Heutter, and two other dashed away in pursuit. They worked a pace line to bridge the gap up to Kingsbury.

Howard and Allis saw them go and realized they had missed a crucial move. Chauner and Heutter were CRC of A-Raleigh teammates, which meant the role of Howard and Allis was to work with other teammates in the peloton—including Waldteufel, Gromek, and Humphries—to go to the front and block. But if Howard and Allis chased, they risked towing the entire peloton up to absorb the breakaway, which would leave Kingsbury alone and closer to the finish. So they worked with Waldteufel, Gromek, and Humphries at the front to slow the pace and block any chases. Then Howard and Allis drifted together to a flank of the peloton and shot away. Their remaining teammates blocked. It was a tricky maneuver.

Howard and Allis made it up to the break and got in their draft when Kingsbury and another rider who had made the chase found the pace overwhelming and drifted back to the peloton, which still trailed by a minute. That made seven riders in the breakaway, four of them CRC of A-Raleigh riders, with 15 miles to go.

Over the next few miles, Howard tried to flee, but Neel was shadowing him and caught his rear wheel, which drew the other five, and Howard's move was checked. Then Neel made a similar dash, which prompted Howard to chase with the others in tow until Neel saw it was futile. The closer they got to the finish, the more it looked like the 115-mile national road racing championship would be a showdown sprint over the last 200 yards.

Officer lacked punch in his sprint and knew his best prospect for winning was to surprise the others far enough from the finish line that they would let him go but close enough that he could play to his advantage. "Neel and I were non-Raleigh riders, so I knew that if I jumped ahead, he wouldn't chase me—but a Raleigh rider would, and probably just one, to cover the break."

With two miles left, Officer pedaled away furiously. "Allis got on my rear wheel and we went for it," he said.

"Chauner and I went to the front and blocked," Howard said. "We watched Allis and Officer go up the road, and we prayed that Allis could beat Officer."

Allis, 32, was the workhorse who always finished, always rode well in any tour team. But in major one-day races, someone else always had quicker legs. He never won a big race when it came down to a sprint. Suddenly he was now only one rider away from winning the national road title. His teammates left him to a *mano-a-mano*.

Officer towed Allis away and then swung out for Allis to take the lead, but Allis refused to move from Officer's rear wheel. Officer looked over his shoulder and saw Howard, Chauner, and others in CRC of A-Raleigh team jerseys cruising about the length of a football field behind. He put his head down and hammered the pedals for another half-mile before he yelled at Allis to take the lead.

"Tom was yelling, but it was more like pleading," Allis said.

"He knew what was going on, and he was pissed."

Howard and Chauner were close enough to hear, close enough to spurt up to them, but they bided their time.

"Allis was someone we all had great respect for," Howard said. "I admit that I was tempted to catch him and Officer. We could see them just ahead of us. But I really wanted Allis to win. I had seen how clever he was. He really wasn't a one-day rider because he couldn't sprint. But he was out there with Officer, and we were working for Allis that day. Allis was the kind of guy I would work for any time."

Officer tried everything he could think of as he pedaled to shake Allis from his rear wheel. "The last guy in the world I wanted on my wheel like that was Allis," he said. "I always looked up to him. He was always very helpful in coaching advice, in giving me encouragement. I was in a tough situation."

Up a small rise that was the last hill, which led down to the finish where spectators gathered, Officer tried one last desperate move. He touched his brakes and swerved sharply—a cyclist's equivalent to a boxer's sucker punch. Allis, a veteran of more than a thousand races, easily avoided the hook.

"I tried to knock him over," Officer said. "But it didn't work. Then I tried to wind it up for the finish, and John [Allis] came by me to win. I was happy for finishing second in my first nationals, but I was also real happy for John. He deserved it."

Thundering behind, Chauner won the dash for third, with Neel in promptly for fourth, Howard fifth. CRC of A-Raleigh riders kept the national champion's Stars and Stripes jersey, and they took seven of the top eleven places.

Back in Dorset, Kim Howard asked Allis to lend her his Volkswagen van for the morning so she could go shopping. Allis was tying his perforated black cycling shoes as he prepared to leave for a 100-mile group training ride. His van had enough miles to circle the globe at least a half-dozen times. Winning the new Ford Pinto in Montreal the previous summer hadn't made him want to give up his van. Instead, he sold the Pinto back to the race promoter for $1,600 and bought new tires and shock absorbers for the van. When Kim asked him for the keys, he gave them to her and pedaled away with Howard, Ochowicz, and others for a five-hour workout.

The shopping that Kim and Annie Cram had in mind was to buy paint to transform Allis's beloved van to match his national champion's jersey. "We wanted the memory to last," said Ochowicz. "It's one thing to shake a guy's hand for winning a race. [But] Allis really earned his national championship and we wanted to do something extra. So we decided to paint the Stars and Stripes on the van."

First came the daunting task of washing years of dirt, grime, and road bugs from the outside. After Kim and Annie spent the morning scrubbing it with a garden hose and Comet, they let it dry in the sun. Then they painted the forward half of the van red, leaving the roof white to reflect heat, and painted the back half with vertical white-and-blue stripes.

"We already had white contact paper cut into big stars that everybody at the camp signed without John knowing about it," Annie said. "Kim and I put the stars on the front of the van. It turned into a huge autograph album." But as she and Kim looked at their product, Annie had misgivings. She was worried that Allis would take offense to his van being repainted. "John is such a straight arrow," she said. "We all though his van should look like his jersey, but he didn't have to see it that way." Later, after supper, Allis and others in the training camp were sitting on the front porch of the annex on Church Street when he saw the van drive up the street for the first time since he had lent it to Kim. "All of a sudden, he let out that soprano giggle of his," Annie said. "And I knew we were home free."

Allis was in wonderland. So was everybody else at the Dorset training camp. New groups of campers arrived every two weeks. They mingled with Allis, Howard, and other national team members. Swaim took campers out on local dirt roads to practice drills designed to teach handling skills and develop confidence. Campers received classroom instruction on training and tactics, then went out on the roads to practice what they had learned. Classes concluded with Swaim and everyone driving to a weekend race in New England to apply the lessons.

Butch Martin had gone to Dorset right after the nationals to work the remaining three weeks with riders he had picked for the Montreal world championship teams. His lineup for the team time trial squad was Howard, Stetina, Ochowicz, and Rich Hammen, who had recovered from the Tour of Britain and won the southern California road racing championship. Riders for the 109-mile amateur road race were Allis, Chauner, Neel, and Marc Thompson of Kansas City.

Martin drove a motorcycle and introduced his riders to

motorpace riding behind it. "Our riders were strong, but they needed to be faster," he explained. "My idea was to get them riding one or two miles an hour faster and doing it comfortably."

Ochowicz was sensitive to Martin's effort. "We had a lot of guys who could ride 25 or 26 MPH all day, but they couldn't handle 28 MPH very long. That difference might not sound like much, but it is. That is what separated us from competing against the big teams in Europe who did race at 28 MPH."

Martin's choice of Ochowicz for the team time trial drew criticism, but ABL officials stood behind Martin.

"Butch was really pushing us," Howard said. "He had the ability to push us to new levels. He was upbeat and made us believe that we could beat those Europeans. American riders then had a feeling of inferiority when we went to international competition. But Butch pushed us through that. The motorpace training helped. We were thinking positively about winning a medal in the team time trial."

Teams from across the Atlantic and Pacific started arriving in early August in Montreal. The worlds opened August 14 with track events for amateurs and professionals, and continued through August 25. Women's defending sprint champion Sheila Young was eliminated early in the track races, but Sue Novara of Flint, Michigan, came through to reach the finals where she faced Tamara Piltskova of the Soviet Union. Novara lost to Piltskova but still won a silver medal. Novara's performance under pressure was good news for Americans.

Owen Mulholland, covering the four-man 100-kilometer team time trial for *Competitive Cycling*, reported that attendance was a private affair limited to the press, team support, and a horde of police who roared back and forth on their throbbing 750 cc motorcycles.

Twenty-two teams competed in the team time trial on August 21, a typically hot, humid day. The course went 25 kilometers (15.6 miles) out on a gently undulating highway to a turn-around, then doubled back, and was repeated once more. "We had the best team we ever had," Howard said. "Wayne Stetina usually wore himself out in other races leading to a big event, but he was ready in Montreal. We all were. I really wanted to win a medal and approached the race determined to give 110 percent."

Teams went out at two-minute intervals. Howard took double and triple pulls at the front of the foursome before dropping back to recover behind Stetina. Ochowicz took over before swinging out for Hammen in the rotation. Martin rode in a car following behind to keep track of times.

By 50 kilometers (31.75 miles), the squad had moved up to 12th place. Soviet riders led, with the Swedish team—which included Bernt Johansson and Tord Filipsson from the Tour of Britain—snugly behind in second.

But drama unfolded in the second half as some teams wilted under the heat and sun. Czechoslovakian riders, who had been third through the first quarter, fell behind the U.S. team and ultimately finished 15th. The Swedes overtook the Soviets to carry on for victory and uphold the highest standards of the Pettersson brothers.

Howard's long pulls caught up to him in the last 25 kilometers. "I was in deep anaerobic debt," he said, although he held his own in the rotation.

By the final 25 miles, the Americans overtook the French and Italian teams to move up. Their speed training behind Martin's motorcycle was showing. They rose to ninth place—the first time the American time trial team ever cracked the top 10 in international competition.

"In the last 10 kilometers (6.2 miles)," Martin said, "Ochowicz was our real spark plug. He took the longest and hardest pulls."

The American team finished together and held on to ninth. Besides beating the Czechs, French, and Italians, they rode faster than traditionally strong teams from Belgium and West Germany. Their time of 2:19:15 was seven minutes (about two miles) behind the victorious Swedes, but they were less than a minute and a half behind the fourth-place team, from Holland.

"Fourth place through 12th were bunched within a span of two minutes," Martin pointed out. "We didn't win a medal, but we were definitely closing the gap fast."

Chapter 8

"My heroes have always been cowboys."
—Willie Nelson

Howard knew he had overextended himself during the team time trial, but he didn't realize the full extent until three days later when he was some 40 miles into the 110-mile world amateur road racing championship. He was one of six U.S. riders among the 172 starters from 33 nations. The race started more aggressively than usual. The first lap was the fastest of the entire race, faster than any lap the professionals rode the next day on the same course. The speed strung the peloton out in a pace-line file three blocks long. A pileup toward the end of the file effectively axed Mike Neel and Dave Chauner on the first lap around the rugged 7.9-mile circuit through Mt. Royal Park. On the second lap, Wayne Stetina and Marc Thompson couldn't ride fast enough up the grinding 1.5-mile ascent to the top of Mt. Royal—the mountain that overlooks the city of Montreal—to stay with the peloton and they dropped out. That left Howard and Allis as the only U.S. riders in the race. Allis wisely stayed in the shelter of the peloton when a breakaway of about 20 riders went up the road. But Howard bolted away on the fifth lap up Mt. Royal on Camillien-Houde Highway in an excited but suicidal chase. He lasted alone for less than three miles. When the peloton caught him, Howard felt the entire summer's preparation for the team time trial and the time trial itself overwhelm him all at once. "I was blown," he said.

Kim was shocked to hear over the loudspeakers that Howard had pulled out. "I couldn't believe it," she said. "John never pulled out of races."

Howard, who had turned 27 the previous week, had been confronted with his physical limit. "My legs just couldn't respond when my mind wanted to go," he said. "I remember watching Tom Officer down in Florida, riding so hard that he fell off his bike at the end of the 10-mile time trial, and I rode the worlds team time trial with that kind of intense effort. I put so much of myself into the team time trial that I shouldn't have started the road race. I was looking forward to mixing it up with the big shots, but when the crunch came, I was completely flat. I reached that certain point physically where my mind couldn't any longer take my body."

Allis fared only slightly better. He faltered up Mt. Royal with five laps left in the race. After the summit, he took advantage of the following vehicles to draft behind them and leapfrog back to the peloton. On the next ascent he dropped off the back and repeated this chase pattern for the next four laps until he completed the race, finishing 64th, nearly 13 minutes behind winner Janusz Kowalski of Poland. Allis explained, "My legs just exploded."

To continue the sport in the face of such adversity was a measure of Howard's dedication. Yet even this had boundaries. The climax of the 12 days of world championships was the professional road race. Pros competed over 20 laps for 164 miles. It was vintage professional racing. Eddy Merckx (it rhymes with works) and Freddy Maertens of Belgium, Raymond Poulidor and Bernard Thevenet of France, Gösta Pettersson of Sweden, and Giovanni Battaglin and Constantini Conti of Italy were among the 70 pros competing. Particular favorites among the spectators were Merckx—nicknamed "The Cannibal" for his voracious appetite for winning everything—and Poulidor—nicknamed "Eternal Second" for his second-place finishes in the Tour de France.

The pro road race was highly tactical. Thevenet, destined to win the Tour de France twice, made a courageous solo that lasted 80 miles. With two laps to go, about 16 miles, his lead was two minutes—nearly a mile. He was caught five miles from the finish by a chase group that Merckx led like a locomotive. Catching Thevenet, Merckx tore past, crossed the line alone, waving his arms high. It was his third world pro road championship. Poulidor, two seconds behind, was second—again. Thevenet rallied to finish fifth, two minutes later.

Howard appreciated the sophisticated tactics, the daring of Thevenet, the heroics of Merckx, and the raw horsepower of all the pros. But Howard wasn't tempted to make the jump from the amateur ranks. Professional racing was virtually nonexistent in the United States, and he wasn't interested in moving to Europe, where the sport thrived on the roads.

"Amateur racing in the world championships had a lot of

problems," he observed. "The pros were more controlled. They rolled very fast and didn't have nearly as many attacks, or crashes. "I have great respect for the guys who race professionally. But I saw the games they played, the way the results were sometimes manipulated. At the finish of the 1973 worlds in Barcelona, for example, I saw Freddy Maertens in the pro race put on his brakes in the finishing sprint so that Felice Gimondi could win. Gimondi was a great road rider, one of Italy's best, but he was never the sprinter that Maertens was. Gimondi rode for Bianchi, one of the big Italian teams which, of course, equipped their bikes with Campagnolo components. When I asked my boss, Giomeccelli of Campagnolo, about what went on in Barcelona, he just smiled.

"There was a certain purity that the amateurs had that the pros didn't. I was in the sport because I truly enjoyed the spirit of competition. When I raced, I was out there to win. When I was beaten, it was by whomever was better, or smarter, that day. We didn't make deals. The spirit of competition was very much part of what I was doing out there. It was part of me, and it still is."

The Montreal worlds were a turning point for Howard. He had put everything into trying for a medal, but fell short. Yet his passion for the sport was as strong as ever. He was America's leading cyclist, and he had a comfortable deal with Campagnolo, who mailed him his paycheck regularly. American cycling was growing, and he was in demand. After the worlds, he and Kim flew out to Colorado for the seventh annual Aspen Alpine Cup race.

The Aspen Alpine Cup challenged riders up towering mountains and provided luxury accommodations in ski resorts. A three-day weekend event, August 31 to September 2, the race went 272 miles in six stages of a counterclockwise route over the Rocky Mountains. Riders crossed the Continental Divide, rode through the White River National Forest, scaled two-mile elevations beyond the timberline, and had an overnight stop in the resort of Breckenridge. Race promoter Bert Bidwell joked that his race was so high up in the mountains that riders who dropped out would get a ride back to the finish in a snowmobile.

Bidwell, a retired racer and proprietor of the Mountain Sporting Goods Shop in Aspen, had organized a prize list of $5,000 in merchandise. Charging an entry fee of $5.25, he provided meals in first-class restaurants as well as accommodations for all three days, plus a post-race picnic, for another $20. Bidwell sent airline tickets for Kim and John Howard as well as John Allis.

Bidwell's race attracted adventurous riders. One of the boldest was George Mount, a brash 18-year-old who rode for Pete Rich's VeloSport team. Mount came from a long line of Princeton graduates but when he graduated in May 1973 from Acalanes High School in Lafayette, near Berkeley, he passed up the chance to attend the Ivy League campus for the itinerant life of a bicycle racer.

Mount became a protégé of Pete Rich, who hired him to work part-time in his bike shop to give Mount a little income and flexible hours to train and travel to races. Mount lived upstairs in Rich's two-story shop, where there was a hot plate for cooking meals and a shower. Mount relished racing. The harder the pace, the more he liked it, which brought a smile to his face when others around him were grimacing. He became known as Smiling George.

Smiling George and three other Bay-area riders packed their bikes and spare wheels in a beat-up Peugeot sedan and drove 1,250 miles to Aspen. There he challenged Howard up the mountains. He wasn't ready for prime time, but he showed promise.

Howard dominated the event, winning five of the six stages for overall victory. Teammate Allis was second. Mount, sixth overall, got in some licks. He learned from Howard and Allis what he was going to have to do to get to the top of American racing as preparation for going to Europe. "I went to Aspen for the experience, " Mount said. "It was an epic adventure."

At the end of the summer John and Kim Howard returned to Houston, where they moved into an apartment in the River Oaks area off Memorial Drive. Howard went to work at the Campagnolo USA warehouse downtown, relieved to get into an office routine.

Howard's departure from Monarch Crescent for Campagnolo USA was well-timed. Bicycle sales had started to slip from the all-time peak of 15.2 million in 1973 to 7.3 million in 1975. Campagnolo products were expensive, but that only added to their prestige. When Campagnolo USA opened its warehouse in Houston, demand for Campagnolo derailleurs, hubs, rims, and other parts started strongly and then increased. Howard worked that autumn and through the winter of 1975 helping to set up an inventory system for the various components.

"Our staff only knew that these were bike parts," Howard said. "I told them what the parts were for, how to tell a front-wheel hub from a rear-wheel hub, brake cables from gear cables, and so on, to send the proper parts to fill orders correctly."

Campagnolo's popularity in America also became a nuisance

as entrepreneurs went to Italy to visit the company's founder, Tullio Campagnolo. A gregarious man, Campagnolo was still involved in the family business when he wasn't tending his vineyard in northern Italy. A good racer in the 1920s and early 1930s, Tullio had invented the quick-release hub after an agonizing experience. (The quick-release hub releases a bicycle wheel from the frame with a flick of a lever that fits to the hub axle.) In a late-1925 race that went up the Italian Alps where snow covered the roads, Campagnolo had a flat tire. He quickly got off his bicycle and tried to unfasten the wing nuts that locked the wheel to the frame, but the wing nuts were frozen and wouldn't budge. He didn't finish the race. That wounded his pride and he was determined never to have that happen again.

He experimented with parts until he perfected the quick release. Right away, his hubs were in demand from every racer and nearly all recreation cyclists. In 1933 Campagnolo founded his company and applied his ingenuity to other components, which over the years set industry standards. When U.S. business representatives visited him, they returned home with a load of Campagnolo parts that filled orders from friends with bicycle shops in the United States. The visits created good will for Tullio Campagnolo, but they undercut Campagnolo USA.

"After spending months setting up inventory, we had to see about sealing off the outside competition," Howard said. "Business was good, though. Occasionally we had million-dollar months. They were always cause for celebration. We would break out Campagnolo wine. Mr. Campagnolo had become tired of small corkscrews, so he made his own. We all had big, gold Campagnolo corkscrews."

Howard settled into a routine of working during the day and training during the late afternoon and weekends. He and Kim went out to popular night spots, like Gilley's Club in suburban Pasadena, a club so huge that it sprawled for several city blocks under the same roof.

Texas oil money gave the state a big injection of cash that propelled spending. Music from Austin helped rejuvenate a national cowboy chic. City folk who never saw a cactus unless it was on a movie screen wore cowboy boots and Western shirts.

"We were drugstore cowboys," Howard said. "When we lived in Houston, we really wanted to soak up the culture there. We went to the Houston livestock rodeo, wore cowboy boots. At Gilley's, we had a grand old time."

Houston was a conservative corporate city unlike Austin, whose artistic ambiance appealed to Kim and Howard. Austin had a blossoming blues scene. Clubs on Sixth Street were jammed with SRO performances. The Fabulous Thunderbirds with Jimmie Vaughan on guitar and Lou Ann Barton belting out songs attracted an avid following that was spreading to Chicago and New York. From all around the South, musicians were moving to Austin. The city ranks first in Texas for musicians and artists per capita.

Howard's cycling season wound down, but it wasn't over. Promoters David Balkan and Joe Avalos invited him to the November 2 and 3 weekend of racing in the Tour of Coconut Grove, a suburb of south Miami. Balkan and Avalos raised funds from the Coconut Grove business community to donate $6,400 in merchandise prizes, including a $1,000 U.S. Savings Bond to the winner of the main event, the second day's 50-mile criterium.

"I went to Miami every chance I got to race there," Howard said. "I loved Florida." He had no difficulty winning the opening day's 7.4-mile time trial. He eclipsed Wayne Stetina, who was followed by his younger brother, Dale, in third. Their father, Roy Stetina, made it a family affair when he competed in the veterans' 9-mile race. He was third.

Wayne Stetina and John Allis rode aggressively to escape from the peloton of 70 Category I and II riders. But when Stetina took off, Howard chased until Stetina was caught. When Allis attacked he couldn't ride fast enough, even with Howard blocking, to open a crucial gap. Their efforts to break away proved unsuccessful, but the speed of the race and the technical demands of the course trimmed the field nearly every lap, mostly from crashes.

Meanwhile, Steve Woznick rode at the back of the peloton to preserve the snap of his sprint. Every time a rider dropped to the back, Woznick moaned, "Get in front of me. I've been lapped."

Howard tried to force the speed high enough to drop Woznick, who drafted snugly in the shelter of the back until the final laps, when he quickly moved up the peloton to the front.

Out of the final turn, Woznick surged ahead to win by three bike lengths over Bobby Phillips of Baltimore, a noted pack sprinter whose nickname was The Baltimore Bullet. Howard was fourth, followed closely by John Chapman, Jim Montgomery, Stetina, and Allis.

The following weekend, Howard ended the season on an upbeat note in the Wurstfest Festival in Austin and nearby New Braunfels.

His main rival was national junior champion Mayer-Oakes of Lubbock. Against Howard in the 70-mile road race from Austin through Texas hill country to New Braunfels, Mayer-Oakes found Howard granted no quarter. "John creamed me," he said.

The 15-mile time trial and criterium of 30 miles in New Braunfels the next day played to Howard's strengths. He won the overall event by more than four minutes. Howard's cycling year ended symmetrically, with wins at the beginning and end of the season.

Howard and Allis shared *Competitive Cycling's* Rider of the Year honorary award. They were the kings of the road in American cycling. But California was harvesting talented riders who would challenge Howard and overwhelm Allis.

When Allis had competed in the early 1960s for the French team Athletic Club Boulogne-Billancourt (ACBB) outside Paris, he was the rare U.S. rider. In the early spring of 1974 another American joined ACBB. Jonathan Boyer of Carmel, California, bypassed the entire ABL system and went to France. Boyer, 19, went native, learning fluent French, answering to the name of Jacques, and winning six Category I races in the 1974 season. He didn't represent the United States in the Montreal worlds, which many observers felt was an injustice. Boyer's absence from American racing, augmented by his poker face published in infrequent features, gave him a mystique in his homeland.

In the winter of early 1975, Howard's training was lax but steady. For variety, he ran—usually two miles—did calisthenics, and stretched. It was a good time for surgery to take care of a deviated nasal septum. "My nose was getting worse, and I talked in a nasally twang," he said. "[The surgery] helped me breathe easier."

He also studied yoga and meditation as an antidote to the emotional tension that came with long stage races, and which he had first encountered in the Tour of Ireland. Howard's disposition is shy, his manner relaxed. But for races he changed character to become highly aggressive, sometimes to the point of being high-strung. Like most successful athletes, he learned to feather his aggression. During competition, he was ready to unleash a furious, all-out physical effort jazzed up by an adrenaline explosion, but most often that fury was carefully controlled and the energy was meted out to meet the physical effort required as the demands and strategy unfolded. But after a few days' action in the Tour of

Ireland, Howard had lain in bed at night preoccupied with upcoming demands. A long way from home and unable to sleep properly, he couldn't shut off the pump of adrenaline.

"I wasn't resting right," he said. "Our trainer gave me Seconal, and that worked well. I fell asleep right away and woke up the next morning feeling refreshed, ready to concentrate on the next day's race. That got me through the Tour of Ireland. But then I was addicted to Seconal—couldn't sleep without it. I had a big bottle of Seconal, which lasted till I got back to Houston. Then I went cold turkey. But I decided that I had to do something about relaxing. It sounds simple, but in a stage race it's not. There's a lot of pressure, day after day. That got me into yoga and meditation. Kim and I read books on them and practiced a lot."

Jim Ochowicz—now a dedicated road racer—settled in Austin early in the year. His victory in the 1974 Canadian classic from Quebec to Montreal convinced him that he had made the transition from the track to the roads. (Ochowicz won the final Quebec-to-Montreal race, which ended after 41 years.) Ochowicz took John Allis's offer to ride on the team going to the Tour of Britain. Ochowicz succeeded Tom Officer, who struck out for France, along with David Mayer-Oakes and Jonathan Boyer.

Mike Neel signed back on for a second Tour of Britain, then shipped out to Europe for the winter indoor season on wooden tracks from Antwerp, Belgium, to Cologne, Germany, before settling in Florence, Italy, where he earned a berth on the Groupo Sportiva Sipa team for the regular season. "I liked Italy over France," Neel said. "Italians were friendlier. They made sure you always had something to eat, and the jokes were better."

Howard didn't heed the siren call to Europe. "I much preferred racing in America," he said. "And the sport was changing and improving so much in the 1970s."

Some of the changes included the ABL board of directors voting in 1975 to officially change the organization's name. It had been the Amateur Bicycle League of America since its founding in 1921, but board members and a majority of the more than 10,000 members felt that "amateur" had a negative meaning, "league" was archaic, and "America" was offensive to cycling organizations in Canada, Mexico, and other Central and South American countries. On January 1, 1976, the organization was renamed the United States Cycling Federation. Another name change involved *CycleNews*. Publishers Barbara and Robert George re-christened it *VeloNews*.

A bold change was the national team's preparation for the 1975 Tour of Britain. The Mexican cycling federation invited the ABL to send a team to the 12-day Transpeninsular de Mexico race in April that went 1,000 miles north up the length of the Baja California peninsula. "We realized that we needed a big stage race before the Tour of Britain as a tune-up," John Allis said. "The race in Baja looked just right for us, one month before the Tour."

Howard was anxious about the prospect of returning to Mexico. His three previous trips there to race had been gastrointestinal calamities. "I had to learn to eat and survive," he said. So he studied how to prevent problems with Mexican food and water. Finally he learned, and he and Kim joined American cycling's early-spring migratory flow to south Florida where he won both the Tour of Coconut Grove and the Cross-Florida Tour, the latter for the fourth time.

The Mexican government spent nearly $1 million on the Transpeninsular de Mexico race, April 14 to 27, to promote the new highway that links the 800-mile peninsula in northwest Mexico—between the Pacific Ocean and the Gulf of California—with North America, where it abuts the state of California.

Twelve teams of six riders each entered from Colombia, Cuba, Guatemala, and the United States, along with six regional Mexican teams and the Mexican national team. The Transpeninsular de Mexico paid cash prizes to the first 40 finishers and top five teams. The winner and his team would collect more than $10,000. That spurred the national cycling federations to send their best talent, which represented the best racers in the northern and southern hemispheres.

Because the Canadian cycling federation declined their invitation, the Mexican cycling federation invited the ABL to send two teams. The ABL, limited to a modest budget, could afford only one team of six riders, a mechanic, and a manager. But Pete Rich in organized a second U.S. team, composed of northern California riders, a mechanic, and a manager, and bore most of the costs.

Howard flew to La Paz, on the southern tip of the peninsula, where he joined teammates Chauner, Ochowicz, Allis, Rich Hammen, and Marc Thompson, mechanic Bill Woodul, and team manager Butch Martin. They made up the ABL national team, designated as the USA-A team. The USA-B team included George Mount, Flip Waldteufel, and Dave Boll.

The Transpeninsular de Mexico went from La Paz and serpentined north to finish in Mexicali, near the border of California. The route coursed over mountains and across deserts. Riders endured burning sun, cold rain, and stinging hail. It was one of the most demanding efforts of Howard's career, pushing him past his physical limits as the race leader's yellow jersey changed hands six times. It became one of his greatest achievements.

A rousing criterium prologue of 17 miles in downtown La Paz set the tone of the race. Motorcycle police gunned their engines and blew whistles in front of the peloton to clear the roads around the 3.4-mile course. Riders went five laps, followed by a long caravan of honking vehicles with international commissaires, team vehicles, and assorted dull-green Mexican Army trucks loaded with tents, bedding, and food, and a portable bar for the police.

"The criterium had a huge crowd turnout," Howard said. "They filled the sidewalks around the course. They all cheered like crazy. It was free entertainment and they loved it. They really went wild."

Responding to the excitement, riders raced furiously, with constant attacks off the front of the peloton of 72 riders. None gained a significant lead, but they kept the pace frenetic. On the final lap, three Cubans dashed away together, promptly pursued by two Colombians and two Mexicans. Jim Ochowicz and Dave Boll fled after them to cover the break by five seconds, a small margin that made the spectators jump up and down in excitement.

Cuba's Antonio Madera won the sprint for the privilege of being the first to wear the yellow jersey. Ochowicz finished fifth, Boll eighth, to put riders on the two U.S. teams in the top 10.

La Paz, the capital of Baja California Sur, one of Mexico's 31 states, is a modern city with high-rise buildings of glass and steel. But most of the race up the peninsula ended in remote locations where the Mexican Army soldiers erected a tent city and riders slept on cots. The remote locations made for early-morning starts for stages to conclude by early afternoon. The media promptly filed their stories by couriers who flew in a small plane to Mexico City where the stories went over the wires or satellite feed for afternoon news.

The next day, the race arced northwest for a rolling 100-mile stage to Ciudad Constitucion, midway across the peninsula width. "The style of racing was what we called chicken chasing," Mount said. "We would ride real hard in the gutter of the road, everybody bent over his bike, head down, our tongues practically wrapped around the handlebars to keep them from getting caught on our front tires. The entire field strung out in a pace line that was gnarly. Then, suddenly, we would all slow down. Everybody would sit up. We were constantly chicken chasing, then sitting up."

Howard and his teammates were ready for the action. On the road to Ciudad Constitucion were three premiums, of which Howard won two, and Ochowicz won one, with Chauner right behind. They gained a remarkable one-two-three lead in the points classification, a subplot in the greater race. Their dashing after premiums on top of the erratic chicken chasing, however, left the ABL team without a rider in a break of five that finally went clear. Waldteufel from USA-B made that break, which gained 45 seconds on the peloton. Manuel Ceja of the Mexican national team won the sprint, but was penalized five seconds for zig-zagging in the last 200 yards and endangering the other riders. Waldteufel, in second, became the new race leader.

Waldteufel kept the jersey another day, over the 87-mile stage up and down the Sierra de la Giganta mountains on the Baja's east Gulf of California coast. But his race leadership put a strain on his team as the numerous Mexican teams alternated working the leader's team over with attacks and chicken chasing.

On the fourth day, a rugged 84 miles over more of the Sierra de la Giganta mountains, Waldteufel's teammate, Tim Parker of Berkeley, suffered food poisoning and exhaustion and was forced to drop out. The team, overextended early in the race, was unable to keep Waldteufel in the break that went away. He finished 11th, 38 seconds behind stage winner Raul Vazquez of Cuba, who became the new race leader, two seconds ahead of Waldteufel, now in second place overall. Within striking distance were Howard, Chauner, and Ochowicz, all in the top 10. The next day's twin stages—an early-morning time trial and a mountain road race—would favor Howard, but Waldteufel's experience would be valuable.

Stage racing is bicycle racing at its most complex, with daily sacrifices that are like small tiles that make up the overall mosaic. Martin had been reluctant to include John Allis on his USA-A team, despite Allis's reigning as national road champion and his past record. Martin was planning ahead to the Pan American Games and the Montreal Olympics. He was looking for a rising 19-year-old, like Mount. Allis, 33, was regarded as an elder statesman by the peloton.

Worst of all, Allis candidly admitted he was inadequately

trained. Cyclists need at least 2,000 miles of riding to begin to meet the rigors of competition. "He told me he had only about 900 miles in his legs," Martin said. "But he was our most experienced stage race rider. I knew he would finish well and inspire the other riders."

Allis, with red hair and a fair complexion, was badly burned by the sun. "John really suffered down there," Martin said. "He got sunburned so badly that he had to ride with creams all over his arms and legs. [But] he was an old war horse and he pulled through."

Allis was riding into shape just in time to help his team, so Howard pulled out all the stops on the fifth day. It began with a time trial of 15 miles, held into a lively head wind. Howard successfully drew upon his time trial strength to win the stage. He gained 1:03 over Vazquez to become the race's fourth leader.

Martin was apprehensive that Howard took the lead too early in the race. "I had looked at the topographical map of the race course before the start and saw that it was going to be a hard 12 days of racing," he explained. "The course was tough, and the competition was really tough as well. The Mexican national team was managed by Augustino Alcantara, who was a very good racer and knew what he was doing with his riders. He had an excellent all-round rider named Rudolfo Vitella, who basically took Alcantara's mantle of Mexico's top road rider. Vitella climbed better than Howard and he could sprint pretty good, although he wasn't a burner. Then there was the Cuban team, which was strong, and the Colombians could really climb the best of any team. I wanted Howard to cool his jets in the time trial. Save something for the last days. But he went out and blasted."

"That made things more difficult for us," Howard agreed. "But I couldn't ride the time trial any other way than to win."

Hours later, riders lined up for the day's second stage, 48 rolling miles interrupted by a steep, five-mile climb. The Colombian team, accustomed to riding in the Andes, led over the top of the day's hardest climb. Only four Mexicans and Howard could keep up. Over the summit, the breakaway was aided by a tailwind. Francisco Vazquez of the Mexican national team won the stage, with teammate Vitella in second, Howard third.

Howard, wearing the yellow jersey, and his team faced eight days of defending it. "That put real pressure on the team," he said. The green points jersey and other individual classifications that his teammates might pick up along the way were subordinated to keeping Howard in the yellow jersey.

While Martin, Howard, and the others planned their team strategy and evaluated their opposition, Mexican soldiers set up a temporary base for the night in rural Mexico.

"It was a wild race," Howard said. "Some nights we stayed in luxury hotels. Other nights we were in army tents. Every day, at every meal, we ate Mexican Army food—beans and rice, sometimes with chicken. The food was always the same, three times a day. I was taking garlic capsules to keep me going. In that race, I found that eating lots of garlic was the way to avoid getting sick."

"We called him Garlic John," Woodul said. Woodul, originally from Waco, Texas, was accustomed to eating beans and rice, but he was surprised to discover the Mexican Army served watermelon juice. "That was an exotic drink," he said.

Out in the Mexican desert that night, Howard came upon his first cactus, many of which exceeded 40 feet in height. "They had flowers blooming on them, and they were much bigger than I expected. In the darkness, they appeared to be alive and moving."

The next morning was a stage of 100 miles of flat and rolling desert to Guerrero Negro, on the Pacific coast. A dozen riders on Mexican regional teams, none of whom was in the top 20 overall, sneaked away while Howard, Vitella, and other leaders let them go. The peloton rode casually under the burning sun.

Despite the newness of the highway, the pavement was coarse. "Portions of the road were washed away from floods," Woodul said.

With 40 miles left in the stage, Martin and Woodul drove their team car up to the peloton and reported to Howard and his team that the breakaway was 20 minutes ahead. "John was riding at the back of the peloton when he should have been up front," Martin said. "The race leader has responsibilities. He has to be up in the front third, showing the colors and acting as a deterrent for challengers. When riders don't see the leader's jersey, they put their heads down and go. Those guys gained a lot of time.

"Our guys went to the front, with John. They had to work a pace line while the whole peloton enjoyed the ride. Our guys brought back the breakaway, minute by minute. Jim Ochowicz and Dave Chauner really put out. They sacrificed themselves, and paid the price by losing places in general classification over the next few days. But it was what we had to do to keep John in the yellow jersey. If he could hold on to it all the way to Mexicali, we were going to make more than $10,000. That was a big incentive. But 20 minutes is a hell of a lot of time to bring back."

They narrowed the gap to within three minutes—close, but

still short. Tito Lugo of Mexico's Regional Centro team was in the break and gained national attention as a result. He finished fourth that day and catapulted from obscurity to first overall. Howard dropped to second place, nine seconds behind.

Emotions ran high as Martin, Howard, and their team worked on their strategy to gain back the yellow jersey. They had a day to work on it, since the next day was Sunday, the race's only rest day.

On this rest day riders didn't race, but Howard and others pedaled for a couple of hours to keep their legs loose. That evening they were treated to songs, poetry, speeches, and folk dancing on an outdoor stage the soldiers had erected.

Two days later, Howard recaptured the yellow jersey by one second. In the 81-mile stage to Santa Ines, near the peninsula's Gulf coast, time bonuses were awarded to the top three. Howard finished third, which earned him a deduction of 10 seconds from his time—enough to take back the lead. The yellow jersey fitted easily over his shoulders, but it was difficult to keep.

The next day was a 100-mile stage across the peninsula and north to San Quentin on the Pacific coast. Howard, chastened by experience, rode at the front of the peloton with teammates and responded to a break that went off the front. He and Marc Thompson joined six others while Lugo took it easy in the peloton. Howard finished second, leading by 1:21. Four days of racing remained.

While Howard's lead was significant, Rudolfo Vitella had moved up to third place, and was a formidable threat. Vitella had been biding his time, skulking in the peloton and the occasional breakaway. Team manager Augustin Alcantara was wise to stage racing. He adhered to the philosophy that it is better to be the hunter than the hunted. Rivals can capitalize on the leader's misfortune—a flat tire or mechanical failure, a bad day in the mountains, or missing a crucial breakaway. Vitella, in third, was ready to overtake Howard.

Howard was a Yankee—an outsider with shrinking support. Teammate Jim Ochowicz was forced to withdraw with food poisoning. Allis, his skin burned and lathered with creams, was riding into shape. Compatriots on the USA-B team suffered the loss of Dave Boll, who had food poisoning, which left Mount, Waldteufel, and two others all riding just to finish.

"The Mexican teams ganged up on Howard," Martin said. "They outnumbered us 7 to 1. Alcantara waved the flag at them, yelling that they shouldn't let a gringo wear their yellow jersey. Our guys did a lot of grunt riding to chase down breaks."

On the 100-mile stage up the Pacific coast to Ensenada, the first big city since they left La Paz, Howard and his teammates spent the day chasing breakaways. The stage finished in downtown Ensenada where more than 250,000 spectators turned out to watch and cheer. Howard finished in the pack to keep his jersey for another day. But he wasn't feeling as if he could keep it much longer.

"With three days left, I was feeling dead," Howard said. "I had lost my appetite. I wasn't eating enough to keep my strength up. The awful part was that the next day we were going to face the nastiest hills of the race. The day after was going to be even worse—we were going over the Rumo Rosa Gap, a grinding climb that was 14 miles long, starting at sea level and going up to 4,500 feet. If I had been feeling up to strength, I would have looked forward to it. But I was dreading it."

Howard felt strained in the rainy, 63-mile stage up the Pacific coast to Tijuana. "The Mexican teams kept attacking," Martin said. "One after the other, and they had so many teams."

Howard and his teammates alternated in countering the attacks. Eventually, Vitella went with a break of five others, including Rich Hammen, and rolled up a two-minute lead. Howard, Allis, Thompson, and Chauner chased with the peloton in tow to bring back the break, or to limit the damage. Allis had found his racing legs and was a strong piston in their pace line.

On the outskirts of Tijuana, 10 miles from the finish downtown, crowds began lining both sides of the road. Spectators stood shoulder to shoulder, cheering for the breakaway and the chasing peloton, propelled by the U.S. team. As riders neared the finish, crowds deepened to three and four deep, yelling at the top of their lungs.

Vitella's breakaway stayed together 1:30 ahead of the peloton. Vitella rewarded his partners by not contesting the sprint, won by his teammate Manuel Ceja. Hammen finished a few lengths down for fourth. Vitella, in sixth, achieved what he wanted—he advanced to second overall and took a chunk out of Howard's lead, now pared back to 44 seconds.

The strategy that Alcantara devised for the penultimate day's 100-mile stage east across the peninsula to Mexicali was for Vitella to attack with teammates up Rumo Rosa and drop Howard. All that was left afterward was the final day's criterium in downtown Mexicali, and its fast pace would check any breakaway and preserve the overall order. That made the stage to Mexicali a showdown.

"I remember the Tijuana newspaper had a headline that said Rudolfo Vitella was going to destroy John Howard," Chauner said. "At stake for us was $1,500 each. That was the biggest payday of my cycling career, and it beat the hell out of winning bicycle parts and then having to fence them for gas money. We were going to do everything we could to help John. He had the juice. But he was going to have to get over the Rumo Rosa on his own with Vitella."

Howard felt like a boxer getting pummeled against the ropes. "I was so tired I had no adrenaline left," he said. "After the stage to Tijuana was over, I had a shower and went for a walk. I passed the Mexican national team, sitting outside on folding chairs. Their team doctor was with them, and I got to talking with him. He spoke some English, and I spoke some Spanish. I told him I was tired. I said the racers knew I was tired. I don't know why I leveled with this guy, but he said he could help me, and he did. He took a syringe and needle out of his medical bag and gave me an injection of vitamin B complex."

Vitamin B complex is an important group of water-soluble vitamins containing vitamins like thiamine, riboflavin, and folic acid, all essential for normal functioning of the nervous system, production of iron, and digestion of food. European stage racers had long been taking injections of it, but they were new to Howard. Right away he felt much better. His appetite returned.

"At dinner, one full meal wasn't enough," he said. "I had to have another, then another. My body just suddenly exploded with power. I was ready for the Rumo Rosa."

Another rider eating his way up Rumo Rosa was George Mount. He and teammates drove their team car across the border to a suburb of San Diego, where they found a restaurant offering a smorgasbord special: all you could eat for a fixed price. Mount and his teammates ate like piranhas.

Martin expected the worst for the crucial race to Mexicali when he discovered where he and his team were billeted for the night in Tijuana. "Our hotel was next to a brothel," he said. "It was noisy all night, with raucous laughter and screaming."

The race was as much a showdown between him and Alcantara as it was between Howard and Vitella. "Alcantara would really yell and wave the flag at his riders," Martin said. "Of course, I did that with my riders, too. Alcantara and I used to have raging arguments in the heat of the moment, screaming at each other from our cars on the road, or on the side of the road at the feeding stations. But afterward, we would have a beer together and talk about how the day went."

The next morning's start did little to calm Martin's nerves. Riders began in a chilly seacoast mist under a lower layer of gray storm clouds. As the race went east up and down over rollers that led to Rumo Rosa, a cold rain poured. "Then hailstones came down on us," Chauner said. "The hailstones were the size of marbles. They hit us so hard we were getting welts. We tried to ride in a tight huddle for as much protection as we could get. That wasn't easy out on the open road, especially with the hills getting longer and higher as we headed for the Rumo Rosa."

Howard, who is uncomfortable in cold, wet weather, went to the back of the peloton, which infuriated Martin. "I remember getting rather heated," he said. "I drove the vehicle up to the peloton and yelled to the other riders to get Howard up there. Vitella had a lot of help, and they were all trying to get him away."

While the confrontation was unfolding through all the rain and hail, George Mount was feeling frisky. He was not even in the top 30 overall and posed no threat to Howard or Vitella. He had nothing to lose and gamely attacked up the hills. Mount was out alone when he reached Tercate but was caught on the downhill by Vitella's teammates and the Colombians. Twice more Mount broke away and was pulled back.

By the time they reached the base of the climb leading up Rumo Rosa, the hail and rain stopped. Mount knew that his efforts had caused others to tire. He decided on a fourth attack. "I gave them the biggest smile I could and blasted off," he said.

Mount gained seven minutes by the summit, earning the red jersey for King of the Mountain. Alone, he faced a steep 10-mile descent and then 30 miles of flat, windswept desert that led to Mexicali. He was far from finishing even in the top 20 overall, but he still had a chance for a stage victory, and he went for it.

Behind him, Vitella was leading the charge for the whole race. He and teammates opened a gap on Howard up Rumo Rosa.

"Howard handled the climb fairly well," Martin said. "Vitella was ahead with some help, but their lead wasn't much—less than two minutes. Howard and Chauner were close together, with Allis and Hammen nearby. Marc Thompson had a flat tire at the wrong time, but we still had good support for Howard when they reached the top. But the rest of the field was completely fragmented."

Down the other side of Rumo Rosa, the sky was bright and clear. A warm breeze blew off the desert. The race became a duel in the sun.

"When we reached the desert floor, John turned into a freight train," Chauner said. "We were chasing like crazy after Vitella and his teammates, who were chasing Mount."

Martin drove back to give Thompson a wheel change, then sped forward to watch Howard, Chauner, Allis, and Hammen work their pace line. Allis motivated his teammates. "Once the race got on the desert floor," Martin said, "I felt a little more comfortable. Vitella's group didn't have the horsepower our group had. Time trials are not Vitella's strength."

Vitella's group of seven caught Mount on the edge of Mexicali, but then were caught by Howard, Chauner, Allis, and Hammen. Antonio Madera of Cuba, who had won the opening criterium, won the sprint for stage victory into Cali. Hammen and Allis went fourth and fifth, with Mount in eighth. Howard and Vitella finished right behind at the same time, which effectively kept Howard in the yellow jersey. "Howard got off his bike in Mexicali and said, 'I feel great!,'" Chauner said.

All that remained was the 40-mile criterium on the final day around downtown Mexicali, the capital of California Baja Nord. Alcantara's last strategy for his team—to box Howard in and launch Vitella with teammates in a break that would pick up a minute around the course—failed to happen. Howard crossed the line in the middle of the pack to win the Transpeninsula de Mexico.

"Vitella would have won if I hadn't bounced back," he said.

At the awards presentation, Howard and his teammates received their individual prize money and more for the team's second place. Alcantara's Mexican national team won, with the Cuban team in third. The Colombians were fourth, with the USA-B team fifth.

Howard and his teammates and Martin and Woodul took the money back to their hotel room to split it between them like cowboys after a rodeo.

Chapter 9

"After seeing John Howard and George Mount
riding all out up and down the mountains,
I wanted to be a bike racer."
—Greg LeMond

Everyone on the six-rider team that John Allis organized for the 1,066-mile Tour of Britain from May 25 to June 7 seemed to benefit from riding in the Transpeninsular de Mexico except its winner, Howard. "I had never ridden so hard in my life," he explained. "It took me longer to recover than I expected."

Howard failed to perform up to expectations in England, but was part of the team that rode against formidable international competition. Before the race was over, Allis grew frustrated over near misses for a stage victory, and gave his teammates uncharacteristically stinging criticism. That motivated Chauner to win the day's stage into Blackpool in front of 10,000 spectators. The American team ended in fifth place among the 11 teams from nine nations.

Dave Chauner was the first of the 66 riders going to set off from Brighton in the race against the clock. As the first rider, his time of 4 minutes, 19.9 seconds on the windy, flat course wasn't taken seriously until England's national road champion Bill Nickson finished in 4:25.4. Race officials and the 10,000 *tifosi* who turned out to watch realized the Americans had come to take something back home for the first time in the 24 years of England's national tour.

Howard struggled in 32nd, slightly faster than teammates Allis and Waldteufel, slower than Chauner, Ochowicz, and Neel. After the last rider finished and times were ranked, Chauner was eighth, the top U.S. rider.

On the next day's 95-mile stage, west along the Channel coast highway to Bournemouth, the American team rode at the front of the peloton and attacked frequently. Five miles into the day was a "Hot Spot" premium. Neel came third in the first Hot Spot, claiming a one-second bonus, points, and respect—a far cry from his first Tour of Britain.

Race director Phil Liggett called the Americans "a different team, always attacking and fearing no man or team."

Heading into Bournemouth, Chauner and Waldteufel suffered from a bad move in the sprint. Knocked down within yards of the finish banner, they were caught in a tangle of bicycles, legs, and arms. Neel, well up at the front, finished ninth to score another top-10 finish for the team.

From Bournemouth, the race arced northwest across England, through Wales, back into northern England to end in the Irish Sea port of Blackpool. "Allis, Howard, and Chauner were often seen at the front of the bunch and they certainly were not feeling outclassed or overawed by the competition," Liggett observed. Yet Chauner's early success was abruptly wiped out. He crashed again and suffered more scrapes. Then, during a stage of 92 miles to Birmingham, he was suddenly struck with fever, diarrhea, and vomiting. He lost 27 minutes, which pushed him back to 52nd place overall.

On the seventh day, Howard was riding well over the Pennines, the mountains that form the backbone of England. He had a good day and scored points in the King of the Mountain competition. But he missed a key breakaway, and Ireland's Sean Kelly, who had turned 18 the week before the race, went away with Bernt Johansson of Sweden and another rider. Kelly won the stage.

A cold spell and rain two days later gave Howard a virus. "I got so sick I was just riding to finish the race," he said.

With three days left, the American team was exceeding expectations. But Allis saw that to gain genuine respect, they had to win a stage. He was frustrated that they were coming close but not winning.

"Allis was so intense that he would get quite upset," Chauner said. "Usually it was at himself. He wasn't the type who would blame his teammates. But this was one of those rare occasions where he got really pissed off at the team. We'd finished the stage with four or five guys in the lead group, but none of us won. Allis came in disgusted, and let us have it. 'You guys had a chance to win, and you blew it,' he said. 'What's wrong?' "

On the night before the last stage, Chauner looked closely at the map. "With 3.5 miles to go, there was a sharp turn after a bridge that crossed a creek, and that was the place to break away," he said. "I was planning to retire from racing after the race anyway.

I was 26, and had a job lined up. My strength was pursuit racing, which is sustained speed. I knew I could pull it off."

The race to Blackpool featured a critical climb 30 miles out of town. "Kelly fell, or was knocked down, going up the hill," Howard said. "When he went down, every one of the English riders attacked. They were all out of there in a flash. They wanted to dump Kelly real bad." The attack caught a number of others off guard. Chauner made the break, with Allis and Waldteufel. They survived the pace up the hard climbs and moved to the front. They were ready as they neared the bridge and the sharp turn Chauner had memorized from the map.

"At the turn in the road, I attacked from one side of the road to the other," Chauner said. "Phil Liggett started speaking into the handset of his car radio that an American had broken away. He said, 'This is history in the making.' That really got my juice going. It made me bear down on the pedals even harder."

Blackpool, the largest resort in northern England, is celebrated for its Middle Walk Promenade. The English, ordinarily restrained, are excited and demonstrative supporters of cycling. At least 10,000 *tifosi* lined the promenade leading to the finish banner.

"The crowd was really exciting, but the roadway was awfully rough and full of potholes," Chauner said. "I could see the finish banner a long way off. It seemed to take an eternity to reach it. I decided to concentrate on the banner. I figured if I punctured, I would keep going until my wheel collapsed. It was all or nothing."

Behind him, a chase group led by a Swiss rider was trying to catch up. Allis and Waldteufel did what they could to block in the peloton, which trailed by less than 30 seconds, about 600 yards. But Chauner stayed away to finish alone, three seconds clear of the Swiss. Allis finished the Tour of Britain as the leading American, in 16th. Howard was 35th, Waldteufel 41st, Chauner 42nd, Neel 53rd, and Ochowicz 57th of the 59 finishers.

"The Americans, so popular with everyone, gave the race the sort of ending one would wish for," Liggett wrote in his coverage for *Competitive Cycling*. "This was proved later in the evening at the final banquet when John Allis was voted by the press as the most sporting and likable rider in the race."

For Chauner, the Tour of Britain was the end of his racing career. "I felt we were knocking on the door of international cycling, but I had to get out and get a job. All of us on the national team had a real passion for cycling. It became part of us.

We thought we were part of a pioneer effort."

Chauner followed other Olympic teammates who had ended their athletic career on a high note and joined the work force.

"Dave's stage win was a great way to go out," Howard said. "Others I had raced against, like Rick Ball and Bob Schneider, were retiring. Every time a national team member left, it made me think about retiring. There was no pressure to keep going. That had a lot to do with why I stayed in. To me, cycling is a lifetime sport. In the time I had been in it, opportunities were opening up. It was still a lot of fun to travel and race."

On June 9, two days after the Tour of Britain, Howard lined up with Allis, Waldteufel, and some 50 others on scratch in the 28-mile Willaston Handicap, which opened the 14th annual Isle of Man Festival. Many were from assorted national teams from the Tour of Britain. "I was really out to prove myself," Howard said.

Another 150 others, mostly English, went off in groups with leads of up to five and a half minutes. "We really jammed over the course," Howard said. "It was my kind of course. I was feeling great that day." Howard won in a solo ride, 30 seconds ahead.

At the awards ceremony, the loudspeakers blared "The Star Spangled Banner." It was the first time it had been played in the Isle of Man Festival. "Listening to our national anthem playing after I won made me feel fantastic," Howard said.

"The Star-Spangled Banner" was being heard more frequently.

Returning to the United States for Howard meant going back to the Dorset Training Group in Vermont. The training camp, now in its third year, had gained a national following in the burgeoning subculture of American cycling. Bicycle racing was developing a mystique. The training camp drew men and women cyclists from all over the country. Group rides of 30 cyclists, all wearing leather hairnet helmets and pedaling two abreast, were a common sight on the narrow two-lane secondary roads that wended past pine and birch forests and stone fences. Routinely bringing up the rear of the group rides was someone driving the Crams' Volkswagen van with license plates that read "BIKES."

Howard traveled around New England with others in the Dorset Training Group competing in criteriums. He was looking for another stage race when he was invited to fly out to Boulder, Colorado, for a new three-stage weekend race, June 21 and 22.

Mo Siegel of Boulder was sensitive to shrinking oil reserves and increasing air pollution, especially around nearby Denver. Siegel, 26, was founder and president of a new company, Celestial Seasonings. Since naming the company in 1968 and nurturing it as a cottage business, Siegel had taken the company past $1 million in sales in 1974. He wanted to put on a bicycle race that would help promote his young company, draw attention to cycling and encourage people to leave their cars behind and commute on bicycles.

"I was a total bike jock," Siegel said, enthusiastically recalling his race. "I thought that with the proper promotion we could put on a bicycle race that would become an important international event. Cycling was still so small then. We did some research and found there was almost no prize money in bike racing. The biggest prize list in 1974 was $7,500 in merchandise. So we put up $10,000 in merchandise. We figured the best racers in the country would come if we had the biggest prize."

Siegel underwrote the event as title sponsor, naming it after his best-selling brand of herbal tea. Local merchants donated prizes that ranged from ski trips in Colorado resorts to stereo equipment.

Usually, the term "classic" in cycling applies to long-standing races, typically one-day European events dating back to around the turn of the century. To introduce an event and call it a classic is an oxymoron. But Siegel had grand things in mind for his race. He boldly announced it as the Red Zinger Bicycle Classic. "We figured we could preempt all the other American bicycle races and become the No. 1 race almost instantly," he said.

One way to give his race credibility was to guarantee that he had the biggest names in the sport. "Mo Siegel paid my expenses out to Boulder," Howard said. "He had a great appreciation for cycling. Celestial Seasonings did a lot to promote the race, and Boulder was quite a cycling town. People everywhere seemed to be riding bicycles. Really good crowds turned out to watch."

They were treated to top riders like John Allis, Wayne and Dale Stetina, George Mount, Dave Boll, Marc Thompson, Alan Kingsbury, Ron Skarin, and Rich Hammen, nicknamed Captain America. Some 80 riders competed in the original classic.

What made the race an official big-game American event was the arrival of Bill Woodul in the silver Campagnolo van to provide neutral support for the riders. (After the Transpeninsular de Mexico, Woodul had started working for Campagnolo USA.)

"I had a van I cut the top out of to install a clear Plexiglas bubble for looking out during the races," Woodul said. "I rode behind the field to do wrench work when it was needed, pass up spare wheels to replace flats, and generally keep the racers pumping on their bike. After the van was outfitted with the proper tools and equipment and a bed, I drove across the country to Somerville, New Jersey, for the Memorial Day race there. That was my first race as the new Campagnolo technical support. From then on, I was a vagabond, going from race to race around the country."

Boulder sits on a plain that sprawls against the base of the Flatiron Range, which juts up precipitously as part of the Rocky Mountains. The opening day's morning race of 65 miles over the Rockies was what Howard looked forward to as a challenge. "I was really climbing well. By then I was recovered from the hard spring of racing in Mexico and England."

They left Boulder for the Flatiron Range where they climbed uphill for most of the first 19 miles. Howard took the first mountain premium, with Mount right behind, followed by Dale Stetina. The trio eased up after the premium and soon were caught by 13 others, with the rest broken into groups that trailed. Mount was comfortable riding in the mountains: the twisting roads and switchbacks were like those he was accustomed to riding in northern California. He broke away for the second mountain premium, at the mid-point of the out-and-back course. Mount tried to take advantage of his lead and build on it with his descending skills, but he lacked teammates in the breakaway to block. Howard was aided by teammate Dave Boll. Dale Stetina had two teammates, Thompson and Kingsbury. The local Allegro team had two riders who knew the roads well. Together they overpowered Mount down the winding mountain roads at speeds topping 50 MPH, hitting their brakes and leaning at a steep angle through the hairpins, then barreling past 50 MPH.

"I was riding in the press vehicle, and we had a terribly hard time staying ahead of the riders going down the canyon," Siegel said. "I never realized that bicycles went that fast. Our press vehicle was a pickup truck. Its tires squealed on the roads. We bounced from one side of the truck to the other through hairpins. We were really worried there was monster danger ahead. I remember a reporter put a blanket over his head to keep from looking."

After a long and fast descent, the course leveled off briefly before a final uphill where the last premium was contested. Howard made a lightning jump ahead of his breakaway partners and won it. Down the descent, Howard stayed away. The press pickup truck strained to keep ahead of him.

"We made the mistake of stopping at a set of railroad tracks," Siegel said. "Howard was roaring down the road and never let up for the tracks. When he reached them, he jumped his bike right over the tracks. I had never seen anything like that. I figured he would stop, or at least slow down. He nearly landed in the back of our pickup. As he went by, he shouted at us not to stop like that."

Howard was overtaken by the other leaders on the run into Boulder for the finish. Dale Stetina and his teammates did what they could to block the others in the hope that Wayne Stetina could win the final dash. But they were too far in front. It came down to a sprint until Howard went past him in the final yards to win. Dale Stetina, then Mount followed at a bike length.

They were all credited with the same time. That made the late afternoon's time trial of nine miles even more important. Howard was the last rider to hit the course. The wind had picked up, which put Howard at a disadvantage. In the final miles, his face contorted in fierce effort and concentration. He blitzed across the finish line in 21:38. That gave him 15 seconds on Thompson, 18 on the Stetina brothers, and 25 on Kingsbury—all of them teammates riding for Follis-Pasadena. They intended to gang up on Howard to usurp his lead in the next day's 50-mile criterium. Howard and his teammates had to defend his lead.

North Boulder Park, where the criterium was held, has a road with square corners that measures eight-tenths of a mile around and features a slight hill for variety and good sight lines for spectators. Several thousand Boulder *tifosi* filled North Boulder Park to watch the race and cheer. Team tactics were critical in the criterium. The 62-lap race, where only seconds separated Howard from five rivals, turned the competition into a confrontation between Howard's Raleigh-CRC of A team and the Follis-Pasadena riders. Soon after the starter's pistol cracked, the Follis-Pasadena riders took turns shooting off the front of the fast-moving peloton. They forced Howard, Boll, and Allis to alternate chasing.

"At one point, Howard, exhausted from chasing, swerved violently across the road at attacking Captain America," reported *Competitive Cycling.* "He hit Hammen's front wheel, nearly putting Rich to the pavement, along with Marc Thompson. Wayne Stetina, disgusted with the dirty tactic, came back at Howard on the backstretch with a similar move. Thereafter, the racing cleaned up considerably."

Thirty-five miles into the race, Wayne Stetina bolted away, soon afterward chased by his brother. Dale gained a gap on the peloton and screamed Wayne's name to get his attention to wait for him to join. They forged a 10-second lead which they kept for 10 miles. Howard hollered at Allis and Boll to help him reel the Stetinas back. With five miles left, Allis and Boll brought Howard up with the rest of the peloton to the Stetina brothers.

With all the riders bunched and speeding at 30 MPH, it looked like the finish would be a mass pack sprint. On the final lap, Dale Stetina sprinted straight off the front and gained 40 yards as he made the turn down the back straight. Ron Skarkin, who had been riding defensively in the peloton, suddenly came to life and dashed after him. Skarkin caught Stetina at the end of the straight and passed him on the final turn, leaning over so sharply in his speed that *tifosi* shrieked in fear that he would fall over.

Skarkin survived the turn to win the criterium by four lengths ahead of Dale Stetina. A dozen lengths behind surged Boll, Howard, and Wayne Stetina, in that order. Everyone else thundered in right behind. Howard defended his margin over Thompson to win the first Red Zinger Bicycle Classic.

"I was a big fan of John's," Siegel said. "He was held up as a champion, and he certainly lived up to it in that race."

Howard returned to Texas for the June 29 district championship road race through Texas hill country near Austin. No longer national champion, he had to qualify for the nationals coming up in Milwaukee by finishing in the top three of his district.

The course was 33 rolling miles Howard was familiar with from previous races, including the Texas Primavera. Early on the second lap he initiated a series of short sharp attacks. They broke up the field of some 50 starters. Four others stayed with him for the rest of the lap. At the start of the third and final lap, Howard burned the other four from his rear wheel. His solo ride took 10 minutes from his previous course record.

As Texas champion, he qualified for the nationals where the ABL would introduce a 25-mile time trial championship.

Preceding the nationals was Super Week in Milwaukee, where Butch Martin would select a dozen riders for the long team to go to Lake Tahoe, Nevada, for three and a half weeks of altitude training. There Martin would make final cuts for the team who would travel to the Pan American Games in Mexico City.

Super Week's excitement was enhanced by the arrival of the four American expatriates who came to try for berths on the Pan

American Squad. Mike Neel, Jonathan Boyer, Tom Officer, and David Mayer-Oakes flew in at the ABL's expense to show what they had gained from competing on the Continent.

The week's races started on July 12. Dale Stetina and George Mount attacked early in the opening 25-mile criterium, going away up a hill to seize a 10-second lead. Mount was less adept around corners on flat terrain than Stetina, who yelled at him for jeopardizing their lead. Stetina took over and made Mount follow his line through the turns. Mount made a quick study and caught on. They worked more smoothly together over the five-mile course and stretched their lead to 30 seconds by the finish. Stetina won the sprint. Jim Ochowicz won the field sprint for third, with Neel right on his rear wheel. Howard finished in the pack.

As the races went on day by day in and around Milwaukee, Dale Stetina alternated winning with brother Wayne. Among the expatriates, only Neel pulled off a victory—in the 98-mile road race over the Lake Michigan waterfront nationals course. Neel had broken away with 10 miles to go, but the peloton caught him with four miles remaining. In the field sprint, he beat Ochowicz by a wheel, with Howard and Boll close behind.

The anticipated dominance of the expatriates fizzled. It reinforced Wayne Stetina's desire to keep racing in the United States. "I could get just as tired racing here, without going to all that extra trouble."

Howard scored a victory in the 60-kilometer (37.5-mile) team time trial with Wayne Stetina and Jonathan Boyer. "Boyer was really smooth and calculating to ride behind," Howard said. "Wayne was rough by comparison. As soon as I finished my pull and swung off, Wayne hammered hard, without letting me get back on first. Wayne was very strong."

Just how strong didn't become apparent until the finish of the national championship individual time trial in suburban Port Washington, where they finished $^{46}/_{100}$ of a second apart.

The inaugural national time trial championship was held July 24 on an undulating out-and-back course along the shore of Lake Michigan, north of Milwaukee. Howard prided himself on his time trial strength. He rode to win. But the wind coming off the lake created greater resistance that may have affected the outcome. Howard favored big gears. Stetina preferred smaller gears and spun them more quickly. Howard's bigger gears favored him with the wind at his back, but into the wind Stetina's smaller gears were an advantage. When their rides were finished and times were compared, they nearly tied. But Stetina's 56 minutes and 6.65 seconds was slightly faster than Howard's 56:07.11. In third was Bill Gallagher, nearly a minute behind.

"I was really frustrated when I learned that Wayne had beaten me," Howard said. "Neither of us knew we were so close—less than half a second. I figured I rode hard enough to win. I remember passing a lot of guys on the course. Looking back on the race, I'm not sure I could have ridden much differently. Wayne rode better than I. That summer, he was riding in his best time trial form ever. Wayne inspired me to win the road race."

The July 27 national championship road race of 123 miles was held in Milwaukee for the third time in four years. Howard had won the previous two nationals there, and was determined to win again. Working against him was the added depth the Follis-Pasadena team had over Howard's Raleigh-CRC of A team. Moreover, the four expatriates were expected to demonstrate Continental savoir-faire and ride away with the national championship. One of the biggest fields ever lined up—240 riders.

The course rolled over nearly 4.4 miles a lap, for 28 laps. There was a steep hill about 400 yards long under a shroud of towering oak trees that lined the road through an elegant residential community. Shortly afterward was a twisting descent, followed by another short, sharp uphill, then a gradual descent to the lakefront for the flat run to the finish. With 123 miles to cover and the burning July sun sending the temperature into the upper 90s, the race would demand handling skills, stamina, and speed.

Promptly after the start, Mark Pringle of Seattle took off with Mike Neel and two others. On the second lap, Neel and the two others abandoned the breakaway for the security of the peloton. Pringle continued alone and later explained that he saw his effort as self-defense: "When I'd see fallen riders on the ground or riders being taken away in an ambulance, I knew I did the right thing."

Four others saw it Pringle's way and bridged up to him. By lap six, about 25 miles, they had a 40-second lead. That tantalized defending champion John Allis. He and Gallagher and three more broke from the peloton and linked up with the leaders. The pace and toil in the heat caused some of the early leaders to wilt, paring the breakaway to Pringle, Allis, and three others. They stretched their lead to one minute as the race reached 40 miles.

Mayer-Oakes, feeling the sting of criticism for not doing much in Super Week, flew down the twisting descent to make contact with the breakaway. By then Allis was picking up the pace with others who wanted to stay away. Mayer-Oakes was like a runner in baseball caught between bases with time against him. The breakaway was pulling ahead to stretch their lead to 1:30 over the peloton. Mayer-Oakes gamely kept trying.

As the race approached the mid-point, Neel, Ochowicz, Thompson, Waldteufel, Mount, Boll, and Hammen took off from the peloton. They caught Mayer-Oakes and kept going to catch Allis's breakaway. Tom Officer chased solo.

Howard remained cruising in the peloton with the Stetina brothers. "I believed I could close a 1:30 deficit, especially since we had not reached the half-way point yet," he said.

Riders in the break wanted to take advantage of Howard's absence. Ochowicz took explosive pulls at the front when it was his turn. Neel policed the break by ordering anyone who couldn't pull hard when his turn came to get off.

On lap 14, the middle of the race, Roy Stetina stood on the side of the road and caught the attention of his sons. He warned that the peloton trailed by 1:45. Both young Stetinas and teammate Kingsbury went to the front and tried to reel in the break.

Howard moved behind the Follis-Pasadena trio but declined to participate in their team effort. The three Follis-Pasadena riders forced the pace which shattered the peloton and left them as part of a group of 20, including Howard and Boyer. This new chase group was clipping 15 to 30 seconds every lap from the leaders.

By lap 18, with 45 miles left, the two leading groups merged to form a new front peloton of 35 riders. It was a new race. Allis, Mount, and Officer attacked on the hill, which precipitated counter-attacks. The lead group split into small fragments.

Howard bided his time until the 21st lap, about 30 miles to the end. For the first time in the race, he attacked, at the base of the course's main hill. Only Officer and Thompson caught him. That was enough help. Howard could outsprint his companions and wanted them to help increase his lead over sprinters like Ochowicz and Neel, who were among those left behind.

The breakaway of Howard, Officer, and Thompson worked efficiently for the next five laps, which took them through the bell lap together. "I was determined to win," Howard said.

He had reduced the race to only two rivals. Then he waited for an opportunity to drop them. After they crested the course's main hill for the last time, Officer took a hand off the handlebars to reach for the water bottle on his downtube. Howard got out of the saddle and sprinted away. He flew down the twisting descent and picked up a lead of 60 yards. Officer chased but saw that Howard was going away and revised his plan to race for second.

With 500 yards left, Howard was 30 seconds clear of Officer and Thompson. He had time to sit back and cross the finish line with both arms up for his fourth national road championship.

The outcome of Super Week and the nationals was that Butch Martin left Milwaukee with the names of the dozen riders he selected to prepare for the Pan American Games, and the ABL officials agreed to fly the four expatriates back to Europe.

Howard, assured a berth on the long team, packed his bike and spare wheels in his Datsun. He and Kim drove 1,000 miles east to Dorset, where they stayed for the rest of the summer.

Toward the end of the summer, Belgium hosted the world championships, but Howard, now 28, sat them out. "The ABL didn't have a lot of money. Much of the year's budget was going for the Pan Am Games," he explained. "We couldn't afford to send a time trial team back for 1975."

Women representing the United States at the worlds made an impressive showing. In the matched sprints on the outdoor cement track in Liege, Sue Novara beat Iva Zajickova in two straight one-mile races to win the gold medal and the world champion's rainbow jersey. Novara's training partner, Sheila Young, beat Linda Stein of Los Angeles for the bronze medal in the matched sprints. Miji Reoch of Philadelphia won a silver medal in the 3,000-meter (1.9-mile) pursuit on the same track.

In the men's amateur road race, Tom Officer was the only U.S. finisher, in 68th.

For those attending the Pan American Games training camp high up in the Sierra Nevadas, life off the bicycle was lived at the edge. "There was a lot of craziness," Howard said. "The track guys were completely unhinged, like wild fraternity boys.

Riders enjoyed lovely weather, breathtaking scenery up among the evergreen forests, fresh air, natural spring water, and fine cooking. Martin said, "People back in New York City never knew a place like this existed." Martin coached his road warriors with morning rides that included a 115-mile circuit around Lake Tahoe with mountains and flat stretches for variety—a few times a week on days when they weren't doing speed work—and afternoon workouts with shorter pace-line drills. The track coach was Jack Simes, back from a career of professional six-day races, assorted short races, and world records on stationary rollers. Simes had his charges pedal most mornings up Brockaway Summit, a steep climb lasting more than a mile, as part of their morning routine. Afternoons he devoted to specialized work on sprints, the kilo, and individual and team pursuit. All the track workouts were on the road, as the nearest cycling track was 250 miles away.

"There was more depth in the riders than ever before," Howard said. "I thought the Pan Am camp was much harder than what we had for the previous Olympics. Butch Martin had to make some hard choices on who was going to make the road team. That didn't stop anybody from having a good time, though."

Contributing to the fraternity-house atmosphere was an absence of women. Kim Howard had returned to Houston, where she was planning a move to Austin. Howard had been approached for a new job after the Pan American Games that would give the couple freedom to live wherever they wanted, and they chose Austin.

The big disappointment for those at the training camp was the lack of racing. Neither Martin nor Simes wanted to risk descending from the 7,000-foot altitude to sea level. They turned down several invitations from promoters for most of the camp's duration. During that time, rivalry steadily built up between the road and track riders over who was superior. They finally had the chance to find out in the Nevada Cup races on the weekend of September 27 and 28—a weekend that would resonate with permanent effects on American bicycle racing.

Before they left, however, Martin had to pare the road team down to eight—four each for the road race and the 100-kilometer team time trial. One of the cuts involved John Allis. "I had to tell him he wasn't on the team, even though he had won the national championship the previous year," Martin said. "It wasn't easy to do."

"Butch told me I was too old," Allis said. "I wasn't entirely happy with that, but I had had my share of the fun and games, and I could understand that he wanted somebody younger to take my place. That was my last year for serious competition."

With Allis packing his bags to go home to Cambridge, an era was ending. Since he had entered the sport in the early 1960s, the standards of competition had risen every season, and he had been a prime mover in that rise. Now he was told his ride was over. Howard was watching another road warrior go home to stay. "That made me think about retiring," Howard said.

George Mount, who came from a long line of Princeton alumni but passed up Princeton himself, took Allis's place on the team. Mount said, "It was clear that Butch was going for young blood, looking ahead to the Montreal Olympics."

Martin's road team of Howard, Mount, the two Stetina brothers, Kingsbury, March Thompson, Rich Hammen, and Dave Boll loaded their bicycles and extra wheels on top of the team van and headed out with the eight track racers in another van for the short trip to Reno, just over the Nevada state line, for the Governor's Cup Criterium, 60 flat laps around a one-kilometer circuit in Reno's tree-lined Idlewood Park. They were going to settle who was superior—the restrained road team or the boisterous track squad.

Spectators were sparse, and only a few dozen other riders felt up to competing against the Pan American team. Wayne Stetina rode with his left hand in plaster, after he broke his wrist in a fall. Brother Dale didn't start because of an inflamed knee. That made 15 of the Pan American team riders in the event, and they rode away from the others in their own contest.

It was a dynamic race. Nearly everyone on Martin's and Simes's teams had a turn trying to forge a breakaway—singly, in pairs, and small groups. All that most of the extras who bravely lined up against them got for their trouble was to get burned off the back of the pack, which soon led to their being lapped and pulled out.

"The trackies were fresh and dominated the early part of the race," Howard said. "But the roadies kept forcing the pace in the second half to even things out."

On the final lap, George Mount planned his sprint behind track rider Carl Leusenkamp of Lafayette, California, who led them across the line as the bell rang. As Leusenkamp wound up for the finish, Mount shot past, followed by Ron Skarin. Mount won cleanly. It was an important victory for Martin's road team—all seven of his riders finished in the top 10.

Howard finished ninth. He was going to have his day on Sunday—115 kilometers (72 miles) north out of Carson City, Nevada's state capital, and back, in a mountainous road race. Carson City, famous for the nearby Comstock silver-ore lode, was about to reveal a gold-ore lode for American cycling.

Fourteen-year-old Greg LeMond had seen the northern California district road racing championship the month before, when the race went past the LeMond home on the outskirts of Reno. "I said, 'Wow! I would like to try that sport to see what it's like," LeMond explained. "I went to a ski camp immediately after, up in British Columbia. I learned that skiers ride a bike in warm weather to get in shape for skiing. So when I came back home, I started riding." Soon afterward, he read in the local newspaper about the Pan American team competing in the Nevada Cup races. "My dad drove us down to Carson City to watch."

The course favored climbers, with a grueling ascent up 10,766-foot Mt. Rose. From the start, the mountain loomed ahead, looking high enough to touch the sky. (Within a week, five inches of snow was to fall on Mt. Rose.) On the early flat miles leading to the mountain, several riders attacked off the front, hoping to gain an advantage before gravity controlled the race. The peloton of about 50 riders hammered their pedals to keep up. When the road reared up for the first stretch of an eight-mile ascent, Howard and Mount rode away in a two-rider race.

"We broke away early," Howard said. "Dave Boll was the last of the others who tried so hard to go with us. He was thrashing his bike from side to side to keep up. But we rode away."

Driving behind in a white Dodge van were Bob LeMond and his son, Greg. Incidents that capture the imagination and set careers into motion often come in surprising ways. Howard began wanting to become a bicycle racer when he watched a film clip of Jack Simes competing in the 1964 Tokyo Olympics. Greg LeMond made up his mind to become a bicycle racer when he and his dad followed Howard and Mount in their breakaway. "We followed the whole race by van," LeMond said. "It was really fascinating."

Howard and Mount were out of sight from the peloton by the time they crested Spooner Summit. After a long descent to the eastern shore of Lake Tahoe, the race started up the short, steep side of Mount Rose in Incline Village. The climb offered a spectacular view of Lake Tahoe, though the breakaway pair didn't have time to look. But they were cheered by the LeMonds.

"I remember that Bob and Greg would pass George and me uphill," Howard said. "They would pull over and stop to get out of their van and cheer for us. Greg had such bubbly enthusiasm. They were our only spectators in practically the entire race." In many ways, the scene represents American bicycle racing in the 1970s—great talents competing virtually alone in the wilderness. Greg LeMond would take American cycling out of the wilderness in the 1980s.

"My dad couldn't keep up with Howard and Mount down the descents," LeMond said. "They passed us, and we would try to stay with them. But my dad wasn't used to the speed they went. They were hitting near 60 MPH. That was the first time I saw all-out racing. After watching John Howard and George Mount riding all out up and down the mountains, I wanted to be a bike racer."

After the breakaway passed the LeMond van, they had one last climb left, about two-thirds of a mile long, before the road leveled for the final 12 miles to Carson City. Howard dropped Mount up the hill and rode solo to the finish. He won by two minutes over Mount and 15 minutes over Kingsbury in third, followed closely by Thompson and Boll. Hammen and Wayne Stetina came in next to make it a sweep for Martin's riders.

The Pan American team headed soon after for Dallas where they started their processing for the Pan American Games.

The LeMonds returned to their home in Reno. American bicycle racing would never be the same.

Chapter 10

"I'm a man and I'm way past 21."
—Muddy Waters, *Mannish Boy*

Rudolfo Vitella and his three Mexican teammates crossed the finish line of the 100-kilometer Pan American Games team time trial smiling proudly, riding shoulder to shoulder. They rode under 2 hours 10 minutes to set a new Pan American Games record and win a gold medal. The U.S. team, however, finished with only three riders together, their faces strained and grim. The USA team of John Howard, Alan Kingsbury, and Rich Hammen was 5:30 behind, in fourth place.

A number of factors contributed to the disappointing place. After the training camp in the Sierra Nevadas, the cyclists had spent three days in Dallas with the 500 U.S. athletes who were given inoculations, then posed for team photos, and received team-issue clothes. From Dallas, they flew to Mexico City to compete against athletes from 32 other nations. But the pollution of Mexico City was hard to take after the clear mountain air of the Sierra Nevadas. Riders joked that Los Angeles with its smog would have made a better training site.

"Mexico City looked much worse in 1975 than it had in 1968," Howard said. "In 1968, the factories were shut and the air was clean. Big cement sculptures that lined the Periferrico, the main road through the city, were fresh and looked really good. The Mexicans work well with structural cement. But in 1975, many of the statues were cracking. The factories kept going during the Pan Am Games, which made the air really bad—filthy, actually."

Days after the team arrived, illness overtook many of Howard's teammates. Coach Butch Martin was forced to revise his selection for the 100-kilometer team time trial and road race daily, which hampered his ability to sharpen the riders. Finally, Martin replaced the Stetinas in the team time trial with Kingsbury and Hammen, who joined Howard and Marc Thompson. "The course had a monster hill we couldn't climb as a team," Howard explained. "Our ride was a disaster. Again, I wanted very badly to win a gold medal. I thought we had the team to do it, too. We showed that at the 1974 Montreal worlds. Wayne Stetina was on that team and was riding very well—until we got to Mexico City. Then he started having problems and was replaced."

During the team time trial, Thompson had difficulty breathing because of bronchitis, and after the first quarter he rode at the back of the team rotation. "Kingsbury was a dynamo," Howard said. "We were working well together, and Hammen was holding his own when his turn came at the front."

Through the first half of the race, the U.S. team was in third place, headed behind the Mexican squad and the Cubans. The Colombian team was in fourth, 43 seconds behind. But in the final quarter, Thompson dropped off the back, Hammen's pulls weakened, and Howard's rear tire punctured. He stopped to get a wheel change, breaking up the team's rhythm and costing them 30 seconds. The Colombian team took the bronze medal.

For the 175-kilometer (109-mile) road race a week later over the same course, Martin worked out a strategy to control the race by making sure that a U.S. rider was in every breakaway. "It was a good plan," Howard said, "but it went right out the window from the beginning." A group of five escaped from the 66 starters up the first long hill on the Periferrico. The breakaway riders were considered non-threatening to the rest of the riders cruising the first of seven laps. But after 25 miles, the breakaway gained a lead of 3:30. A more dangerous group of Mexicans, Cubans, and Colombians took off in pursuit. Their teammates went to the front of the peloton to block defending champion Howard and the USA team.

After the race's midpoint, Martin drove up in a team vehicle and got the attention of his riders. He commanded, "Let it loose now or forget it." Howard, Dave Boll, George Mount, and Dale Stetina took over the front of the peloton and worked together to bring the peloton up to the breakaway. Howard and his teammates chipped the lead down to 1:30. But Mexican, Cuban, and Colombian riders became aggressive in blocking, boldly interfering with the U.S. team rotation at the front. The peloton began falling behind again. With 25 miles remaining, the peloton was 2:30 behind, which put the U.S. team at a major disadvantage.

Just when the race looked hopeless for Howard and his teammates, Vitella decided to make it up to the breakaway because two of his teammates couldn't sprint well on the uphill finish.

Colombian Alfonzo Florez also learned from his coach that a teammate in the break was weakening. "With one lap to go, Howie and I went with Vitella and Florez and a Cuban," Boll said. "We got up to the break with about eight miles to go."

That changed the race radically. The three Mexicans and two Colombians were rivals and tried to spring one of their own away to increase their chances for the gold medal. "Howie and I were alternating covering breakaway attempts," Boll said.

Meanwhile, the three Cubans in the breakaway were spared having to do any extra work. Nicholas Reidtler of Venezuela tried to take advantage of the Mexican-Colombian rivalry and attacked with 3.5 miles left. Within a mile he was caught, precipitating the decisive move for the gold. Aldo (Buffalo) Arencibia of Cuba dashed away. Howard tried to go, but found he was spent. "Howie yelled at me to chase the Cuban," Boll said. "I had it in my legs, but I didn't have it in my head. I didn't respond like I should have."

Arencibia was away, with Florez on his wheel as the others pursued. Arencibia won with a comfortable margin of seven seconds over Florez. Behind them was a battle for the bronze medal.

Cuban Carlos Cardet won the sprint for the bronze, 34 seconds behind his teammate Arencibia. Vitella was fifth. Howard was the first U.S. rider, in eighth. Boll was 12th, Mount 26th, Dale Stetina 28th of the 44 finishers. "We should have ridden smarter," Howard said.

On the outdoor board Olympic Velodrome, Jack Simes's track riders made up for the road team's disappointments with two gold medals and two bronzes. The four-rider team pursuit of 4,000 meters (2.5 miles) was won by the U.S. team of Ron Skarin, Roger Young, Ralph Therrio, and Paul Deem of San Pedro, California. Steve Woznick took the bronze in the 1,000-meter (two-thirds of a mile) individual pursuit. Woznick also produced the greatest drama in the matched sprints to upstage all the cycling events of the Pan American Games.

Woznick, nicknamed "the Bull" as much for his appearance as for his strength and temperament, charged through qualifier heats in the one-mile matched sprints. His performances encouraged teammate, Carl Leusenkamp, a bronze medalist sprinter at the 1967 Pan American Games in Winnipeg, Canada. In the semifinal, Woznick defeated Jose Lescay of Cuba to advance to the final; Leusenkamp beat Octavio Dazzan of Argentina to also advance to the final and thus make it a U.S. race for the gold medal.

But U.S. riders were unpopular with the highly partisan crowd, which booed and whistled derisively at them. A special favorite with the crowd was Dazzan. He was 18 and in June had won the junior world sprint championship in Lausanne, Switzerland. Now, the judges announced that they had reversed their original decision in the Leusenkamp-Dazzan match, which went to Dazzan.

Frustration soared for the U.S. track riders. None of the judges on the jury of review spoke English, which added to their frustration. Then the announcer broadcast that Woznick's ride against Lescay was being reviewed. Woznick retaliated. He stalked to the board track's start-finish line with his bicycle and jabbed a knife in each of the tires. They exploded before the audience of 3,000 spectators like pistol shots. Then he shocked spectators and officials by taking off his warm-up suit and throwing clothes on the track. He stood in his cycling shorts and jersey and loudly proclaimed he wouldn't compete again. Then he strode angrily away.

Officials eventually persuaded him to return to the track, where he faced Dazzan in the final—the best of three matches. Woznick won two straight for the gold medal. Leusencamp similarly shut out Lescay for the bronze. Woznick's final match became his last race. He had been U.S. national sprint champion for two years and national kilometer champion for four years. He stood on the victory podium and announced his retirement.

Howard was beginning to think of retirement, but he wanted to make one more Olympics.

After riding in a stage race in Guadalajara, Howard accepted a job as a consultant for Exxon. The giant oil company had recently bought the Composite Sports Line, which made sports products— golf clubs, tennis rackets, fishing rods, and bicycle frames—out of a new lightweight composite metal. The new metal, called carbon fiber, was a breakthrough—lighter than steel yet at least as strong. Exxon marketed the product line under the name of Graftek and wanted a name to give their line of bicycle frames credibility. Howard's new job meant that he and Kim could leave Houston.

"Austin was a much better environment for cycling than Houston," Howard said. "Houston lacks hills and open spaces, which Austin has in abundance. I had three serious accidents on training rides in Houston. I was glad to move to Austin."

Starting to work for Exxon meant resignation from Raleigh-CRC of A. "I called Fred Kuhn to tell him I was going to leave his team and he was pretty understanding," Howard said.

Howard spent most of the winter and early spring commuting

from Austin to Graftek's offices in South Plainfield, New Jersey, where he rode the new frames to test them on the roads. "I was working with the Graftek engineers to design the geometry and composition of the frames. One day I would take a new bike out with one kind of frame, and then the next day a bike with a different frame and a different composition of metal."

New Jersey's winter made for harsh cycling conditions. "It was freezing cold, and the streets were ripped up," Howard said.

Part of his work involved helping Skid Purtle, the engineer in charge of marketing Graftek products, to prepare a brochure to introduce the product line of frames at the February cycling show in the New York City Convention Center. Skid Purtle was a chain smoker who probably had never ridden a bicycle after he was a kid. But he wanted to learn about bikes and asked Howard a lot of questions, priding himself on knowing his products. Laying out and designing the brochure, writing copy, and seeing the brochure through production appealed to the artist in Howard.

"Our pre-marketing strategy involved flying down to Florida to attend a golf tournament in Orlando. Skid Purtle and I met with golfers using the Graftek golf clubs and asked them about how the shafts were working for them."

One of the golfers using Graftek shafts was Hubert Green, who had recently won the Bob Hope Open and was to achieve lasting distinction for winning the U.S. Open despite a death threat that prompted the FBI to provide security during the tournament.

When they left Orlando, Howard and Purtle agreed on what they wanted in the brochure and continued discussing the formation of a team of riders to compete with Howard on Graftek frames to help promote the product. At the bike show they met David Jacobs, who had a new line of cycling clothing called Cool Gear. Jacobs, originally from Montreal, had been Canadian national downhill ski champion and coach of the Canadian national ski team before he moved to Boulder. "I offered to supply all the clothing for a team that John Howard was putting together," Jacobs said. "Ski companies had already been doing that sort of sponsorship for a long time, and I was influenced by that."

When Howard returned to Austin, he wrote proposals for Exxon and Cool Gear that defined expectations and included budgets for extensive travel. Exxon promptly approved the proposal and provided a budget of $25,000. Cool Gear signed on to provide clothing. Next came the team selection.

"My biggest rivals in 1975 had been the Stetina brothers, who were going to be even better in 1976," Howard said. "So I figured I wanted them on my team." Others added were Bill Gallagher and Tom Doughty, from Indianapolis.

Rules governing sponsorship had loosened, but the U.S. Cycling Federation still required a sponsored team to be affiliated with a local club. With the Stetina brothers and Doughty riding for the Indianapolis Speedway Wheelmen, the team was officially designated Exxon/Cool Gear/Indy.

Howard's new team had a generous supply of Cool Gear cycling uniforms and warm-up suits, lightweight frames, and a travel budget. They were ready for the new season and the Montreal Olympics.

Howard was confident of competing in his third Olympics. He understood the great physical and psychological demands inherent in cycling. But he was getting restless to push his limits behind cycling.

Kim also was anxious about his racing past his prime. "I used to tell John not to stay in the sport too long—to go out on top."

In an interview with *Competitive Cycling*, Howard expressed concern with how time-consuming training, traveling, and competing were. "I think 1976 will be my last year on the international scene," he said. "I'm definitely going to continue bike racing beyond 1976, but I'm planning on de-emphasizing the bike over the next four or five years and doing other things."

That was still a long way off as he began serious preparation for the Montreal Olympics. He drew up an itinerary of Olympic development races to accrue enough points to qualify for the Olympic trials. After missing some early-season racing in Florida and Louisiana with Graftek commitments, he got back in for the three-stage weekend race in St. Louis.

Howard dominated the opening day's 12.5-mile time trial, out and back along the Mississippi River. Teammates Doughty and Gallagher went one-two in the 50-mile criterium later in the day. On the final day, in the 114-mile road race outside St. Louis, Wayne Stetina, Howard, Dale Stetina, and Doughty swept the first four places. The race concluded with Howard the winner, followed by Wayne and then Dale Stetina, Doughty in fifth, and Gallagher in eighth. "People started to wonder if we were winning because of our bikes," Howard said.

In contrast to the previous two years, America's top riders passed up the Tour of Britain because it conflicted with the Olympic trials in early June in upstate New York. After several

Olympic development races, Howard had enough points to qualify for the Olympic trials, and he and Kim drove back to Austin.

Training around Austin in the spring is ideal. Riders pedal past fields of bluebonnets and Indian paintbrush, and peach orchards redolent with the scent of ripening fruit. Near Austin, the Texas hill country goes from sea level up to 1,000 feet, with a variety of quick roller coasters and long gradual grades. The steepest is the Balcones Fault, a geological quirk jutting up 1,000 feet, which separates the eastland pines from the blackland prairie. Howard was descending the precipitous fault west of Austin when he suffered the worst crash of his career. "I was going downhill at warp speed on one of the prototype Graftek frames," he recalled. "It was a very light frame, not stable downhill at speed."

Spinning wheels generate centrifugal force that acts as a gyroscope to keep a bicycle stable as the rider and bicycle go faster. But if the front and rear wheels are not aligned in a perfect plane, or if the frame has other design imperfections, the bicycle can shimmy like a washing machine with a load imbalance.

Descending the fault line on Ranch Road 2222, Howard's bicycle started shimmying around 50 MPH and grew worse as the speed rose. Riding without a helmet and wearing only wool cycling shorts and a short-sleeved wool jersey, Howard was thrown to the pavement.

"John was knocked unconscious," Kim said. "He was just lying there beside the road, knocked out and bleeding from losing so much skin, even from his face, until two guys in a pickup found him. They threw him and his bike in the back of the pickup and drove him to Brackenridge Hospital. In two days, he was out of the hospital and back riding his bike."

Howard spent time recovering from his abrasions before commuting to one of the last national-class races before the Olympic trials, the Miami 100. Wind and rain discouraged spectators, but the racers were undaunted. Howard, Dale Stetina, Skarin, and local rider Dave Ware broke away early to deliberately eliminate Roger Young, who could outsprint them all. The four breakaway riders lapped the field half-way through the race. Stetina broke away and rode solo to win by a minute. Skarin finished second, with Howard third, and Ware fourth. Young won the field sprint for fifth.

Howard, 28, was among the oldest of the 60 elite riders who arrived in the town of Saranac Lake for the Olympic road trials. The trials were three road races of 106 to 118 miles, through lush evergreen forest in the Adirondacks, and a 50-mile criterium downtown. Butch Martin was there to select riders for the 100-kilometer team time trial and the Olympic road race.

In large part due to his drive of some 3,000 miles, Howard's riding at the trials lacked sharpness. Worse yet, when he tried to race up a hill in the final miles of the opening day's 106-mile race, he broke a toeclip. He finished in the middle of the peloton as 19-year-old Tom Schuler of Milwaukee scored an upset victory. In the second race, Howard managed ninth as Neel authoritatively won the sprint from Stetina. Riders knew what Howard was capable of, but he wasn't showing it. *Competitive Cycling* called Howard, "A mystery wrapped in an enigma."

"The courses were rolling, but not hilly enough to break up the field and make a difference," Howard said. "I was still confident that I was going to make the team. Butch knew that I wasn't 100 percent. He was supportive of me."

In the last day's road race, in a chilly rain, Howard rode impressively to finish third, behind George Mount and Dave Boll.

Martin overlooked the traditional points system to determine his road team for the Olympics. He made his decision based on what he saw in each race and what he saw and heard about the spring campaign. He picked Howard and Exxon/Cool Gear teammates, Wayne and Dale Stetina, who rode consistently well. Tom Doughty was chosen as alternate for the 100-kilometer team time trial. Neel, winner of a road race and the criterium, was selected with Mount, Boll, Marc Thompson, and Alan Kingsbury. Upstart Tom Schuler was named alternate for the road team.

"I wasn't even close to a supreme effort," Howard told *Competitive Cycling.* "I'm saving what I have for Montreal, which is the only thing that counts."

The Olympic cyclists moved to a private junior college, where they set up their training camp. Six weeks remained until the opening of the Montreal Olympics.

When support counted most from the sport's governing body, the U.S. Cycling Federation, Martin and his cyclists found they were left alone. Officials had promised a van to transport the riders and their equipment, as well as a motorcycle for motorpace training. But the vehicles didn't arrive. Nor did money for food. Martin and his Olympic cyclists were paying out of their pockets.

Martin assigned Howard, Kingsbury, Wayne Stetina, and Thompson to the team time trial, and the rest to the road race. Martin had them all working out twice daily to make them ready for their assigned race. Their routine was to train, eat, and sleep.

The last U.S. riders to win an Olympic cycling medal had competed in the 1912 Stockholm Olympics, when riders pedaled one-speed bicycles with wheels made of wooden rims over 200 miles of rough roads that ground their tires to the wood. Beginning with the next Olympics, the road race was shortened to nearly half the distance, which became the Olympic standard, and over the next six decades, technology improved substantially. Bicycles were equipped with derailleurs that by 1976 gave riders a panoply of 12 speeds. Lighter metals replaced the wood and made bicycles more responsive. But none of the developments had helped younger American riders match the Olympic feat of the older generation. Winning an Olympic medal became each generation's quest.

Of Martin's team, Howard was the most likely. His gold medal in the 1971 Pan American games road race had whet his appetite for the Olympics. Neel and Mount had set their sights on doing well in the Olympics as a step towards moving to Italy and racing professionally. Boll dropped out of Stanford University to race full-time for a year to make the Olympic cycling team. American cyclists were criticized for racing well at home but falling flat internationally. Winning an Olympic medal would quell that criticism.

Howard was back at top strength by the time they went to Montreal for the Grand Prix Cycliste Chatequay on June 20, a 55-mile criterium around a 1.7-mile course. After two laps, he and Schuler powered away from the other 75 starters. The Stetina brothers went a few laps later in pursuit. Martin, following the race on a borrowed motorcycle, drove up to Howard and Schuler to tell them to wait for the Stetinas. When the four U.S. riders linked forces, they made a team trial out of the race.

Twenty miles later, however, Dale Stetina's front tire punctured. Despite a fast wheel change from the Campagnolo support van, the peloton promptly engulfed him to reduce the breakaway to three. Then Neel chased on his own and bridged up to his teammates to keep the four-rider team time trial going. They stayed away to the end. Neel outsprinted Schuler for victory, with Howard third and Wayne Stetina fourth. Boll and Kingsbury led the pack in for an impressive run of the top six places.

The victory—and the prize money—helped boost morale while the Olympic team riders kept up their training regimen.

Through television, the XXI Olympics in Montreal had a worldwide audience of nearly 1 billion. Howard and his 425 U.S.

Olympic teammates joined 7,000 athletes from 95 countries participating in the opening ceremony before 72,000 spectators.

"I was looking forward to the Olympics, but some of the thrill of marching in the opening ceremony was gone," Howard said. "I had been disappointed by the political things I had seen in the previous Olympics in Munich and Mexico City. Montreal had its politics, too, with the African nations' boycott."

As many as 18 African countries pulled out of the Olympics in an 11th-hour protest of a New Zealand rugby team playing in South Africa, a nation banned from the Olympics for its apartheid policy.

Overcoming the imbalance of politics were individual performances that captured the imagination of the media and the public. The star of the Montreal Olympics became Nadia Comaneci, the 14-year-old gymnast from Romania. American's Bruce Jenner, a graduate of tiny Graceland College in Lamoni, Iowa, became a national hero for running, jumping, and throwing his way to a gold medal in the decathlon.

Martin's 100-kilometer time trial team had cracked the top 10 two years earlier at the Montreal world championships, and expectations were realistic for improving their finish in the Olympics. Two of his original four—Howard and Wayne Stetina— were returning with Kingsbury and Thompson. In training on the Trans-Canadian Highway, the U.S. squad matched the times of the Soviet riders, the pre-race favorites. Pressure rose steeply.

"It's so hard to maintain your head in that kind of environment," Howard said. "To train, we had to ride through crowded Montreal traffic. We were living in crowded conditions in the Olympic Village, as many as seven to a room. The media was everywhere, making the place like a circus. Our preparation at the end was stalemated."

On July 18, Howard lined up with Wayne Stetina, Kingsbury, and Thompson for the team time trial. A hard, steady wind of 25 MPH blew east over the cement highway, which glared under the bright sun. Riding into a head wind on the first out-and-back leg, repeated twice, forced the U.S. foursome to begin raggedly.

"We got off to a terrible start," Howard said. "It got worse from there."

"We had a miserable race," agreed Stetina. "I had slammed my knee in a crash a week before and wasn't riding as strongly as I could have been."

Martin said that once his team reached the turn-around and had the wind at their back, they rode with class. "It was a matter of horsepower," he rationalized. "Into a wind like that, it's not your fastest but your strongest riders that make the difference. Our riders had 50 kilometers into the wind, and it sapped them. They couldn't make it up on the fast sections with the tailwind."

The Soviet team lived up to their expectations as pre-race favorites to win by two minutes over the defending world championship team from Poland. The U.S. finished 19th of 29 teams. "We had it in the Montreal worlds in 1974, but we lost it by the Olympics," Howard said.

Despite improvements in American cycling, European countries made off with all the cycling medals. The last chance for an America medal was the 110-mile road race on July 26. Coach Martin entered Howard with Mount, Neel, and Boll. "There was enough time between the team time trial and the road race to fully recover," Howard said. "I was ready to do something."

The Olympic road race was 14 laps around the rugged 7.9-mile Mt. Royal course. The first lap was fast right from the starter's pistol—about 30 of the 134 starters dropped off the back of the peloton on the first climb up the steep 753-foot Mt. Royal.

George Mount's strategy was to ride constantly among the first five riders and go with every break away. He promised to finish in the top 10. Lap after lap, he was busy chasing breakaway attempts. Howard, Neel, and Boll also rode prominently at the front.

None of the early forays from the front was successful, although the flyers and immediate chases kept the speed high. Small groups of riders continually splintered off the back of the peloton like wood shavings. On the seventh lap up Mt. Royal, Mount went with six others who broke clear. Another seven riders—including Bernt Johansson of Sweden, Peter Thayer of West Germany, and Guiseppe Martinelli of Italy—pursued; they joined the first breakaway by the time they crossed the start-finish line to begin the eighth lap and the second half of the race. Johansson was particularly aggressive in keeping the break going to avoid a crash like the one that had knocked him out of the Munich Olympics road race four years earlier. Riding in the breakaway with 14 riders was safer than taking corners at speed with the entire peloton.

The sunny sky over Montreal on the morning of the race had turned cloudy by the start and grew dark as the event went on. When the racers started the eighth lap, a light rain fell. Soon it was a heavy rain that made the temperature fall. By then the breakaway had a lead of 1:20—about a half a mile.

"We had real promise with George up in the break," Howard

said. "The rest of us were riding support. I remember thinking that if I went, I would have to go alone to avoid taking anyone with me. But then I crashed."

Howard went down on the ninth lap. Neel and Boll also hit the pavement on that lap. Neel suffered injuries that forced him to abandon, but Howard and Boll got back up and kept going.

"A New Zealand rider fell in front of me on a descent," Howard said. "I went down hard and hit my head on a metal crowd barrier. I remember thinking this was one too many crashes for me. But I got back up and chased with a Czech rider. We were two minutes behind the field. We kept chasing and caught the field on the final laps. By then the break with George Mount was way up the road."

Mount stayed with the leaders as their breakaway dwindled to 10. "It was a hard and miserable race because it was raining," he said.

On the last climb, Johansson rode at the front of the breakaway and attacked at the summit to zoom down the descent and surprise the others. Mount, near the rear of the break, charged after until he saw he couldn't catch Johansson. Mount decided to wait for the others to contest the sprint for the remaining two medals.

Several thousand spectators lining the road behind steel barriers gave Johansson a thunderous ovation. He sat up and waved both arms high to acknowledge the crowd as he crossed the finish line.

Thirty seconds later the group of nine that included Mount sped by. They were whipping from one side of the rain-slick road to the other like a frenzied snake. "It was so hairy that one gendarme literally dove head-first over the barrier into the crowd," reported *Competitive Cycling*. Leading them across the line was Peter Thayer of West Germany. Italy's Guiseppe Martinelli followed closely, then Mieczysl Nowicki of Poland. Mount was seventh. Judges ruled that Thayer had interfered with Martinelli by weaving and demoted Thayer to ninth. Mount moved up to sixth. Howard finished in the peloton, in 42nd place, seven minutes behind Johansson. Boll finished 56th, 18 minutes behind.

George Mount smiled into the cameras of photographers and talked to reporters who wrote about the American cyclist who had cracked the top 10 in the Olympics. His ride didn't win a medal, but it showed a standard of performance that was on track to win one. Some of the race was broadcast on television, which helped broaden cycling's exposure in America.

"George created his own luck in that race," Howard said. "We were getting better. It wasn't going to be long before American riders would pull through and win Olympic medals."

Howard, the cornerstone of the team time trial and road race team in three Olympics and two Pan American Games, was disappointed that an Olympic medal had eluded him.

But nobody on the cycling team had time to dwell on the Olympics. The center of attention shifted too rapidly. Mo Siegel had invited Commonwealth riders from England and Australia to travel to Boulder after the Olympics and ride in his second annual Red Zinger Classic. Siegel had expanded the race to three days. Mount, Boll, and other Olympians left Montreal for Colorado.

The Datsun took the Howards 2,000 miles southwest to Boulder, where Howard was well-known for his Red Zinger Classic victory the previous year. Posters to help promote the race featured a cyclist resembling Howard, sweeping a turn at speed.

The Red Zinger Classic adhered to the same format as the first edition, but held the three stages one day at a time. The competition started with a 10-mile time trial east of Boulder on fast, flat roads. Howard blasted through the time trial to take out his frustration from the Olympics. He was on his own, free to pedal as hard as he could on dry roads. He poured himself into his ride and averaged 30 MPH, winning by more than a minute over teammate Tom Doughty and Dudley Hayton of England. Howard was back on the podium as champion.

The next day's 70-mile road race over the Flatiron Range broke up the field. "John Howard looks awesome riding in the mountains," said David Jacobs. "He would get such an intense look in his eyes when he climbed. He had such power, and it showed when he was in the mountains."

Howard rode to protect his leadership and was content to let others take the stage. Clyde Sefton of Australia won over Mark Pringle of Seattle and Hayton of England. Howard's lead was not threatened.

On the final day's 50-mile criterium in North Boulder Park, Howard rode defensively to protect his leadership. George Mount, Dale Stetina, and others were all taking shots to try to gain a lap. Howard stayed at the front. "It was raining and there were lots of crashes," he said. "It was a hard, fast race. I was very fatigued. I saw a crash in front of me, which got me to thinking again about retiring."

In the pack sprint for the finish, Bill Nickson of England beat Dave Boll for the criterium victory. Howard prevailed to take the overall race, winning an expensive stereo outfit.

"Winning the time trial pretty much sewed up the race for me," Howard said. "It felt so good to win again. Winning took the edge off some of my frustration from the Olympics."

Over the next dozen years, the Red Zinger Classic expanded. In 1980, it became the Coors International Classic. The race grew into 19 stages and became America's national state race, until it ended in 1988. Only two other riders, Dale Stetina and Greg LeMond, won the race twice, but Howard remained the only rider to win it twice in a row.

Howard was riding a hot streak, and wanted to crown his season by taking the national time trial championship from Wayne Stetina. The road nationals started five days after the Red Zinger Classic concluded, in Louisville—1,150 miles from Boulder. He was living life in the fast lane. "John decided that he wanted to fly to Louisville," Kim said. "I would drive."

"I really wanted that time trial," Howard said. "After the previous year when I lost by so little, I definitely wanted to come back and win it."

The national 25-mile time trial was held on an out-and-back course along the banks of the Ohio River north of Louisville in Carrollton. Time trials usually generate little spectator interest. But the 1976 national time trial was a re-match between Howard and Wayne Stetina, which got the attention of the *tifosi*. Howard had been national road champion since 1968, but what he wanted most was to win the national time trial title.

He also wanted to go out of racing as national time trial champion. "I'd like to follow through on other interests, such as sculpturing and business ventures," he told *Competitive Cycling*.

Part of time trialing's appeal to Howard was its individual effort. The disk wheels and aerodynamic, low-profile frames identified with time trial bicycles today were still to be introduced. Howard, Stetina, and others all competed on their road bicycles.

A tailwind aided riders going out on the first half of the time trial. As Howard approached the turn-around point at the Markland Dam, he caught George Mount, who started a minute ahead. "I thought I was going to win when I caught Mount," Howard said.

On the way back a head wind buffeted riders, but Howard cut through it like a razor blade through Styrofoam to win. His time of 55 minutes, 36.6 seconds was 30 seconds faster than Wayne Stetina's winning time the year before and became the new national 25-mile time trial record. Finishing second was Tom Margevicius of Philadelphia, more than a minute behind. Defending champion Stetina was sixth, in 57:23. Mount was 18th.

Howard's victory gave him his sixth national championship

in three disciplines—time trialing, road racing, and cyclo-cross.

He watched the other national championships in the events held in Cherokee Park in Louisville. Greg LeMond, 15, competed in his first nationals, in the boys' intermediate division. LeMond was active at the front with Jeff Bradley of Davenport, Iowa. Their attacks and counter-attacks trimmed the peloton from 63 starters to about 24 by the close of the 25-mile race. Bradley was superior and won, with LeMond fifth. LeMond was hooked on cycling.

In the women's 40-mile road race, Connie Carpenter of Madison, Wisconsin, displaced Mary Jane Reoch as the queen of the road. Carpenter was a new face in the sport. She and LeMond would lead American cycling to the top of the world.

For the men's 114-mile road race on August 15, Mount was the pre-race favorite with Howard among the 140 starters. But Mount and Howard were watched closely. When each made a move, several dozen others immediately followed. Wayne Stetina broke away early in the race of 28 laps with Tom Schuler, Dave Boll, and six others. "Dale Stetina and I went to the front of the field and blocked for Wayne," Howard said.

As the miles under the summer sun accumulated, chase groups fled from the peloton, but none made up the distance to the breakaway, whose members dwindled one by one. With 20 miles left, the breakaway was down to Stetina, Boll, and Schuler. They were four minutes ahead—at least a mile and a half.

By then Mount saw the race was virtually over and pulled out. He was criticized for quitting and lashed back. "I've given the nationals a lot of publicity just being here," he told *Competitive Cycling*. "They should pay me to race. They didn't, so why put out?"

With 20 miles to go, Howard broke away with Dale Stetina and Mark Pringle. They clipped the lead to 3:00 on the final lap.

Wayne Stetina worked Boll and Schuler over with attacks to test their legs—and his—on the final laps. Boll and Schuler could parry his feints, but they couldn't counter. When they went up Fountain Hill the last time for the finish banner, Stetina's legs pumped slowly in the sprint. He lumbered over the line with Boll on his wheel for second. Schuler was a few lengths behind for third. Howard won the contest for fourth, with Pringle fifth and Dale Stetina sixth. "If it weren't for John Howard, I wouldn't have been as good as I was," Stetina said. "He was the guy we had to beat. I couldn't accept it when he beat me. That made me train harder. I came back and beat him. John helped me become the national road champion."

Howard's Exxon/Cool Gear team had garnered first, fourth,

and sixth in the national road race and first in the time trial. More people started talking about the advantages of the lightweight Graftek frame. David Jacobs said the team's performances helped sales of Cool Gear clothing.

Howard's business venture with the team had panned out well. That gave him confidence to push his limits in another business venture. The day after the road race, he turned 29—a pivotal age for an athlete. "Karl Barton of Raleigh said if I was interested in touring pro with the Raleigh team in Europe, he could fix it up," Howard said. "I would be mid-level domestique and ride to help the team leader. Cycling is something that I like doing, but I didn't want to have to do it the way the pros do—all the time. So I turned down the offer."

It was a summer of permanent change for Howard. Mickey Cohen, who kept a scrapbook on Howard's early career, had been released from prison in 1972 and died during the time of the Montreal Olympics. In Dorset, Vermont, Anne Cram was preparing to sell the Dorset Training Group to a local bicycle shop proprietor.

But Howard was still a national champion and addicted to winning. He and Kim drove north to Dorset for one last visit and two more national-level races. Professional racing in Europe didn't appeal to Howard, but it did to Mike Neel.

Neel competed in three professional races before his team manager got him a last-minute entry into the world championships in Ostuni, Italy. In the final miles, past olive and fig orchards of southern Italy, Neel was among the leaders. Belgian Freddy Maertens was in a duel with Italian Francesco Moser. Neel, shrewdly riding on Belgian Eddy Merckx's rear wheel, was in an enviable position in the last half-mile.

"With 300 meters to go, (Felice) Giamondi pushed me off Eddy Merckx's wheel," Neel said. "We were flying at that point, and suddenly I was pushed into the wind. That cost me places."

Nevertheless, Neel finished a respectable 10th place, and the first U.S. rider to finish the professional road race and make the top 10.

His accomplishment was a significant addition to the gold and silver medal final that American Sheila Young and her sometime training partner Sue Novarra in the women's matched sprints.

Howard's season and career ended on an upbeat. Since he had won his first national championship and made his first Olympic team in 1968, he had exerted a significant influence on American cycling. He was going out on his own terms, and as national champion.

Chapter 11

"When you get to a fork in the road, take it."
—Yogi Berra

In early 1977, Howard excused himself from the U.S. Cycling Federation national road team to pursue a business venture and to try other sports. *Competitive Cycling*, acknowledging his scaling down of racing, said Howard "has been the standard that the riders have been shooting for since 1968, and that's not a bad legacy."

The business venture he had in mind was a waterslide park, modeled after the ones he saw in Vermont's Green Mountains. He discussed the prospect with Paul Monroe, a recreation cyclist two years younger, whom he had met in Houston.

"Waterparks were a new fad," Monroe said. "In the Ozarks, they attracted families traveling through the mountains. John thought a waterslide park was the business to go into. I had a wonderful idea to make a skateboard park. So we talked about making a combination waterslide and skateboard park."

From living frugally, regularly setting aside a portion of most of his paychecks, and selling bicycle equipment and other merchandise he won in races, Howard and his wife had managed to save $25,000. Monroe had recently come into an inheritance. "Altogether, we had about $120,000 in capital," Howard said.

Early in the year, Howard and Monroe began scouting around Austin for appropriate sites. Meanwhile, Howard still had obligations with Exxon Enterprises as a consultant for Graftek frames. Skid Purtle started moving Graftek's operation to Solana Beach, near San Diego. Howard went west to test new prototype frames to determine what the new year's product line would be.

Howard was getting in good training mileage while testing new frames when he heard about a three-stage weekend race in Fresno, April 9 and 10. The Tour of San Joaquin radiated out of Fresno into central California's fertile San Joaquin Valley.

"A lot of the best southern and northern California riders were going to be there," Howard said. Among the entrants were a rare father-son team, Bob and Greg LeMond. The younger LeMond, still two months away from his 16th birthday, received special permission from race director Harry Morton to compete against 75 Category I and II riders. The permission was based on impressive performances that LeMond and other northern California junior riders (under age 19) were achieving.

Fresno was an appropriate setting for Howard, who was winding down his cycling career, and Greg LeMond, who was rising meteorically, to overlap wheels in a race. Fresno was also home to author William Sayoran, who wrote, "As I rode my bike, music began to happen to me."

The tour opened Saturday morning with a hilly 55-mile road race. A fast pace from the starter's pistol split the lead pack to 25 riders, led by young LeMond, his hair sticking through the straps of his black leather hairnet helmet. Up a long hill 22 miles into the stage, LeMond broke away with Dan Nall of Berkeley. Howard charged from the main lead pack and bridged up to the breakaway pair. Nall faltered near the summit and lost ground.

Suddenly, Howard was on a breakaway nearly midway through the opening race with a 15-year-old who had finished fifth in the national intermediate division.

"Junior riders usually ride strong early in the race and then die," Howard said. "So I did the bulk of the work and started to pull him around the course. I was doubtful of our chances when we started the second lap. Our lead then was 1 minute 30 seconds. I thought this kid would die on me at any moment."

When told recently about Howard's anxiety that day, LeMond laughed good-naturedly and nodded his head in agreement. "I can see how he thought that. If I had a junior rider do that to me, I would be disappointed, too. But I felt better and better as we went on. But I also remember suffering so hard to stay with him. I was at that age, when you first get into cycling, when you are able to push yourself beyond your limits. As you get older, you realize it is not always healthy to push yourself as much."

LeMond, riding under U.S. Cycling Federation rules governing junior riders, was restricted to pedaling gears that were significantly less than those Howard and the other seniors were riding. Junior riders didn't ordinarily compete against senior riders, and were restricted in their gears to develop leg speed rather than rely on muscling their way through races. That only added to Howard's anxiety about being out front with young LeMond. "But on the second lap, he surprised me," Howard said. "LeMond actually got stronger. Then he started pulling too hard when it was his turn to come through and it was though he was trying to drop me. We lost our rhythm. I had to warn him that if he kept that up, he would jeopardize our lead. It had begun to shrink, to 45 seconds. So Greg let up a little and we got our pace-line rhythm back together. We opened the lead to a minute and a half."

Behind them, the lead chase group diminished to eight, with the rest strung out in small groups in their wake. "I wasn't quite 16, was racing in junior gears, and ended up staying with John the whole way," LeMond recalled with a proud smile. Then he shrugged. "John beat me in the sprint."

Three hours later, they began the second stage—a 10-mile time trial. Riders pedaled on a flat road into a 20 MPH head wind to the turn-around, then doubled back with a tailwind. Young LeMond reinforced the promise he had shown in the morning's opening race. Despite riding restricted gears, he finished second, six seconds behind Howard, who won. "I still remember the time trial," LeMond said 15 years later. "I was real happy that I was even close to John Howard, and I ended up second."

On Sunday the final stage was a 68-mile road race north of Fresno—three laps of a flat-to-rolling course of about 22 miles each, around the Friant Dam. It was a popular course where the Fresno Cycling Club and Montrose Cycle Club had been putting on races for at least five years. Crosswinds and a one-mile climb up a mountain pass in the foothills of the Sierra Nevadas made the race tactical, augmented by an aggressive pace on the first lap. Riders set a new course record. Only two dozen riders—including Howard and Bob and Greg LeMond—survived the first lap in the lead pack.

Over the last two laps no serious moves went off the front, although the fast pace, crosswinds, and toil up the mountain pass reduced the leaders to a pack of 17. Greg LeMond tried in the last miles to break away. His incentive was a time bonus for the stage winner that would be enough to reduce his overall time and make him the tour winner, a coup for any junior rider. But a tailwind pushed the other leaders up to a higher speed than usual and worked against his restricted gears.

Howard spent the last miles at the back of the leaders, drafting to conserve his legs, until the finish line was close. Then, with 250 yards left, he sped to the front. As he rolled briskly forward, several riders were quick to catch his draft. One was Rick Baldwin of Palo Alto, who caught the sweet spot behind Howard's rear wheel. Baldwin took advantage of Howard's accelerating speed and with 100 yards left shot passed Howard like a slingshot. On Baldwin's rear wheel was Calvin Tramplepleasure of Berkeley. Moving up fast was Bob LeMond. Howard had to kick it in hard.

Baldwin surged ahead with enough margin to sit up on the saddle and throw his arms up in the air in a victory salute at the line. Howard held off Bob LeMond for second. Tramplepleasure finished fourth, a few places ahead of Greg LeMond.

When the Tour of San Joaquin's results were compiled, Howard was the winner, Greg LeMond second, Baldwin fifth, Dan Nall seventh, Tramplepleasure ninth, and Bob LeMond 10th.

From being inspired in 1975 while watching Howard and George Mount break away riding up Mt. Rose near Carson City, young LeMond had progressed rapidly to finish second in his first major senior race. He had outclassed strong regional riders like Baldwin, Nall, and Tramplepleasure, and finished second to Howard. That Greg LeMond rode so exceptionally while still a high school sophomore was not lost on the *tifosi*. They immediately began heralding him as "that phenom from Nevada," a phrase that soon reverberated across the United States and the world.

"I've always liked and appreciated John Howard's dedication to cycling," LeMond said as he looked back on the Tour of San Joaquin. "He was one real class cyclist from the 1970s who opened up doors for guys like George Mount and myself."

For the waterslide and skateboard park, Howard and Monroe found a four-acre section in industrial south Austin, near the intersection of Ben White Highway and South Congress Road. Howard and Monroe decided to pool their $120,000 capital to buy the property directly from Charles Goodnight III and construct the amusement park the way they wanted.

"We both put our life savings into the venture," Howard said. "I always felt that it takes money to make money. I felt we had a worthwhile investment. Kim and Paul and I were willing to take the risk."

Once the land purchase was final, they organized their plans for the park, named Flomotion, and set about constructing it. They hired contractors to level the land and pour acres of cement. Their hill for the waterslide descended more than 50 feet. Howard studied the heavy-equipment operators to see how they worked, then started operating equipment himself, to save costs.

As the two entrepreneurs caught on to what they were doing, they did more of the construction themselves until they took over completely. They rented the equipment they needed and operated it. "Running the cement machine took a lot of physical effort, and John ate that up," Monroe said. After the two entrepreneurs had labored for 12 to 14 hours a day all summer, the park was completed shortly after Howard's 30th birthday.

"The real fun part was building the amusement park," Howard said. "But after that, I wasn't really interested in running it."

"We figured that it would work all right and practically run itself," Monroe said. "I was going to be the supervisor. But it didn't work out that way." He sighed at the recollection of what they thought would happen and what did happen. "We put in tons and tons of hours to help keep the payroll down."

When they opened for business shortly after Labor Day, weekend traffic was lively, and the after-school crowds kept the cash registers running. Flomotion employed as many as 18 people, mostly part-timers, including skateboard professionals who were interested in keeping the skateboard park going, and lifeguards.

Venturing into the amusement park enterprise had its compensations. "Business was good that first year," Howard said. "We took some of the profits and invested them in the business. We installed pinball machines in the clubhouse, which was another source of expenditure, but they generated another source of revenue. We kept the amusement park open through the winter and expected to see a return on our investment the next year."

In late 1977, Graftek headquarters' move to Solana Beach foreshadowed problems for Howard in 1978. The Graftek frames that he and Wayne Stetina had ridden to national championships were seen as high-tech improvements that were pushing the limits of technology in a sport reluctant to try anything new. Wool clothing and steel frames had been used all century, and cyclists were bound by tradition to keep things as they were. But the success of the Exxon/Cool Gear team gave the new frames credibility.

After Graftek moved to Solana Beach, however, the frames were never the same. They started falling apart where the tubes fit together. Exxon Enterprises stood behind the frames and replaced them, but even the replacement frames fell apart. Quality control became an issue. Two years of magazine advertising and winning results by the racing team were being overcome by the perception that Graftek frames were high-priced junk. Then, David Jacobs announced that he wouldn't continue Cool Gear sponsorship.

Mike Neel's professional cycling career in Italy also ended

in late 1977. He returned to the United States.

New developments that would take the sport forward and draw Howard back to it were transpiring. Polish immigrant Eddie Borysewicz (pronounced Bory-SHAY-vitz) was hired by the U.S. Cycling Federation in 1978 as the national cycling coach. Poland was a major international cycling power, and Borysewicz had been a coach of the national junior team, which is a crucial source of new talent. Borysewicz was the Federation's first salaried coach. He was put in charge of the men's and women's road and track teams as well as the junior team, which included Greg LeMond.

Federation officials also hired Neel as the national road coach for 1978. He took the national road team to race in Italy that spring, and to the Tour of Britain, in which George Mount finished fourth.

Meanwhile, Howard was confronted with rising difficulties at Flomotion which was sued by parents whose children chipped teeth while descending the waterslide. "Instead of going down the waterslide on their backs with their feet forward like they were supposed to, luger-style, some kids were standing up and trying to surf down," Howard said. "They were going too fast into the hard turn and some chipped a tooth."

"Then two other waterslides opened up for business in Austin," Monroe said. "We were splitting business three ways. In 1978, the fad for waterslide was beginning to taper off."

As if to make a point that nothing is a sure bet, news came from Europe that May that Eddie Merckx had abruptly announced his retirement. Merckx, who had dominated professional road racing from 1969 to 1975, had won more than 550 races.

Howard could see that the amusement park was in a downward spiral through the summer he turned 31. "Running the business was taking all my energy," he said. "We were having a tougher and tougher time making our monster mortgage payments. Our cash reserves were slipping through our fingers. On weekends, I tried to get out on the bike, to pedal through Texas hill country. The rides were therapeutic relief from the pressure at work."

As Howard was beginning to look for an alternative move, Congress authorized an unprecedented $30 million package, for the fiscal year beginning October 1, to fund development of Olympic sports, including cycling. The U.S. Olympic Committee and the Congress were sensitive to the term "weekend athletes," which described many athletes who had to work daytime jobs to earn a living. The $30 million was to convert an abandoned Air Force base in Colorado Springs, Colorado, into the new Olympic

Training Center. The money also was to be divided up among the two dozen sports federations to hire staff and purchase needed equipment. Rules governing prizes were also relaxed so that athletes could accept cash without harming their amateur status.

Other events pushed the sport forward. George Mount won $4,000 for first place in a 75-mile race in New York City. Greg LeMond and three junior teammates won a bronze medal in the team time trial at the junior world championships in Washington, D.C. American cycling was maturing.

Late in 1978, Howard and Monroe missed a mortgage payment. Goodnight promptly foreclosed on the property. "Our business went right out from under us, and we got slapped with $6,000 in back state and federal taxes," Howard said. "That was pretty tough to face—especially after two years of hard work and investing all of our money. It was an awful situation. The irony is that it was all over an amusement park."

Monroe decided to enroll in law school at the University of Texas in Austin. Howard turned back to what he knew best: bicycle racing. "John found a niche in cycling," Kim said. "I understood early with John that everything he did revolved around bicycle racing—he ate, drank and slept for training and racing. The bike came first. I called his bicycle an iron mistress."

"Fortunately, my consulting with Exxon didn't take up a lot of time, and I got an income from that," Howard said. Essentially he had to attend the New York City Bike Show in February, which he enjoyed, and test new frames for the season's product line. That put him in a good position for a comeback.

His connection with Exxon Enterprises helped him put together a new team for 1979. Howard prevailed upon his contracts with Campagnolo USA in Houston, which had acquired a subsidiary called Ultima, a consortium of Italian manufacturers that made cycling apparel, tires, and other equipment. Ultima signed on as a sponsor for Howard's team. Exxon/Ultima/Indy, tied to the Indianapolis Speedway Wheelmen with the Stetina Brothers. "We basically picked up where we had left off," Howard said.

Howard's first big test was on April 1 in Houston. Back on the starting line, he was ready for the flat 100-kilometer race around the tight one-mile circuit with eight sharp turns per lap in a canyon of downtown office buildings. Howard and the other 42 starters were competing for $3,000 in cash prizes, a new dimension in amateur races and a powerful incentive to do well.

As though he were picking up where he had left off three years earlier, Howard broke away from the peloton after 12 miles with two others—fellow Texan and new Exxon/Ultima teammate David Mayer-Oakes, and Gary Holder of Chicago. They worked a paceline together and stretched their lead to a minute.

But as the miles wore on, Howard became sluggish. "I had lost my leg speed and snap," he said. When the three breakaway riders contested the final sprint, Howard and Mayer-Oakes divided to opposite sides of the road—a mistake that gave Holder a choice of rear wheels for drafting in the final half-mile. With 300 yards left, Howard accelerated for 100 yards to reach his top end. Holder took advantage of the acceleration that took them ahead of Mayer-Oakes, and surged past Howard's rear wheel to win.

Second place after a layoff wasn't bad. Howard felt confident that he could make the Pan American team bound for the Pan American Games in early July in Coamo, Puerto Rico. He set his sights on making the 100-kilometer team time trial.

With Congress appropriating money for Olympic development, more corporate sponsors got involved. The Miller Brewing Company negotiated a sponsorship package of $100,000 with the U.S. Cycling Federation to promote its Lowenbrau beer. They funded the Lowenbrau International Grand Prix-Pan American Series, a nationwide circuit of races that Borysewicz would use to determine his roster of riders for the Pan American Games.

Six weeks after the April Fool's Criterium, Howard felt his conditioning starting to come back. On May 13, he went to south Miami for the Miami 100. When he arrived, the cycling community learned that the jeep Augustin Alcantara had been driving as the Mexican national team coach in the Tour of Cuba had flipped over and crushed him. News of his death saddened many in North and South America.

The Miami 100 drew a fast field of 60 starters, who commuted 89 laps up and down Biscayne Boulevard in front of Bayfront Park. Early in the race, Howard broke away with local rider Chris Carmichael (now the U.S. Cycling Federation head coach) and six others. They lapped the field in 20 miles, then moved up through the peloton and broke away once more to lap the field a second time. At the end, Howard put forth an impressive sprint to win the race.

Part of Howard's incentive to win and make the Pan American Games team was that his arrangement with Exxon Enterprises was about to end. Management at the Houston corporation giant had decided to get out of the sporting goods market. So, as Howard followed cycling's migratory route up the East Coast, Exxon Enterprises sold the Graftek division, effectively dealing the final blow to the development of composite bicycle frames.

"Graftek was onto something," Howard said. "With some more advertising and better luck with the quality control of the frames, they would have advanced composite frames five to 10 years."

In the course of his travel to a Pan American Games qualifier time trial, Howard read a feature in the May 14 issue of *Sports Illustrated* that caught his attention. *Sports Illustrated* devoted 10 pages to covering a new event, the Ironman triathlon in Hawaii. Barry McDermott's coverage told how Tom Warren of San Diego swam 2.4 miles through rough Pacific Ocean water, rode his bicycle —which Howard noted from looking at the photo was not a proper fit—112 miles, then ran a marathon of 26.2 miles, each event right after the other in a day. Warren earned the title of Ironman for his win. The remarkable three-sport event defined pushing the limits of human endurance. Howard was intrigued.

Howard had his own limits to push on May 21 in Warwick, New York. There, he joined national time trial champion Andy Weaver of Miami, Wayne and Dale Stetina, George Mount, and other national team riders as well as others hoping to make an impression in the 14-mile time trial. Borysewicz was going to use the results to help pick his long team of riders for the Pan American Games. Howard was under pressure to do well.

One by one, the riders set off at one-minute intervals. The hills and the distance measured each rider for riding technique, bicycle handling skills, power, stamina, and speed. Howard poured himself into his effort. When he crossed the line, his time was the fastest of the day, earning him a spot on the long team.

But making the final cut was more difficult than in the past. By 1979, the general level of American racing had risen considerably. Speeds for races were going up, times were going down to better the performances of the professionals of American cycling's glory days. (Dave Boll won the 1976 50-mile Tour of Somerville in New Jersey with a time of 1:46, which finally broke the record of 1:49 that professional cyclist Alf Goullet had set on the Newark, New Jersey, velodrome in 1920.)

"In the early 1970s, you could count the people who were likely to win a big race on the fingers of one hand," observed Wayne Stetina. "Then in 1976, you could count the likely winners on two hands. In 1979, you needed another friend so you could use his hands. The increase in the level of racing was important for Greg LeMond. That was the point when he entered the sport. From there, Greg made the leap to European racing."

Making the final cut for the Pan American games team involved a different process than in the past. Butch Martin was displaced by Eddie Borysewicz, struggling to learn English and inclined to be dictatorial and brusque. Critics said he believed bicycle racers knew only two words: "Go!" and "Now!" But he was the head coach, and he selected the Pan American team.

Leading up to Borysewicz's final selections were plenty of races. The Lowenbrau International Grand Prix-Pan American Series had the national team traveling a wide migratory route from coast to coast. The U.S. Cycling Federation, perhaps overreacting to please their first major sponsor, opened the races to too many athletes to ensure large pelotons. Howard and other contenders for the Pan American team complained. George Mount was the most outspoken critic: he called the races "demolition derbies."

"There were 300 riders on half-mile circuits in criteriums," he complained. "By the time we got to the fifth race, most of the riders on the national team had been just beaten to a pulp in crashes in Central Park and all over the East Coast."

Howard's results were uneven. One of his better performances was in the 50-mile Ross Cup on May 26 in Allentown, Pennsylvania. In a field of 150 starters—which included future Olympic medalists Leonard (Harvey) Nitz of Sacramento and Steve Bauer of St. Catherine's, Ontario—Howard made the early break of 25 riders. They sped around the rolling, tree-lined 3.7-mile Lehigh Parkway course. "Greg LeMond came up beside me as we were riding uphill and whopped me on the back to say hello," he said.

Mount tried to break away with Andy Weaver, but with 12 miles left they were caught by a group of 20 who included Howard. With a quarter-mile to the finish, Weaver took off again. Wayne Stetina was quickly on his rear wheel, with Howard catching his draft and the others trailing in a tight file behind. With 200 yards left, Stetina and Howard peeled off Weaver's rear wheel and drove past. Howard tried to sling-shot past Stetina, but Stetina caught him in a wheel-to-wheel contest. In the last yards, Stetina was sharper and pulled ahead to win by a wheel. "I could tell I was going to have to dedicate a couple of years to getting back to where I was before I quit," Howard said. "The races were very hard. More riders than ever were fit. The races were faster than ever."

As they went from city to city in the Lowenbrau International

Grand Prix-Pan American Series, Howard's roommate was Steve Wood of Albuquerque, New Mexico. Only 18, Wood had seen his first bicycle race three years earlier when he watched coverage of the Montreal Olympics.

"John was one of the big names in American cycling," Wood said. "I was in awe of him. He was a hero of mine. I was honored to be rooming with him. Watching him attack in a race was like seeing Godzilla the Monster on a bike—he could go awfully hard."

So could Wood go awfully hard, which is one reason Mike Neel had Wood rooming with Howard. Wood was the youngest rider on the long team; Howard was the oldest. Only one of them was going to survive the cut and go to the Pan American Games.

Wood was moving up in the selection process. He won the 100-kilometer Tour of Nutley (New Jersey) criterium against a field of 200. Howard was holding his own. Borysewicz continued scrutinizing his riders and making notes. When asked recently about Howard, whom he hadn't seen since 1979, Borysewicz replied without missing a beat, "John had incredible strength. I don't think he had reached his potential as a cyclist. But I didn't have the chance to work with him. He had the right body for cycling—tall and lanky, with a narrow torso and power quadriceps—like a satyr's build. But he had no coaching or proper training. John was absolutely out there as a bike rider. But he was in the middle of nowhere. He was past being the right age for the national team, and didn't have the right preparation for turning pro. It was John's time to end."

Yet Howard's power and experience were assets for the time trial. Borysewicz kept him on the long team that went to the Olympic Training Center for the final preparation for the Pan American Games, which would open July 2.

The Olympic Training Center lies in the shadow of Pike's Peak in central Colorado. It was a new facility for the U.S. Cycling Federation, which had moved offices in there only months earlier. Previously an Air Force base, it still maintains cookie-cutter neatness. Riders share small rooms.

"It was rather Spartan living," Howard said. "Not much for frills, but it was long overdue for a place for training."

The riders on the long team arrived in the middle of June and stayed for a week. They did little training, as Borysewicz and Neel had them riding at maximum performance in races that Borysewicz devised to test them. Just as the riders were under pressure to perform and make the team, Borysewicz was under pressure to produce medal winners and keep his job. Neel was his assistant, but also was a back-up to replace him in the countdown for the 1980 Moscow Olympics in case their team came back empty-handed from the Pan American Games.

Howard had previously doubled up in the team trial and the road race. But for 1979 he was focused on the team trial. "I felt we could win a gold medal in the team trial," he said.

With less than two weeks before the Pan American Games opened, Borysewicz flew his team to Quebec for a three-day stage race. Howard performed well, but none of his results sparkled. At the end of the race, Borysewicz made up his mind. His final roster of riders would be announced the next morning. "I remember it was raining that morning," Wood said. "Mike Neel knocked on the door of our tiny hotel room. Both John and I stood up when he came in."

Neel said: "It was hard to wake a guy up at 6:00 in the morning to tell him that he isn't going to be on the team. But I had to give John Howard the bad news. I always regretted that the team time trial didn't have him on it. But when you are building a team, sometimes you have to make tough decisions."

Howard, who had been a fixture in American cycling, reached the end of the line on the national team in a cramped hotel room.

"John was upset," Wood said. "He gave Mike an incredulous look that said, 'You picked this kid over me?' Then he recovered and looked at me and shook my hand. He said, 'You did good.' We had a couple of races left to do, but he packed his bags right away and left."

Of the six cycling events in the Pan American Games in Caomo, Puerto Rico, the 100-kilometer team trial of George Mount, Wayne Stetina, Tom Doughty and Tom Sain won the only medal for the United States—a gold.

By the time of the medal ceremony, Howard was busy planning what next to do.

Chapter 12

"You can check out any time you like,
But you can never leave."
—*Hotel California*, The Eagles

When the Greek messenger Pheidippides ran 24 miles from the Mediterranean coast to Athens in 490 B.C. to deliver the crucial news that the Greeks had defeated invading Persians at the Battle of Marathon, he left a legacy later called the marathon. This prompted many who follow sports to assume that marathoners are the ultimate endurance athletes. Cycling *tifosi* argue that bicycle road racers are the ultimate endurance athletes. Ocean swimmers who negotiate sea swells while swimming vast distances contend they are the ultimate endurance athletes.

Many spirited debates were held over this issue. Finally, John Collins of Honolulu decided to settle it.

Collins's inspiration reportedly came while he was drinking beer in front of the Primo Brewery after running in Honolulu's Around the Island Relay Race. He had heard about swim-bike-run events, held in that order, in San Diego's Mission Beach. Such events, referred to as triathlons, were made up of short swims, bicycle rides that were only modified warm-up distances, and mid-range runs. Collins challenged all comers in front of the Primo Brewery to combine three separate existing events—a 2.4-mile rough-water Pacific Ocean swim off Waikiki Beach, a 112-mile bicycle ride around Oahu, topped off with a marathon of 26 miles and 385 yards through Honolulu—into a single Hawaiian triathlon.

Some in the crowd may have felt that Collins had enjoyed too much beer. Others may have felt that he had been out too long in the sun. But some listened and heard a challenge they couldn't walk away from. Collins and friends decided that whoever successfully completed the challenge would have to be made of iron to survive and tell the story, so the winner would earn the title, Iron Man.

Early in the morning of February 18, 1978, 14 men joined

Collins in jumping into the warm surf off Waikiki Beach to compete in the first Iron Man Triathlon. They would spend the entire day pushing the limits of human endurance as they swam, rode bicycles, and ran. Collins, a Navy commander with an appreciation of rewards, made sure that they were competing for something more than bragging rights. Each finisher would receive a five-inch, hand-brazed figure of a man made from a pipe (for the body) and a nut (for the head).

One who joined Collins was John Dunbar, 25, a former Navy SEAL who led for most of the race. As a SEAL, Dunbar had endured severe training. In 23 weeks of training, SEALS are not permitted to swat mosquitoes; they spend up to 21 hours a day in mud, which they leave only to sleep for three hours. SEALS like challenges, like the Iron Man. Dunbar splashed out of the ocean swim 20 minutes ahead of his main rival, Gordon Haller. But after about 10 hours of arduous effort under the tropical sun, Dunbar was suffering from dehydration.

Haller, a bearded 27-year-old part-time roof repairer in Honolulu and full-time fitness fanatic, chased Dunbar down as they pedaled their bicycles against strong off-shore head winds. Haller, also a Navy veteran, ran as much as 500 miles a month and had completed several marathons. He enjoyed running and talked of some day running across the United States. His support crew, a gaggle of friends who followed in a van, served him water and soft drinks to keep him going.

Haller caught Dunbar in the marathon, but Dunbar rallied and took back the lead. Back and forth they dueled. After 16 miles, Dunbar's support crew ran out of water. Badly dehydrated and starting to hallucinate, Dunbar guzzled two cans of beer. Instead of refreshing him, the beer made Dunbar drunk. He started stumbling into cars parked beside the road.

Haller pulled away for the fourth and final time at 21 miles and won the Iron Man in a time of 11 hours, 46 minutes. Dunbar struggled in 34 minutes later for second place. Collins, who stopped in a roadside diner for a bowl of chili, was among the 12 finishers. Only three of the starters had dropped out.

The battle between Haller and Dunbar was the stuff of legends. Collins and the other finishers were credited with accomplishing a feat that acquired an instant following.

Although coverage of the event was limited to a brief write-up in a Honolulu newspaper, word of the Iron Man spread from the island to the mainland like an electrical charge. When Collins announced Iron Man II would be held on January 13, 1979,

Sports Illustrated dispatched associate editor Barry McDermott and photographer Peter Read Miller to cover it.

A gale blew in and nearly canceled Iron Man II. Collins postponed the race for a day, but conditions didn't improve on Sunday. Five feet of rain had fallen in six days, and the storm was still going strong. In the eerie early-morning darkness, 16 determined athletes assembled on Waikiki Beach to discuss what to do. Wind gusted to 40 MPH. Palm trees bent over like macaroni. The ocean frothed with swells of four to six feet. Rain stung exposed skin. "We took a vote to decide whether to hold the Iron Man," recalled Tom Warren of San Diego. "The vote was 13 to 3 to race."

A woman who had dropped out of college to train for a year for the event decided her health was more important and left the beach to return home. The 15 men stayed.

Warren was one of those who voted to go on with Iron Man. Warren, an unknown, was 35 that year, and had spent $1,000 to fly to Honolulu. Haller was the pre-race favorite and came prepared to defend his title. He had seen the movie *Superman* twice, and went to the start of Iron Man II wearing a Superman costume. Another entrant was Lyn Lemaire of Cambridge, Massachusetts. She had won the women's 25-mile time trial championship in 1976 when Howard won the men's, and she set the women's national record on the way.

Warren still has the brown mustache he had then and still weighs the same. His blithe spirit masks an intensity that engulfs him when he turns his attention to the task at hand. At Mission Bay High School, he wasn't the fastest swimmer on the team, but he was selected Most Valuable Player. At the University of Southern California, he earned letters in swimming and water polo. He kept swimming when faster classmates retired. In his 30s, he won eight masters national medals and set a national age-group record. Warren also pedaled a bicycle from Vancouver, British Columbia, 1,650 miles down the Pacific Coast to San Diego. In 1976 he ran 75 miles from Tecate, Mexico, to Ensenada. He was preparing for the Iron Man as part of his own recreational fitness program.

Commander Collins, cautious about the effects of swimming in such rough waters, moved the start to calmer waters near Ala Moana Park. At 7 a.m. January 14, Warren, Haller, Dunbar, Lemaire, and 11 others made the plunge into the Pacific for Iron Man II.

A local ocean swimmer, Ian Emberson, led through the 2.4-mile swim. Warren was close enough to catch him 12 miles into the bicycle ride, up a steep hill overlooking the Pacific. Then the rain stopped, although the wind continued to blow hard. Lemaire got on her bicycle and overtook Dunbar. He wanted to know if she was in the race. She turned and waved to him.

Haller had had a disastrous swim but made up ground on the bicycle. He and Dunbar were relieved when they completed the 112 miles so they could get off their bikes and put on running shoes for the run, during which they finally overtook Lemaire.

But they didn't close on Warren. He jogged along Kalakua Avenue, singing the Southern Cal fight song to keep his mind off throbbing leg pains. He slugged on until he reached Kapiolani Park, where a knot of 20 people, including Collins, stood at the finish.

Warren won in 11:15. Dunbar gave it everything he had and then more, but came in second again, 48 minutes behind. Emberson was third. Haller, the original Iron Man, was fourth. Lyn Lemaire was fifth overall, and the first Iron Woman. Collins didn't enter the second edition. Taking his place was son Mike, who finished at 8:30 a.m. Monday.

Barry McDermott's coverage with Peter Read Miller's photos turned Warren into a cult figure overnight, and catapulted the Iron Man to national prominence.

Howard, three years younger than Warren, scrutinized the magazine photo of Warren on his bicycle. "I thought that no matter how good a swimmer he was, or how good a runner he was, I could outride him with enough of a margin to win overall."

Another cycling-related feat that gained national attention was accomplished by John Marino of Irvine, California, who rode into the *Guinness Book of World Records* for pedaling his bicycle cross-country in 13 days, 1 hour in June 1978. Marino, a former catcher for the Oakland Athletics farm team, turned to ultra-marathon cycling after a back injury cut his baseball career short. In 1979, he was making another well-promoted assault on the record from the pier in Santa Monica, California, to the Empire State Building in New York City. A film crew was following him. In 1973, Los Angeles physician Allan Abbott had ridden 138 MPH behind a souped-up1955 Chevrolet on the Bonneville Salt Flats for the world speed record on a bicycle. Abbott, acclaimed as "The Flying Doctor," sped into the *Guiness Book of World Records,* too.

When Howard returned home after he was cut from the national team in Quebec, he mulled over his prospects. He thought about the Iron Man, the cross-country record, and the speed record. Meanwhile, the cycling season was in full cry and he had obligations as a member of the Exxon/Ultima racing team.

"I had to come to grips with the fact that I didn't have the level of riding that I had before my layoff," Howard said. "I had a good start early in the 1979 season, but I got tired. I could see that it was going to take a couple of years to get back to my previous level of fitness. I wasn't sure I had that kind of time."

Howard had one important opportunity to regain a spot on the national team—the national road racing championships in early August in Milwaukee. An impressive showing, either in the time trial or the road race, could open a door of opportunity.

He had to qualify by winning a medal in the Texas district championship road race in Buda. On July 4, four days before the Texas district championship, he went to Dallas for a 35-mile criterium. In the field of 65 starters, the race turned into a contest between Howard and Mayer-Oakes. Howard won the sprint.

Next came the 100-mile district championship in Buda. "It was a hard race through hill country, and awfully hot," Howard said. "Mayer-Oakes was real strong. We were battling each other up the hills. Another rider cut in front of me at one point and I crashed. But I got back up and caught the leaders. Then I beat David to win the race." His gold medal qualified him for the nationals. But he and other troubles. He and Kim started fighting.

"I started rebelling because there were things I wanted to do besides going on the road to bike races," she said. "I liked going out nights to see the bands. Austin is a great town for music. All the great acts were coming to Austin. I even saw Chubby Checker."

The marriage was on a collision course. One of their last trips together was to Boulder for the fifth annual Red Zinger, July 21 to 29. The event had blossomed to nine stages covering about 800 miles, and had become the international race that Mo Siegel had envisioned. Top American talent competed against riders from Australia, Belgium, Holland, New Zealand, and Switzerland for a prize list of $170,000 in merchandise and cash.

"The speeds were so fast," Howard said. "I couldn't believe how hard the competition was. I remember looking around the pack at Boyer, Mount, LeMond, and the Stetina brothers, and thinking they had made some major improvements. I felt I was still young enough to come back, and I had a lot of ego involved as the previous two-time winner of the Red Zinger."

Mount pushed the pace up the relentless climbs. He loved to play psychological games, which Howard was not used to. Mount's games alienated other riders as well.

The race was a showcase of riders who would take the sport forward into the 1990s. LeMond, now 18, finished fourth overall and was awarded the Youth Classification. Davis Phinney of

Boulder, destined to win two stages of the Tour de France, won the criterium in Vail. Boyer, who would become the first U.S. rider in the Tour de France, won the road race from Colorado Springs to the top of Hoosier Pass above the tree line. Mount won the Estes Park circuit race. Phil Anderson of Australia, a professional, won the concluding 50-mile criterium in North Boulder Park.

Howard failed to crack the top three in any stage, even the opening day's time trial. "I was burned out," he said.

That was impressed upon him in the North Boulder criterium when the peloton was hammering in one long pace line at 30 MPH to chase down Phil Anderson, who was about to lap them. "I was holding on by the skin of my teeth when several riders in front of me got into trouble and crashed heavily. I hit my brakes and swerved to avoid them. The memory of riders tumbling like tenpins on waxed wood remains clear, even now."

A northern California racer, Gary Fisher, suggested one evening that Howard relax by riding a fat-tired bicycle with five speeds, which Fisher had made for pedaling on dirt trails through woods. "I knew Gary from road racing, and he showed me what he called a mountain bike. I didn't think much of it at the time." Howard laughed at the irony of his renunciation of a sport—mountain bike riding—that would become immensely popular in the 1990s. "I should have dropped right out of road racing and jumped into mountain bike racing right then. But I didn't. I still wanted to see what I could do in road racing."

Howard may not have been setting the pace, but he was still a player. He rode support to help teammate Dale Stetina win, and finished 15th of the 80 riders. His Exxon/Ultima team won the team competition, which gave him some satisfaction because the national cycling team was third.

Cycling's migratory route went north to Milwaukee for the nationals. "I felt ready for the time trial," Howard said. "I wanted to go out there and really blast it."

The 25-mile time trial on August 2 was in Wautoma, near Lake Winnebago, northwest of Milwaukee. Howard and 60 others went off at one-minute intervals in their race against the clock.

"I remember catching my minute man in about five miles," Howard said. "I was moving well into the rhythm of the ride. Then my front tire blew out. I had to hitch a ride in a car back to the start-finish," he said.

Defending champion Andy Weaver, fortified with a breakfast of a dozen assorted donuts and two tall Pepsis, won in 54 minutes,

53 seconds to usurp the national record from Howard.

In the intervening days before his road race, Howard watched other events that showed the sport was passing from one generation to another. Jack Simes III, 37, won the veterans' 40-mile race. LeMond won the junior boys' 40-mile race. Connie Carpenter won the women's 40-mile race.

On August 5, Howard was among the 150 riders lining up for the 114-mile road race around the course he had ridden successfully in three national road races. But Howard missed going away with one of the several groups that sprinted off the front after six laps. The leaders formed a group of 20 that galloped away.

Steve Wood dominated the breakaway, which lost several riders in the fast pace. With two laps to go, Wood pulled away with Tom Doughty. Wood dropped Doughty on the last lap to win by 15 seconds. Howard persevered to finish 17th.

Howard, less that two weeks from his 32nd birthday, was confronted with looking for a regular job. He also gave more thought to preparing for the next Iron Man.

Release of the movie *Breaking Away* that summer injected bicycle racing into the American conscience. Even the staid *New Yorker* praised the movie for its "affection for the middle classes, the landscapes of Indiana and bicycle racing."

The 1970s also saw an explosion in the popularity of running. James F. Fixx's 1977 *Complete Book of Running* was one of the most successful in a series of books that encouraged running as a way of life, stressing the enjoyment of participating in races rather than pressure to win or place well.

Recreational swimming also made a big splash as Howard's generation explored ways to avoid the middle-age spread. Taken together, the increased popularity of cycling, running, and swimming was also laying a broad base for triathlons.

When Howard returned to Austin he made a crucial decision. He asked the people at Campagnolo USA about working for them. America's cycling market no longer remained Campagnolo's private domain. Shimano, a Japanese company, had taken a significant portion of their market. Officials at Campagnolo USA were interested in rehiring Howard later in the year.

Howard also decided to shift his training regimen for the next Iron Man. "I was casting about for a different challenge. When I read about the Iron Man, something in me clicked. I knew I could win it, but I had to concentrate on running and swimming because they weren't my sports. I calculated that I could chip 45

minutes from Tom Warren's winning time." That got Howard
running short distances, and then stretching his runs to 10 miles
daily. He also took up swimming. He became a regular at the
Barton Springs Pool, an outdoor 25-yard pool fed with spring
water from rifts in the limestone along the Balcones Fault.

"Swimming in spring water is interesting," Howard said. "You
get into a pocket of water that is 40 degrees, and then five feet
away the temperature goes up to 80."

As he continued his triathlon training, he decided to try the
national cyclo-cross championship November 25 in Eugene,
Oregon. "It was a cold day, and the course was wet and slick," he
said. He and 22 others watched Laurence Malone dash away from
them at the start and gracefully continue to win his fifth straight
cyclo-cross title. Howard finished a disappointing sixth.

"The good part was returning to Austin and getting a job offer
from Campagnolo USA," he said. "Julio Marquevich was the CEO.
He hired me as the public relations liaison."

Howard moved to Houston where he found an apartment.
Kim remained in Austin. It was effectively the end of their marriage.

On December 8, Howard entered the White Rock Marathon in
Dallas for his longest-ever run. All his cycling and 10-mile runs
had given him fine cardiovascular training, but they were short
of what he needed to master the marathon. The marathon has
two distinctly separate parts—the first 20 miles, and the last 6
miles and 385 yards. Some scientist attribute the two lopsided
sections to a typical runner burning 100 calories a mile and the
liver holding about 2,000 calories of glycogen (blood sugar), which
gives a range of 20 miles. Runners call the sudden depletion of
calories at 20 miles "hitting the wall." Cyclists have a descriptive
metaphor: "bonking."

Howard hit the wall and bonked at 22 miles. "I had to walk
the last four miles," he said, grimacing at the recollection. "It was
brutal. I just couldn't run any more. My leg muscles seized up."

He finished in 3 hours and 10 minutes, a respectable time for
hobby runners, but nearly an hour behind the winner. Running—
which bears all the weight with each footfall—is also considerably
harder on the body than cycling, since the bicycle takes the
cyclist's weight. "I had a severe case of shin splints. They crippled
me and caused me to nearly buckle in my effort to finish."

He still had four weeks to recover before the Iron Man. He
devoted more time to cycling and to swimming. "I figured the
variability of cycling skills had the greatest potential to influence
the outcome of the Iron Man."

Officials at Campagnolo USA gave him a new Cinelli, an Italian bicycle with Campagnolo components that is to cycling what Hermes is to scarves. In early January, Howard flew with his Cinelli to Honolulu for the third annual Iron Man, set for January 10, 1980.

The Iron Man had turned into a serious event. Valerie Silk, part-owner of the Nautilus Fitness Centers of Honolulu, took over as race director. Her Nautilus Fitness Centers sponsored the event. "ABC's Wide World of Sports" sent a film crew to cover it with Diana Nyad and Jim Lampley as commentators. Now it was billed as the Ironman Triathlon World Championship.

Most of the 108 entrants who went to Ala Moana Park for the dawn start were from Hawaii. Warren returned to defend, as did Haller. Overlooked in the excitement were Californians Dave Scott, a 27-year-old swim coach from Davis, and Chuck Neumann, a former SEAL, from Paradise.

"What I remember most about that Ironman was the camaraderie," Howard said. "We stood together in the dark on the beach in Ala Moana Park. When the sun rose, we put our arms around each other and had a sunrise service on the beach. I remember feeling close to everyone there. The feeling brought to mind what Baron Pierre De Coubertain, the Frenchman pivotal in reviving the Olympics, had said: that the most important thing in the Olympic games is not to win, but to take part. That the essential thing is not to have conquered but to have fought well. This is what had been missing in my cycling. Then I rediscovered that feeling again. That morning, I became a triathlete."

Howard needed that feeling to propel him into the water for the swim. "I was spooked by the surf," he said. "Waves were crashing on the shore. It was a weird experience. Later, I realized that the ocean was calm, but I had never swum in the ocean."

Training in Barton Springs pool had helped him put in the distance, but the placid water had spoiled him. In the Ironman swim, salt water seeped under his goggles and burned his eyes, waves rose and fell like mountains, and everyone was swimming over one another in a flailing of arms and kicking legs.

"I was so unnerved," Howard admitted. "The whole thing was so intimidating. The ocean swells were rollers of three and four feet. We had no lane markers. It was so hard. The swim took me 1 hour 45 minutes, which is so slow that it's a joke. By the time I finished, there were a few swimmers behind me, but not many."

Finally out of the water, Howard quickly ran on the beach to his Cinelli, changed into his cycling shorts, shoes, and jersey, and set off for the 112-mile time trial around the perimeter of Oahu.

"I rode like a man possessed. But the course was open to traffic. We were on our own at traffic lights and all other intersections. Motorists yelled at us all the time."

Results show that Howard zoomed from obscurity to second place. "Tom Warren was the last person I caught. Dave Scott was the only person ahead of me. He was so far ahead that I never even saw him. My bike time trial was the fastest time that day—4:28. That included stopping to change a tire after I had a flat."

Next came the marathon. Howard got off his bicycle, changed into running shoes, and trotted along the course, through traffic past Waikiki Beach and up Kalakua Avenue. "Dave Scott was only about 10 minutes ahead of me," Howard said. "But Dave had a good balance in each of the three sports. I was a cyclist, but Dave was a triathlete."

Howard's legs began to hurt midway through the run. "I had to walk a lot. That was frustrating. But I had no choice. I was shattered."

With about two miles to go, Chuck Neumann caught Howard. "I was walking at that point, with killer shinsplint pains. Chuck was hurting too. He was hobbling. But he could hobble faster than I could walk. We must have been a sight, the two of us struggling with all we had left, no longer able to run."

They made their way into Kapiolani Park, where Scott had won in a new course record of 9:24:33, for the total distance of 140.6 miles. Neumann finished 1 hour and 8 minutes behind for second. Howard, whose marathon took a little more than four hours, was another couple of minutes back for third. Warren was fourth. Haller, the original Iron Man, finished sixth, nearly two hours faster than his original winning time.

Howard's third place boosted the Ironman's legitimacy. "ABC's Wide World of Sports" gave the event exposure into millions of households nationwide. When Diana Nyad interviewed Neumann immediately after he crossed the finish line, he was so wiped out that he fell asleep while answering her questions on-camera. Millions of viewers were enthralled at seeing the coverage of this outrageous new sport.

"I was resolute about winning in 1981," Howard said. "I was going to have a fuller approach by developing my running and swimming. I also thought about John Marino's record for crossing the United States, and Allan Abbott's speed record of 138 MPH on the Bonneville Salt Flats. When I went back to Houston, I told Julio Marquevich that he had a chance to get Campagnolo involved in triathlon. I told him I was going to win the next Ironman Triathlon World Championship, set the record for pedaling across America, and set the new world speed record.

"I wanted to be a triathlete, and I really got serious about training," Howard said. "I got fanatical about training, especially to get a balance in my swimming, cycling, and running."

He got up at 5 a.m. and ran 10 miles, most often in the dark, before going to work at 8:00 a.m. At noon, he went cycling, usually time trials of 30–40 miles in Memorial Park. Four or five evenings a week he worked out with the master's swim team for adults in Houston's Jewish Community Center. "I swam about 5,000 yards in each workout. They helped me get my times down, which was encouraging," he said.

His routine of training in three different rigorous disciplines while working full-time made for a solitary life. "I was living alone. It was probably the most dedicated I have ever been."

During this time, Howard and Kim filed for divorce.

"Living with John was often tough because he was going and going, but in the next breath it was exciting," Kim said. "We traveled all over and met so many wonderful people. But after a while, I wanted something more out of life."

Howard faced a long, hard haul to prepare for the next Ironman. By then the event had become so established that hundreds of smaller versions proliferated nationwide, drawing tens of thousands of new triathletes. On September 14, in Columbus, Ohio, Bud Light sponsored a full Ironman distance of 140.6 miles. "I went to Columbus and kicked ass to win it in a good time," Howard said. "I felt like I was ready to win the Ironman in Hawaii."

His winning the Columbus Ironman Triathlon helped persuade officials at Campagnolo USA to sponsor him fully. "I wrote up a proposal in which I stressed the importance of winning the Ironman, setting the cross-country record, and setting the world speed record. I was drawn to the projects because they're huge challenges. Marquevich had been leery about the whole idea. But Campagnolo was losing more market share to Shimano, and these projects would make Campagnolo look good."

Part of Howard's motivation came from reading Norman Mailer's recent novel, *Executioner's Song*, in which Mailer writes: "No psychic reward can ever be so powerful as winning a dare with yourself." Howard's dare was to win the Ironman Triathlon World Championship and then fulfill his other two feats.

Valerie Silk moved the event to Kailua-Kona, on the big island of Hawaii, because Oahu's traffic had threatened the safety of the triathletes. Her 1981 event on February 14 drew 326 starters, including 22 women. "ABC's Wide World of Sports" was back to cover the Ironman with Diana Nyad, Jim Lampley, and tennis legend Arthur Ashe. The Ironman was a major production.

Defending champion Dave Scott was forced to sit out the event as a result of injury. Howard himself was nearly unable to compete; tendons on top of his right foot had been inflamed for several weeks. By the time he arrived in Kailua-Kona 10 days before the triathlon, he could hardly walk.

"A week before the Ironman, I ran 15 miles and was in excruciating pain," he said. "I went to a doctor there who suggested injecting cortisone. He gave me 14 injections around the foot, then told me to elevate it, ice it eight times a day, and avoid running. I didn't run for six days. The day before the race, I went out and ran three or four miles. It felt great. I knew I was ready."

While at the Ironman, Howard met triathlete Dave Spangler of Ontario, California, whose business partner Gary Hooker and he owned a share in the racing car that Rick Vesco of Salt Lake City drove. Hooker, whose leader systems for hot rodders are standard fittings, and Spangler had connections that would help Howard set his world speed record. "Dave and I had breakfast a day or two before the Ironman," Howard said. "He said he and Gary would do their best to help. I said we would be in touch."

With his foot taken care of and an introduction to professional car racers, Howard was ready to concentrate on his Herculean tasks, beginning with winning the Ironman.

This time out, the surf didn't intimidate him as much, and his training paid off dramatically. The swim in Kihua Bay was out to a boat, then back to shore for a distance of 1.2 miles, which everyone repeated twice. "I took 40 minutes off my time," Howard said.

The Ironman was still so new that officials administering it believed that athletes had to shower off the salt from the swim before changing into their cycling clothes for the bike ride. Howard skipped the shower to shave time.

Howard's improved swim put less pressure on his cycling performance. The 112-mile course on the big island took riders through a lava field where the temperature rose above 110 degrees.

"I rode one of my old Raleighs, which wasn't as fast as the Cinelli. But in 1981 I was better balanced in the three disciplines. The heat riding through the lava fields was tough."

To prevent heatstroke by replacing fluids, riders picked up a new water bottle from a roadside table every five miles. "We also had to dismount and get weighed at various points," Howard said. "Somebody made a big deal about athletes maybe dying from dehydration. This probably was well-founded. But stopping and getting weighed certainly upset our rhythm."

Howard was a study in concentration as he rode, overtaking one cyclist after another. The ABC television film crew followed close enough to capture Howard on camera, riding like a predator, hands on the drops of his handlebars, his back slightly humped.

He took command of the lead after 50 miles. Among the last riders he passed were future Ironman winners Scott Molina and Scott Tinley, and his first inspiration, Tom Warren.

Howard rode a well-paced ride on the out-and-back course. He finished in 5:03—a half-hour slower than the year before. "That left me more energy for running the marathon," he said.

His closest rival became Molina. Wearing his father's white T-shirt and black dress socks, Molina seemed out on a lark. He smiled cheerfully at the television camera as he finished the cycling portion, changed into running shoes and chased after Howard.

"The run was difficult because it was so hot that day," Howard said. "As difficult as a marathon is, the heat made it even worse. It was brutal." Molina was steadily gaining on Howard. "I knew if I ran any faster," Howard said, "I would get into deep trouble. I was trying to keep up a steady rhythm."

Howard's run was considerably improved from the year before—he didn't have to walk. He reached the turnaround still leading, knowing that on the way back he would pass Molina. "I wanted to look as smooth and fresh as possible," Howard said. When they passed by one another on opposite lanes of the road, Howard ran smoothly, and managed a relaxed smile. Soon afterward, Molina collapsed and was taken to an ambulance.

Howard completed the marathon in 3:25 for a total elapsed time of 9:38:29, 26 minutes ahead of Tom Warren, the runner-up. Haller took 11:41:00 to complete the distance in 37th place.

"It was such a tremendous feeling to win Ironman," Howard said, excitement still in his voice a dozen years later. "It helped take away the burning feeling I had when I was bounced from the national cycling team. I felt I had redeemed myself. I felt like I could accomplish anything. Winning the Ironman Triathlon World Championship put me into motion to go after my next projects—the cross-country record and the absolute speed record."

Chapter 13

"His Majesty keeps above 600 horses in his stables:
They are generally from 54 to 60 foot high."
— Jonathan Swift, *Gulliver's Travels*

Going after John Marino's cross-country record turned into a far greater project than Howard expected. He had no way of knowing that a Hollywood agent would get involved. He had no way of knowing that the record assault would turn into a unique four-man bicycle race that drew national television coverage, broadcast in a two-part program, which won an Emmy.

It started simply enough. Marino's successful 1978 cross-country ride inspired him to think about creating an annual cross-country race, to be called the Great American Bike Race. The following summer he set about improving his record of 13 days, 1 hour, and 20 minutes. After leaving the pier of Santa Monica and crossing 14 states, he was within 60 miles of New York City when time ran out. But in June 1980, Marino was better prepared. Following him in a van was Peter Rosten, who filmed both rides for documentaries. Marino demolished his record with a new time of 12:03:41, which gave Rosten a dramatic conclusion to his film.

Marino's new record was dutifully entered in the *Guinness Book of World Records*. Rosten produced a 23-minute documentary, "Psychling," about the record-breaking ride. Rosten's lean script and well-edited film evoked the drama of Marino's solo coast-to-coast ride. His effort meant more to viewers when it was described as the equivalent of doing 1 million push-ups, or 43 consecutive marathons, or swimming the English channel 18 times. The film showed the value of setting a goal and breaking that goal into achievable parts that contribute to fulfilling the goal—with Marino and his coast-to-coast ride as an example.

Marino attracted widespread media attention that extended beyond the cycling community. He drew the attention of a book editor at Houghton-Mifflin who commissioned him to write *John*

Marino's Bicycling Book. His editor connected him with a Hollywood agent, who soon set Marino up with national television talk shows and lucrative sponsorships. In the spring of 1981, Houghton-Mifflin published Marino's book.

Howard's success in the Ironman early that year gained him more recognition than his previous three Olympics, two Pan American Games, and six national championships combined. Howard and Marino were by far America's best-known cyclists.

Whatever chance Greg LeMond, George Mount, and the new generation of cyclists had for winning medals and popular acclaim in the 1980 Moscow Olympics fizzled when President Carter announced the U.S. boycott in protest of the Soviet invasion of Afghanistan. LeMond and Mount turned professional and moved to Europe, where they raced against the giants of the road. But in America they were virtually unknown.

In April 1981, Howard and Marino were featured celebrities at the Cleveland consumer cycling show, BikeAmerica. Another celebrity was Bryan Allen, who recently had crossed the English Channel by pedaling Paul MacCready's Gossamer Albatross—the first-ever human-powered flight over the Channel, which earned him international recognition and a $200,000 prize. Eric Heiden, the speed skater who won five Olympic gold medals in the 1980 Lake Placid, New York, Winter Olympics, had switched to full-time cycling and was at BikeAmerica to sign autographs. Cleveland's bike show created high energy for American cycling.

Howard and Marino knew of one another, but didn't meet until they went to Cleveland, where they had breakfast together. Howard quizzed Marino, three years younger, about the cross-country ride. "Howard was polite and asked a lot of questions," Marino recalled. "I could almost see the cogs turning in his brain."

Seated with them was Michael Shermer of Altadena, California, who was covering the show for *Bicycle Dealer Showcase* magazine. "Howard and Marino talked about a duel between them, racing across America," Shermer said. "Originally, Marino was going to race Englishman Paul Corbett, who set the record of riding the length of England, 750 miles from Land's End to John O'Groats. But that duel fell through. As Howard and Marino talked about racing across America, I got excited and wanted to race, too."

Shermer, 26, was the youngest of the three. The previous summer he had set a new record by riding from Seattle down the Pacific Ocean to San Diego, a distance of 1,500 miles, in 7 days and 8 hours. "I talked them into letting me join their race,"

Shermer said. "I wasn't in their league. But they agreed that I would join the race under the condition that I would break my previous record by a significant amount that summer."

As the breakfast talk continued, the name of Lon Haldeman of Harvard, Illinois, came up. In July 1980, Haldeman, 23, had ridden from New York City to Santa Monica, then promptly turned around and pedaled back to New York City. On his odyssey, Haldeman not only established a round-trip record of 24 days and 2 hours on Marino's route, but also improved the cross-country record by better than a day.

"What Haldeman did was a jolt in the cycling community," Shermer said. "So we decided to include him in the race."

After the bike show, Marino returned to southern California, where he met with his agent. In a spacious office filled with signed photos of celebrities, mounted platinum records, and other show-business mementos, Marino told him of the proposed four-man race across America. The agent listened intently.

"He said he thought it was a great idea and that he would handle getting sponsors," Marino recalled. "Sponsorships are much easier to get when a sports event has television coverage. So he took a copy of Peter Rosten's documentary under his arm and met with executives at ABC-TV. Their first reaction was that four guys racing from coast-to-coast sounded boring. But he told them about the drama and showed them the documentary. They changed their minds. ABC-TV signed on to cover the race."

While Marino and the agent were shaping plans for the Great American Bike Race, Howard was busy organizing a program to set his speed record. He still worked full-time for Campagnolo USA, while he and corporate officials talked about details of a sponsorship package. Howard wrote proposals to other companies seeking sponsorships and talked with contacts in the cycling industry.

Just as important was lining up the proper crew and equipment for the task. Dave Spangler and Gary Hooker agreed to help. They introduced Howard to Rick Vesco, a second-generation race-car driver. Vesco, of the Salt Lake City suburb of Brigham, was vice-president of the Utah Salt Flat Racing Association. Vesco's connections helped provide Howard with access to the Bonneville Salt Flats, timers, and other officials instrumental in making such a record ride take place and gain official recognition.

Howard also needed a special muscle bicycle—one that was as sturdy as a motorcycle for the speed he would ride, yet still handled like a bicycle. "I got in touch with Allan Abbott, who lived in Los Angeles where he had a medical practice, and talked with him about his 138 MPH record," Howard said. "He said I would have to design a different drive-chain system."

Pedaling faster involves using a bigger gear, which ordinarily means increasing the size of the front chainring. Howard usually raced with a chainring of 53 teeth. But Abbott used a chainring of 280 teeth, so oversized that any bigger chainring would become a third-wheel. "Allan Abbott recommended that I use a step-gear," Howard said.

Instead of the standard drive chain of a single chainring rotated by pedals to move the chain connected to the rear-sprocket on the rear-wheel hub, the step-gear has two chain drives. The first chain rises diagonally from the chainring to a small sprocket on the frame behind the seat. When that sprocket turns, it connects to an axle fitted to another large sprocket which drives a chain that descends to the rear-wheel hub sprocket. The step-gear system gives another important dimension to big gears necessary to pedal faster than 140 MPH.

Howard got in touch with Doug Malewicki, who designed motorcycles for Evel Knievel, to help with the design of his bicycle. Howard also talked with Skip Hijsak, a Texas custom bicycle-frame builder, about making his muscle bicycle.

Meanwhile, Howard continued training diligently. One of the Ironman competitors he befriended—Ron Smith of Del Mar, California—invited him to southern California where the weather was even better than Texas for year-round training, but Howard needed to secure sponsorships before he could make the move.

In June, Shermer, inspired by the prospect of joining Howard, Marino, and Haldeman in the Great American Bike Race, greatly improved his Seattle-to-San Diego ride. He boosted his daily average from 208 miles to 301, and reduced his time to 4 days and 4 hours. Shermer earned his place in the line-up of the race.

Howard, Shermer, Marino, and Haldeman met late in the summer in San Francisco at the *CitySports* magazine BikeFest. "We laid down the ground rules and made a pact that no matter what happened regarding sponsors and television, we would race," Shermer said. "If necessary, and as a last resort, we would use our own money to sponsor ourselves—the winner getting a pat on the back from the other three."

"It was going to be a gentleman's race if race sponsorships didn't come through," Howard said. "We were out for a great adventure. I wanted to win it as part of my trilogy."

In the spring of 1982, Howard and officials at Campagnolo USA came to terms for a sponsorship package of money and equipment. The Howards' divorce also became final. "I decided it was time to leave Texas," Howard said. "Ron Smith invited me to stay in his guest house in Del Mar, near San Diego."

A potential sponsorship with Pepsi-Cola USA connected him with the Pepsi Challenge 24-Hour Bicycle Marathon in New York's Central Park on Memorial Day weekend. New Yorker David White had gained considerable media attention for winning the 1981 event and setting a new 24-hour distance record when he pedaled 440 miles. For the 1982 edition, Howard was invited by Lenny Preheim, proprietor of the local Toga Bike Shop, to ride for Toga and set the new 24-hour record.

"I wanted to break David White's record and go farther than anybody had gone," Howard said. "I had never done any ultra-distance before. I figured the 24-hour ride would be perfect preparation for the Great American Bike Race."

Al Toefield, the New York City police sergeant and former ABL president, said he would introduce Howard to an official at Pepsi-Cola USA. When Howard made the trip east, he and Toefield met in Central Park on Saturday, the day before the Pepsi challenge. With Toefield was Joe Block, vice-president of public affairs at Pepsi-Cola USA. Block knew about Howard and his trilogy, but wasn't interested in discussing Pepsi's potential involvement. "He said to wait till after the race to talk about it," Howard said.

The Pepsi Challenge drew a field of 9,316 riders, according to *The New York Times*. They lined up by Tavern on the Green in Central Park for the noon start of the 11th annual event. Howard, the veteran of countless races, had rarely been in a field larger than 200 riders. "It was such a mob scene," he recalled with a groan. "I had no idea what I was getting into."

Helping Howard was a support crew of about a dozen that Preheim put together. They included David White and his training partner Jonathan Cooper. White and Cooper took turns with others leading Howard and threading through the mass of other cyclists around the rolling 5.1-mile course. "We were constantly turning and weaving," Howard said. "We must have gone an extra five to 10 miles to get around people or avoid crashes."

Preheim and friends worked in shifts around the clock to pace Howard and serve up food like chocolate-chip cookies, banana bread, turkey sandwiches, and one of Howard's favorite meals, baked potatoes and sour cream.

All day and through the night, Howard continued riding with shifts of riders Preheim dispatched. They set the pace for Howard to draft behind while others formed a wedge to protect him from the cyclists they were constantly overtaking. By 10:00 the next morning, with the noon finish still two hours away, Howard passed White's record. "David White helped me break his record," Howard said. "He was very generous."

When noon came, Howard had covered 475 miles for the new American 24-hour record. His effort, however, was short of the world mark of 507 miles that Englishman Roy Cromack set in 1969 in Yorkshire, England. "That left me with another goal to shoot for," Howard said.

Winning the Pepsi Challenge with a new national record helped make Howard more attractive to Pepsi-Cola USA officials. Shortly after Howard returned to California after the race, Joe Block arranged for him to fly to the corporation's headquarters in Purchase, New York. "We signed a contract," Howard said, "for Pepsi sponsorship in the Great American Bike Race, to compete again in the Ironman and the Pepsi Challenge, and go for the speed record. Pepsi's sponsorship meant a lot. It gave me revenue— enough for a margin that I didn't have to go in the hole for the Great American Bike Race."

One more sponsor signed on with Howard. Mike Sinyard, president of Specialized Bicycles of Morgan Hill, California, signed on to supply equipment, like the tires Howard was grinding through, and new bicycles.

A major television network's commitment is a considerable plus for any sports event, but somehow sponsors for the Great American Bike Race weren't working out. Early in 1982, the race had been scheduled to begin August 4 from the Santa Monica pier. The riders logged heavy mileage to prepare. ABC-TV committed a crew of 33, including commentators Jim Lampley and Diana Nyad. They were prepared for a staggering marathon of 2,978 miles through 15 states to finish in front of the Empire State Building. But in early July the event was nearly scrapped.

The Hollywood agent called the riders into his office for a meeting and told them that the total race sponsorship consisted of Igloo donating a couple of ice chests for each rider. He suggested they cancel the race. "We could not believe it," Shermer said. "We sat in that office with our jaws hanging open. All those miles and all that planning would go down the drain."

But the four riders had made a pledge to compete—no matter what happened. "We were going to race, come hell or high water, and both had come," Shermer said.

Despite the network's fee of $25,000 paid for the broadcast rights, the riders themselves each had to pay $8,000 to cover the cost of renting Winnebago motor homes, gas, and food. Shermer and Haldeman used all their savings. Marino took a second mortgage out on his four-bedroom home in Irvine. Howard's individual sponsorships helped avoid putting him in debt, but the race wasn't a break-even proposition. The Great American Bike Race was a race of monumental ambition, media hype, and great promise—but a commercial bust.

Nevertheless, Howard was still game. He returned to Missouri to visit his parents and to see about getting Ray Florman as a member of his support crew. In Springfield, Howard was invited by Ed Ruesing, president of the St. Louis Chamber of Commerce, to go to St. Louis to help promote a criterium there.

"Howard pedaled 220 miles from Springfield along Interstate 44 to St. Louis," Ruesing said. "That's a hilly 220 miles, over the Ozarks. They're steep hills. I had arranged an interview with Rich Koster, a sports writer for the now-defunct *St. Louis Glove-Democrat,* for an article on bicycle racing growing in the United States. Howard had his own Great American Bike Race, and we had a criterium in St. Louis—the 50-mile VP Fair Criterium. When he was done, Howard pedaled back to Springfield. We paid him $500 to come and speak. He turned it into a training ride that earned him $500."

Two days before the race across America was to start, Bud Light signed on as sponsor for a fee of $25,000. But the race still remained one with a trophy for the winner.

The riders were four individuals with deep inner strength and convictions. Each rider was determined to ride as long as he could and stop to rest for as long or as little as he needed to.

At 10 a.m. Wednesday, August 4, Howard, Shermer, Marino, and Haldeman lined up by the pier of Santa Monica. Behind them was a fleet of motor homes, vans, and trucks for the support crews and the film crew. Santa Monica Mayor Ruth Goldman was the official starter. The four riders and about a dozen *tifosi* began pedaling east for the Empire State Building through a light haze.

Howard's crew consisted of Florman, serving his last tour of duty for his protégé; Jim Brady of Fort Worth, Mike Hemmit of

Houston; Chris Hardwick of Columbia, South Carolina; and Sandy Daggett, a nurse from Los Angeles. They would take turns driving the motor home, preparing meals, keeping Howard's bicycle operating, and keeping him competitive.

The giant proportions of the Great American Bike Race took some getting used to. "I discovered quickly that I had been cavalier in my approach to a race of this magnitude," Howard said.

Haldeman, a bicycle mechanic with an open face and a quiet manner, had a talent for ultra-distance riding. By Palm Springs, 120 miles after the start, Haldeman and his support crew were so far ahead that all the others could see was the helicopter the television crew had hired to monitor the race, far away in the azure sky.

Howard pursued with determination. Shermer chased Howard. Behind them, Marino's back began hurting. After Palm Springs lay the Mojave Desert, where the riders pedaled through afternoon heat that rose to 113 degrees. Howard, accustomed to winning, faltered in the desert. After dark, Howard was forced to pull over to drink, eat, and rest.

Haldeman rode for 22 hours straight, reaching Prescott, Arizona, 401 miles away, with an insurmountable lead. Shermer moved up to second place. Marino pedaled past a resting Howard for third. Marino's crew had a sign on their motor home that read, "Remember the tortoise and the hare." In the night, Marino moved up to second place, which he held briefly.

After four hours' rest, Howard resumed chasing. He passed Marino. At 600 miles, he caught Shermer. They rode together and discussed how to catch Haldeman.

"I was feeling great and planned to ride all night," Shermer said. "My crew chief pulled out a map and showed me how far we had left to go—more than 2,000 miles, plus the mountains. So I pulled over and slept in the motor home for a few hours. I never saw John Howard after that, although I came close."

Howard had lost ground on the first day, but he kept chasing. In Santa Fe, New Mexico, after being in the saddle for 40 hours, he was forced to give in and pull over in the motor home. "My knees gave out. Every muscle in my body cramped up. I slept for six hours. It was the longest stretch of sleep I got for the rest of the race. When I got back up. I pedaled for 44 hours straight."

Haldeman's lead over Howard stretched to a maximum of 160 miles on the second day. But even Marathon Lon began experiencing difficulties. His hands and feet were numb. In Texas, he traded his cycling shoes for loafers.

Marino suffered back and leg-muscle pains. Blisters prevented him from sitting properly on the saddle. Mechanical problems slowed his progress. He fell back to fourth and steadily lost ground.

The most difficult emotional times were on the third and fourth days. Riders were weary from pedaling 300 miles a day, burning 14,000 calories daily, and sacrificing sleep.

"My race was memorable for vivid hallucinations," Howard said. "In West Texas, I pedaled across the Panhandle in the dark. At 3 a.m., it was pitch black. I was riding by the light of the motor home behind me. Suddenly the road was covered with Egyptian hieroglyphics. I was riding over ancient Egyptian graffiti. The road was perfectly flat, but I kept feeling like I was dropping down long descents and pedaling up steep grades.

"Later, I had stopped and a golden retriever came up and started licking my hand. I blinked and the dog was lying at my feet. I blinked again and the dog was a pile of white bones. After that, I took brief power naps and kept better hydrated."

A heavy rain and head winds slowed the riders across Kansas. Yet the conditions helped them concentrate on the yawning stretches of highway. Mary and Harry Howard cheered their son when he rode through Missouri. "We waved to John and yelled for him," Harry said. "He kept right on going."

After crossing the Mississippi River and then Illinois and Indiana, Howard was weary in the extreme. "It was a contest of sleep deprivation," he said. Frustrated by not closing to within 100 miles of Haldeman and suffering from fatigue, Howard entertained the notion of quitting. But Shermer was trying to capitalize on Howard's weariness, which Howard learned about.

"With Lon so far up the road, the race was for second," Shermer pointed out. "I kept thinking if John Howard took a nap, then I could catch him. That was my motivation."

In Ohio, Shermer's support crew clipped a magazine photo of Howard, fashioned an Old West "Wanted, Dead or Alive" poster, and glued it to the back of the Winnebago motor home. "Every time my crew drove by, I had to chase that Wanted poster of John Howard," Shermer said.

When Howard learned from his support crew about Shermer's poster, his competitive spirit took over. "One of my support crew, reported that John Howard was really going for it," Shermer said. "Howard was out of the saddle and charging the tops of hills in West Virginia. So I had to charge over the hills, too."

When Haldeman pedaled into Pennsylvania, his lead was 100

miles on Howard, 200 on Shermer, and 300 on Marino. In a sport where places often are separated by the width of a tire, riders in the Great American Bike race were spread apart by a state.

Marathon Lon made it look easy, but he admitted that the miles and effort were taking a toll. "I'm fried," he told the film crew. "My mind has been gone for four days."

Howard put on a show descending mountains in West Virginia and Pennsylvania. He passed cars at faster than 50 MPH.

Haldeman succeeded in setting a new cross-country record, reaching the Empire State Building in Manhattan early in the afternoon with a record of 9 days, 20 hours, and 2 minutes. "It was hard," he said. "I feel sorry for the other guys out there."

Howard was still in eastern Pennsylvania. He crossed New Jersey and made his way to New York, pedaling in the dark through Harlem and arriving in Manhattan shortly after midnight for second place in 10:09:35. He broke Marino's old record and Haldeman's record. When Diana Nyad interviewed him immediately after the finish, she asked if he would do the race again. Howard shook his head and spoke thickly. "No," he said. "I am ready to fall asleep for three days."

Shermer arrived in 10:19:54 for third. Marino completed the race in 12:07:21. He was greeted with a hero's welcome. "I'm going to celebrate with my annual beer," he told Diana Nyad. He smiled. "Maybe three."

The budget for ABC's coverage of the race went over $500,000, prompting the network to abandon the more expensive video-tape in favor of film. That lent more freedom in editing and offered a more lyrical quality. The two-and-a-half-hour program was introduced at the January 1983 New York Bike Show in New York City, near where the race had finished.

"It was really moving," Shermer said. "Barry Manilow was singing, 'I Made It Through the Rain.' Diana Nyad was moved to tears. All kinds of ABC-TV executives were at the show, including Larry Kamm, the producer, and commentators Jim Lampley and Diana Nyad. When the program was over, somebody suggested we all go out to dinner. I said, 'Great!' But Howard said he had to get back to his hotel room to do some work."

When the program was broadcast over the national network, it drew considerable praise. Frank Litsky wrote in *The New York Times*: "This is a story of men competing against themselves, striving to reach their limits and exceed them, beating the challenge."

"The bike," Jim Lampley said in his narration of the program, "is a prop."

Howard still had other challenges to meet. "With the Great American Bike Race, I realized I had set my goal too high. I needed to scale it down. For me to give my best effort, I need proper sleep. I decided to go after the 24-hour world distance record."

Going after Englishman Roy Cromack's world record of 507 miles, however, looked daunting at the start of the 12th Annual Pepsi Challenge in Central Park on the Sunday of Memorial Day weekend. Rain poured down, reducing the starting field to 5,000.

"The conditions are a bit treacherous," Howard told an anonymous *New York Times* reporter minutes before the start. "But I've competed in conditions like this before, and I feel confident I've got a good shot at the record."

As for the year before, Lenny Preheim of the Toga Bike Shop put together a team to help Howard. Jonathan Cooper returned with local rider Ambrose Salmini, a year older than Howard and himself a veteran of the Ironman that Howard had won. Salmini, a film producer, also made a film of the Pepsi Challenge.

"Central Park is the worst place in the world to go after a world distance record," Salmini said. "There are lots of turns. The road has potholes everywhere. And the weather was nasty that weekend. So we tried to help John focus so he could stay on the bike as long as possible and ride as fast as he could for 24 hours."

Rain continued all day and into the night. Howard was forced to stop seven times because of flat tires. Preheim had to return to his bike shop in the middle of the night to get more tires. The most difficult time was about 3 a.m. when the rain was heaviest. "I could barely see," Howard said. "Mud was in my eyes and up my nose. The park was dark in many places. But as hard as it was, it also gave me a sense of mission. I was determined to make the world distance record mine."

Finally, shortly after dawn, the rain stopped. On his 100th lap around the 5.1-mile course, at 11:37 a.m., Howard broke Cromack's mark. Riding until the noon finish, Howard set the new 24-hour world record with 514 miles.

Finishing second was Karl Zalenko of Plymouth, Massachusetts, with 401 miles.

Howard considered his effort in the rain one of the most grueling of his career. But it left him free to concentrate on setting the new world speed record.

Chapter 14

"The bicycle is the noblest invention of mankind."
—William Sayoran

Howard's ride to set the new speed record involved considerable attention to detail. His research quickly showed that he needed a leather suit for protection in case he fell. Motorcyclists recommended Bates Leathers in Long Beach, where he was fitted with full-length motorcyclist's leathers. They were made of polished red and yellow leather, featuring Lycra expansion joints to allow movement, and weighed 12 pounds. His leathers were adorned with "Campagnolo" down each arm, and block letters with "PEPSI" across the chest. He also bought a motorcycle helmet, leather gloves, and leather covers for his boots.

"Wearing that suit was hot, but I got used to it," he said.

Howard and officials at Campagnolo USA hired Austin frame builder Karol "Skip" Hijsak to make the muscle bicycle he needed. Hijsak, a frame builder since 1976, worked with a computer to design the frame. He built the bicycle in two weeks in June 1982.

"It wasn't a matter of drafting it out first or welding tubes together to see what worked," Hijsak explained. "I knew that if I had the right parameters, then the frame I designed would work."

Once Hijsak had the design, he and his wife Vicki picked through assorted bicycle and motorcycle parts. Wheels and the front fork came from a motorcycle. The rest came from bicycle tubing. It had one brake, a cantilever rear brake taken from a tandem. Jutting from the front fork was a vertical bar that Howard was to use to bump against the back of Rick Vesco's race car to slow to below 100 MPH. Instead of curved handlebars, the bicycle had straight handlebars with short black grips resembling the throttle of a motorcycle. It looked like a Picasso sculpture.

"It was styled after a motorcycle," Hijsak said. "Its long wheel base gave it stability at high speed. The step-gear we put on it had the big advantage of letting John use ordinary chainrings and sprockets to get the gear he needed without great expense."

Howard tested the 46-pound prototype on the road to see how it handled. "We did some test runs on the Texas World Speedway in College Station," he said. "I pedaled behind a hot-rod Dodge van and we got up to 75 MPH. I felt we had a suitable design."

After returning the bicycle for some adjustments, he did one more test run. "The last one was on a highway near Katy, Texas. We cranked it up to 100 MPH behind the Dodge van." He laughed at the recollection. "We broke 100 MPH on a public highway, like Alfred Letourner did."

Elated and restless, he got in touch with Rick Vesco about going out to the Bonneville Salt Flats to practice together. In mid-July, with the Great American Bike Racing two weeks away, Howard went to the Salt Flats to see about breaking 150 MPH.

For Vesco, two years older than Howard, driving 150 MPH was a cakewalk. At 16, Vesco had driven a 300 c.c. motorcycle 131 MPH on the Bonneville Salt Flats. He then graduated to race cars and became a member of the 200 MPH club. Once he nearly set a world speed record when he roared along Bonneville's timed mile at more than 300 MPH in the Bonneville Streamliner that his father, John, had designed in 1957. On young Vesco's mandatory second timed run, however, his car flipped over. The car crashed before he completed the second run; Vesco walked away unhurt.

When Dave Spangler and Gary Hooker approached him about driving for Howard, Vesco agreed to be part of the project. He recruited his engine mechanic and three timers.

Vesco's car was a thoroughbred machine. Its fuselage was only two inches from the ground, 21 feet long, and 41 inches wide. Car, driver, and fuel all weighed less than 1,500 pounds. For Howard's run, Vesco repainted it, renamed it "Pepsi Challenger," and decorated its body with other sponsors' names.

A crucial component in Howard's effort was a special Plexiglass fairing—a device that fitted over the back of Vesco's low-slung car and shielded Howard from the wind so he could pedal in the draft. The fairing was 5 feet tall and 4½ feet wide, and fitted on the back. Facing Howard on the fairing was a speedometer. He looked through the fairing with a windshield. In case he needed a reminder, a sign below the windshield read, "Faster, you fool."

"Dave Spangler and Gary Hooker made the fairing in their Hooker Performance Factory," Howard said. "They applied their knowledge of aerodynamics to make it. The fairing is what made my record ride possible. Dave and Gary donated the fairing. They were my major sponsors."

All of Howard's sports background and his elaborate preparation for the speed record were coming together. But out on the vast expanse of the Bonneville Salt Flats, he realized he was in another category of experience. Vesco eased himself into the cockpit of his aerodynamic fuselage and fired up his 350 cubic inch Chevrolet engine. Its 650 horsepower growled deafeningly. Howard realized he was shaking like a leaf on his bicycle.

"Everything was vibrating," he recalled. "That engine was like nothing I had ever heard before. The fiberglass body of Rick's car was vibrating. I was breathing nitromethane fumes. Rick gunned the engine and I broke out in huge goose bumps. That first time was a traumatic experience. The ground would shake and shake. The noise of the engine was deafening. Completely deafening. I started to wonder what I had gotten myself into."

Because Howard was turning over such a big gear, which carried him 111 feet with every revolution of the pedals, he and his bicycle were towed by a cable up to 60 MPH. That saved him taking the four miles he would need under his own power to build to that speed. Vesco accelerated smoothly. Approaching 60, Howard disengaged the towline and started pedaling on his own.

Howard's bicycle started to wobble. Granules of salt whirled up, white rain against his visor. Some granules were sucked up under the visor and stung his face and eyes. Yet he pedaled carefully in the protective slipstream, which extended to about seven feet behind the car, and the bicycle became more stable.

For three miles, Howard and Vesco accelerated before they started the timed mile, a section marked for an official 1,760 yards surveyed by the Bureau of Land Management. Electronic eyes at the beginning and end of the mile mark the timing trap.

Howard chased after Vesco's car, careful to stay within the shelter of the fairing. If he fell behind it, wind would rush at him with as much force as smashing into a wall. If he veered outside the breadth of the slipstream, he would suffer the same smash of air. If he accelerated too fast, he would hit the bumper bar on the fairing. His effort required precision riding.

After they whizzed through the first timed mile, Vesco slowed the car. Howard decelerated by banging the vertical bar jutting from his front fork against the bumper bar of Vesco's car—steel against steel. He had to hit the bar repeatedly rather than use his hand brake, which would melt from the friction created by braking at such high speed.

"It was a tricky process," Howard said. "I slammed into the bumper bar. I had to be very careful. It was really violent. I put dents in the back of the bumper bar. Paint cracked and peeled on the bumper and the bike. But after a while I got used to it."

That afternoon they made five such runs, each as physically demanding on Howard as a pursuit race. His heart sped to 195 beats a minute, and his legs spun like an egg beater.

"It was a tremendous thrill," Howard said. "But it also was terrifying because we were doing something dangerous. I could feel the power of the vortex behind me. Let me tell you, that power was tremendous. The margin for error when riding behind Rick's car was so small. We had to do everything just right."

A timer gave Howard a slip of paper stating he had clocked 114.9 MPH. "I felt like we made progress," he said. "But soon it started to rain. The next day, the course was sloppy; salt picks up water like a sponge. I tried riding in it. My tires shot long trails of salt water. Rick's car risked hydroplaning. We had to back off. Day after day, the rain kept coming. Then there was major flooding."

Howard returned to San Diego to make his final preparations for the Great American Bike Race.

Finishing second in that race left Howard with numbness in two fingers of each hand. While he recovered, the Salt Flats remained under water. Periodic flooding has kept the Bonneville Salt Flats level, but waiting for them to dry frustrated Howard. The rest of his 1982 speed quest was literally rained out.

He settled for good in metropolitan San Diego, where the soaring popularity of triathlons put him in demand as a speaker and coach. His performances in the Ironman, which were broadcast on national television, towered over his cycling achievements. Seen as an accomplished triathlete, he was in demand for coaching.

"I liked coaching," Howard said. "It gave me a lot of satisfaction. I especially liked making suggestions and seeing athletes improve."

Restless to set the speed record, Howard and Dave Spangler scouted around that autumn for alternate sites. "We drove Dave's souped-up Camaro 160 MPH on the highway near Edwards Air Force Base in southern California," he said. "The road was smooth enough. We thought it was perfect. If motorpacing on the highway was good enough for Alfred Letourner, it would be good enough for me. We tried to get permission from the California Highway Department to close off the roads for us. They didn't say 'no.' They said, 'Hell no!'"

Spangler and Hooker, both Ironman veterans who liked pushing physical and mechanical limits when they could, suggested that Howard try going south of the border. Spangler and Hooker had connections in Mexico with the hot-rod community there. In early January 1983, Howard and Spangler drove to Tijuana to meet with Pepe Lemon, a hot-rod promoter, and to look around for possible sites. They found a 7-mile stretch of the San Filipe highway, 50 miles south of Mexicali, which looked like what they needed. It was the same stretch that Howard had raced successfully over when he won the Tour of Baja.

"Pepe thought it was a great project," Howard said. "He had clout in the government. He knew who to talk to so we could shut down the highway."

With a new venue taken care of, Howard got in touch with Vesco, who brought his race car, engine mechanic, and three timers to join Howard in Mexico. Others who made the trip were Campagnolo USA corporate officials, including Julio Marquevich; film producer Ambrose Salmini; and journalists including Harry Hurt III, who would cover Howard's attempt for *Texas Monthly*.

On January 9, some 60 people converged on the site. According to the map, they were at Laguna Salado (Salt Lake). Since it was a barren lunar landscape, Howard's group dubbed it, "The Pits."

Assorted Mexican *federales* in police uniform drove up in small trucks. A pair of paramedics in white smocks arrived in their ambulance. *Federales* spread out along the highway. At the appropriate time, they closed off the road at both ends of a 7-mile stretch. Traffic backed up as Howard and Vesco took over.

Even closed to traffic, the San Filipe Highway looked ominous. Elevated 11 feet over the Baja desert, the two-lane road was only 27 feet wide. Although the black asphalt looked smooth, it had numerous swells, which Vesco called whoop-de-dos. Since his car sat only two inches from the pavement, whoop-de-dos launched his car, he discovered, when he drove past 110 MPH.

"I was very apprehensive the whole time we were there," Salmini said. "I followed John's first run from a helicopter to shoot film of his ride. It was wild to watch. They built up their speed and were going 100-plus through the timed mile. But I could see what they were going through on the bumpy road."

Vesco and Howard made runs for two days. Often they were delayed when crosswinds blew too strongly. When the wind was right and they made another run, driver and cyclist relied on an almost mystic communication for staying in sync.

Each run increased the speed another 5 MPH. But after 110 MPH, Vesco's car was becoming airborne. He had to keep the car going as straight as possible to avoid careening off the road to certain disaster. Each time Vesco hit a whoop-de-do, Howard had a difficult—and dangerous—time tracking the car. By the second day, his forearms were aching from fighting the bumps.

Vesco discovered that the bouncing runs had worn out a rubber bushing on the car's right suspension. Without the bushing, which limited the shock of the car landing after a bump, the suspension was rubbing metal to metal. That meant Vesco had to keep the car traveling straight or he would lose control. He said the only way they could try one more run was if they had a head wind or a tailwind. Close to noon, the wind blew across the road.

Everyone else knocked off for lunch. Howard vented his frustration by borrowing a dirt motorcycle and tearing around the desert. Vesco parked his car, got on his motorcycle, and roared away to be alone.

Within a few hours, the wind shifted to a 22 MPH head wind. Vesco announced they were back in action. On that run, Howard looked smoother. He seemed to pedal faster, possibly inspired by knowing he had to make the run count. When Vesco hit a whoop-de-do, Howard recovered quickly. Howard reported that he experienced at least three whoop-de-dos through the timed mile. Each time, paint and debris flew from the belly of the car and was sucked up under Howard's helmet, getting in his eyes.

Past the timed mile, Vesco slowed the car. Howard banged into the rear. Then the car hit another whoop-de-do. Howard abruptly felt his bike jerk out of control. A pedal scraped a deep groove in the pavement. He struggled with all his strength to keep his balance as the bicycle swayed perilously. Then Vesco recovered and straightened his path, and Howard regained control.

When they stopped, Howard discovered he had worn his steel pedal down to the spindle. A timing official radioed that he had gone 124.189 MPH. Moments earlier, Howard had been terror-stricken. Now he was elated. He was still short of his own goal of breaking 150 MPH, and he was short of Allan Abbott's record, but at least he had established a world record for riding on a road.

"We got film footage of that ride and sent it to 'That's Incredible,'" Salmini said. "John's ride was broadcast on national television."

Howard and Vesco agreed they were pushing the outer limits of safety on the highway. Reluctantly, they realized they had to wait for the Salt Flats to dry.

Through 1983, Howard and Vesco stayed in touch. Utah received more rain than it had in a century. Howard expanded his multifitness coaching and trained for triathlons. In May he scored a second-place finish in the Ricoh Ironman U.S. Championship in Los Angeles, behind Scott Molina. "I worked out all winter preparing for the L.A. Ironman," he said. "Once I almost drowned in the ocean preparing for it. I got hypothermia and then was caught in a rip tide. Fortunately, I was with an experienced swimmer who told me to swim cross-current, and guided me to shore."

Howard's network widened in the burgeoning triathlon community. He coached Nancy Hoover, whose son, George, was a promising triathlete. Hoover had an investment business with J. David Dominelli, headquartered in a plush office on Ivanhoe Street in the center of the financial district of La Jolla, in southern California. Dominelli specialized in arbitrage—selling securities, commodities, and foreign currencies in different markets to profit from unequal prices. In the early 1980s, arbitrage was where the action was in finance. Arbitrageurs were fast becoming multimillionaires. Hoover and Dominelli were flush with success.

Team J. David had race horses and branched out to acquire a stable of world-class triathletes, including Scott Molina, Scott Tinley, Mark Allen, and Kathleen McCartney. Howard was hired to coach them. He invested some of his money in the company and reaped financial gains. For the first time in his life, Howard was doing better than skimming along.

The confluence of a heated investment atmosphere and his passion for cycling encouraged Howard to consider producing his own line of signature bicycles. When Dominelli provided him with the capital to start the enterprise, Howard hired Dave Moulton and his assistant, Dave Tesch, who built expensive custom bicycles in their shop in San Marcos. His signature bicycles sold for $1,100 and up, and drew praise in the cycling industry.

"I took a great deal of pride in those bicycles," Howard said. "They had my name on them. I made sure they had no flaws whatsoever. Each one was beautifully finished. They were snazzy. We had a limited edition of 500 which came out over a couple of years. We sold every one."

Howard was ensconced in the triathlon community, which earned him an invitation to teach a cycling class that summer at the Omega Institute in Rheinbeck, in the rustic Hudson River Valley north of New York City. He joined other accomplished athletes like Olympic runner Jeff Galloway and world-class miler Tom Birch in teaching classes to triathletes. It was a lovely place to work short hours and continue training up to eight hours a day for triathlons.

Triathlons had burst into a thriving sport. The United States Triathlon Association was formed as the sport's governing body. Valerie Silk, promoter of the Ironman World Triathlon Championship, was inundated with so many entry requests that she imposed qualifying times for men and women. Publications devoted to triathlons, including *Tri-Athlete* magazine, competed on newsstands. In France, an international triathlon was introduced in Nice in late 1982. In August 1983, Howard and Team J. David triathletes went to southern France to compete for the Nice Triathlon's $75,000 purse. "We swam 1.5 miles in the Mediterranean, rode about 60 miles in the mountains north of Nice, and ran 20 miles," Howard said. "I was mixing it up with Dave Scott, Mark Allen, and French triathlon champion Yves Corridor."

Allen triumphed while Howard and the rest of Team J. David swept all the top places.

Howard's name recognition was growing sharply. Manufacturer's Hanover, the main sponsor of the New York City Marathon, offered him $10,000 to run in the marathon and wear their name and logo. The marathon, however, was scheduled the day after the Ironman in Kailua-Kona. Howard agonized over the choice. Especially tempting was the prospect of competing in the Ironman on Saturday, boarding a jet to fly through six time zones, then running the New York City Marathon on Sunday. That would make an Ironman-plus weekend, and he would earn $10,000. But it also meant crawling across the marathon's finish line in Central Park. He turned down the offer and returned to Hawaii for the Ironman.

The 1983 Ironman is remembered as the year of the tack attack. A saboteur dumped thousands of carpet tacks on the road that cyclists pedaled. Howard swam through the rough water five minutes faster than when he won in 1981, and emerged from the ocean in about 50th place. On the bicycle, he and others battled 35 MPH head winds. He was moving up fast when he punctured. He stopped, changed the tire, and resumed pedaling, only to soon get another puncture. Without another spare tire or a patch kit, he was forced to quit. "I was greatly angered and bitter about the unfair anticlimax to months of training eight and more hours a day," he said. "But I resolved to return the next year to Ironman."

By December, Howard was doing well enough financially to make a down payment on a house in Encinitas, where he still lives. He had a comfortable house, was making more money than ever, his line of bicycles were selling, and he was in demand as a personal trainer. But his success didn't diminish his passion for the absolute speed record.

Howard's persistence with the speed record was consistent with predecessors in that eclectic fraternity who pushed the limits of speed on a bicycle. Back in the early 1890s, Charles Murphy of Brooklyn, New York, pedaled on wooden rollers to stay in shape during the winter and discovered his time for the mile was less than 30 seconds. Like Howard, Murphy had won several national championships. Murphy concluded that without wind resistance, he could pedal 60 MPH, then considered a barrier. Not even a car had come close to a mile a minute.

Murphy came up with the idea of drafting behind a locomotive, which could take him through the mile-a-minute barrier. But his idea was seen as too far-fetched. After years of talking up his plan, Murphy finally attracted the attention of an official of the Long Island Rail Road who thought it would be good publicity for the railroad. A few miles of boards were laid down between rails for a smooth surface.

On June 30, 1899, Murphy paced behind a locomotive and went through the mile in 57^4/5 seconds. Overnight he became a national hero. Some newspapers reported that people fainted at the news. Perhaps that was an exaggeration, but the decade brought the introduction of electric lights, the telephone, movies, and cars. Suddenly a cyclist was the first on two wheels—or even four wheels—to break the minute barrier for the mile. Someone may have felt faint at the prospect of what else might be next.

When Letourner broke the 100 MPH barrier four decades later, observers thought his record would stand for the rest of his life. Instead, it lasted only 10 years.

In 1951 Jose Meiffert, a French orphan like Letourner, topped Letourner's record by less than 1 MPH behind a Talbot Formula One car near Toulouse, France. Meiffert was uneasy about the slim margin he achieved and set out to break the barrier of 200 kilometers an hour (125 MPH). A crash at 80 MPH during one attempt nearly killed him. His recovery took nine years, including time spent as a lay brother in a Trappist monastery.

Finally, on July 19, 1962, Meiffert—now 49—paced behind a Mercedes-Benz 300 SLR along the German autobahn near Freidberg. Meiffert carried in the pocket of his jersey a note which said that, in case of an accident, he didn't want anyone to feel sorry for him. "If doctors can do no more for me," he wrote, "please bury me by the side of the road where I have fallen."

Meiffert pedaled 127.342 MPH (204.778 kilometers an hour) for the new world record. He retired to write his memoir. His record inspired Allan Abbott. Unlike Meiffert and Letourner, Abbott had grown up in relative comfort, and was introduced to cycling at Indiana University, where he competed in the Little 500. Afterward, he raced motorcycles on the road and in the dirt, and became intrigued with seeing how fast a cyclist could pedal behind a pace car. He designed a frame modeled after a motorcycle. He trained in a fierce regimen of hard sprints and grueling climbs up the mountains around Crestline, California, near where he lived. On August 23, 1973, Abbott—29—pedaled 138.7 MPH on the Bonneville Salt Flats. That brought the absolute speed record back to the United States.

In 1984, Howard's project was still on hold. He was impatient to return to the Salt Flats, but he stayed busy. He was writing a book of his own, *The Cyclist's Companion*, to help newcomers to cycling get started and veteran cyclists to enjoy the sport more.

He continued training to remain sharp for when the Salt Flats dried and he could return. In April, he went to east Texas for an unprecedented 520-mile race in Waco, called the Spenco 500. Wayman Spence, a physician who founded Spenco Medical Corporation, a sports medicine company, had organized a race to help test a new line of cycling accessories he had brought out— including padded cycling gloves, saddle pads, and orthotics. The Spenco 500 offered a purse of $25,000 cash and another $25,000 in merchandise, with $10,000 to the winner. More than 300 men and women entered.

England's former national champion, Phil Corley, Australian Neil Stephens, American national pursuit champion Jeff Rutter, and ultra-distance riders like Michael Shermer and Michael Secrest were among the riders who traveled to Waco where Dr. Spence put them up on his 50-acre ranch.

At 9 a.m. on April 20, Spence started the riders off on a rolling 150-mile loop on highways and farm roads, past farms and fields. Howard was a marked rider during the race, which took 27 hours.

He was competing against riders who had been born about the time he started racing. Steve Speaks of Walla Walla, Washington, won. Howard finished fourth.

Howard left Waco with additional sponsorship from Wayman Spence. "I got to know John when he came to my race," Spence recalled. "I also had met his parents, who are the nicest people. Somehow they raised a son who marches to the beat of a different drummer. I signed him up as an endorser of Spenco products."

Howard needed additional sponsors as his expenses mounted. He was caught in the abrupt reversal that Hoover and Dominelli suffered when their investment business went bust. Practically overnight, they lost their business, race horses, and Porsches. But Howard shifted gears and came up with a sponsorship from Wendy's and another deal with KHS, a Taiwanese bicycle manufacturer, to endorse their product line.

Triathlons continued to take up his competitive energy. He won in Carthage, Missouri, and returned to the Nice Triathlon. On October 6, he went to Hawaii for his fourth Ironman, where he finished sixth.

Now 37, he was conscious of the crow's feet deepening around the corners of his eyes. For two years he had tried to set the absolute speed record, which kept him training rigorously. He concentrated on sprinting, which he needed to get up to speed behind Vesco's Streamliner. He lifted weights to strengthen his upper body and gained 12 pounds. But the crow's feet he saw in the mirror were a sign that his time was limited.

In mid-October, he and Vesco talked on the telephone about taking another shot at the record. Vesco reported that the Salt Flats were at last dry. Then Vesco called back a couple weeks later to say that it had been raining for days. Once again, Howard was rained out.

In July 1985, Howard was back at the Bonneville Salt Flats—three years and $100,000 after he started. Also attending were about 50 friends, corporate representatives, journalists, photographers, timers, and Vesco and his crew. Heat corrugated off the brilliant white surface. The temperature rose into the 90s. Salt coated everything and crunched underfoot. It was all a good sign. Howard finally had the right conditions to fulfill the dare he had made with himself about breaking 150 MPH.

"Part of the Bonneville experience is hanging around with the

Bonneville veterans," said Salmini, there to film Howard's ride. "They tell stories that no sane person would believe ever could happen. It's such a unique place. No sound carries out there. Planes don't fly overhead. It's so silent. To get an idea of what John was going to do, I drove my rental car through the timed mile. It's so flat and the area is so vast that you don't have any sensation at all. I couldn't tell if I was going 6 MPH or 60. I've seen guys drive what they think is a straight line, but through my telephoto lens I see they are veering 30 degrees off center."

What guided Howard and Vesco was a dark, biodegradable lane marker that showed vividly against the white salt.

Over the three years that Howard had worked fitfully on the speed record, he had made minor changes on the bicycle. He covered the spokes of the rear wheel with Mylar disks, which reduced drag. Specialized supplied custom tires for his motorcycle wheels, made of Akront alloy rims. Man and machine were ready.

On Friday, July 19, Howard and Vesco went through six practice runs to get back in sync as they increased their speed. Each run had Howard pedaling hard for three miles as they accelerated past mile signposts. Accelerating strained Howard because the tempo went up constantly. Then he would pedal furiously through the timed mile, exerting himself to the limit of his ability. Afterward, he would slam into the back of Vesco's rear bumper as they slowed.

At 125 MPH, Howard discovered weird turbulence called Von Karman Vortex Shedding. "It kicked me violently forward if I began to fall back from the pace vehicle's slipstream," he explained. At that speed, he was in a narrow bubble of air pressure that was highly sensitive to any position change. Fortunately, his Mylar covering of the rear wheel helped the wheel to act as a rudder, and made the bicycle more stable.

Everything was a prologue for Saturday, July 20. Howard was up before dawn to watch the sunrise. "I was too excited to sleep." He and Vesco resumed their pursuit of the record at 8:30 a.m. On their first run, they got up to 134 MPH. The record seemed within reach. The routine was familiar, almost boring, but dangerous.

But on the fourth run, around noon, Howard was smoothly pedaling past 140 MPH when suddenly he had to fight to control his handlebars. They jerked in his grip as the rear wheel fishtailed wildly. He was forced to fall behind the car's slipstream.

"I felt as though I was being sand-blasted," he said. "A wave of air punched me." He put his head down and squeezed the handlebars to keep from being pulled off the bicycle. "I finally managed to remain upright until I could stop."

People raced in cars and motorcycles to where he was in the vast flat expanse to find out what had happened. His rear tire was flat. When his mechanic, John Vaneeckhoutte, took the tube out of the tire, he was surprised to see that the tube still held air.

Doug Malewicki, an engineer, figured out that the culprit was centrifugal force. He calculated that, at the speed Howard was traveling, air inside the tube pushed out through the valve, which lacked a cap. By chance, the front tire valve had a cap. The rear tube was put back in the tire, which was pumped up. Howard borrowed another cap. The quest continued.

"That flat only served to boost my confidence," Howard said.

At 4:00 p.m., on the sixth run of the day, Howard and Vesco knitted everything together. Howard worked hard to stay close to the car's rear bar as they accelerated from 65 MPH to 80 and then 100. At 110 MPH, he heard the roar of the wind around him but felt comfortable with this familiar distraction. Then, past 120 MPH, he hit the Van Karman effect. He drifted back two feet from the bumper bar, then was thrown forward hard.

As he entered the timed mile, his heart was pounding 195 beats a minute and his legs were spinning at 140 RPM. But now, past the Van Karman zone, his bicycle felt lighter and shorter.

"The world was reduced to a streaming white ribbon that I vaguely saw through the Plexiglass window of the car's fairing," Howard said. "It felt like the closing kilometer of a 4,000-meter pursuit race, where you know you must keep going despite the excruciating pain."

Dealing with oxygen debt is one thing for an athlete of Howard's caliber. But fear of losing that sweet spot behind Vesco's car was another matter. "That was a new dimension of this challenge," Howard said.

At the finish line, he streaked past. Friends and officials waited anxiously and quietly. Then an official radioed that Howard had pedaled 152.284 MPH for the new absolute speed record. Everyone let out great whoops. Howard had pulled it off! Perhaps as important was that he had won the bet he made with himself. Friends caught up to him after he stopped and bathed him in champagne.

Chapter 15

"How essential it is to have work that
fits the contour of your soul."
—Gail Godwin, *A Southern Family*

Word of Howard's absolute speed record raced around the world. "I learned about John's record from friends in France who telephoned to say what he did before John had the chance to call," Skip Hijsak said.

"I originally thought that the prototype bike we built would last about 20 trial runs, then come back and we would build another to improve it," Hijsak continued. "But that prototype held up."

Soon Howard was invited to New York City as a guest on Johnny Carson's "Tonight Show." On national television, Carson teased that Howard was such a pure cyclist that his life story could be called, "My Mother, the Schwinn."

Howard was riding high as a public figure—rare for a cyclist or triathlete in the United States. His book, *The Cyclist's Companion*, was excerpted in a new magazine, *Bicycle Sport*. He also co-authored another book, *Multi-Fitness*, with Al Gross and Chris Paul, which Macmillan published. Both books sold out. *The Cyclist's Companion* was revised with Gross and Paul listed as co-authors for another printing.

The publicity that Howard gave cycling—with his speed record, his books, and goodwill to the cycling and triathlons—contributed to the Bicycle Dealers Association naming him Man of the Year for 1985. He was widely recognized for doing what he chose. Rather than coast on his acclaim, Howard used the momentum to create a new agenda. Part of this involved establishing his School of Champions, "to develop better athletes at the grassroots level." His format, still in use, organizes classes for cyclists, duathletes (those who choose a combination of cycling and running), and triathletes, for men and women of all ages and abilities. Accomplished athletes who join him in teaching classes include world and Ironman champion Paula Newby-Fraser, Rob Mackle, Dr. Nick Martin, and Greg Welch. School of Champions formats are flexible, ranging from one-day performance seminars to week-long workshop and skills clinics.

School of Champions grew with Howard's wider recognition. He was hired to coach national triathlon teams from Japan, China, Australia, Canada, Mexico, and Brazil. Triathlons kept him traveling. He ventured to Hondo, Japan, in October 1986 for the Hondo International Triathlon: a 1-mile swim, 25-mile bicycle time trial, and a 6.2-mile run. Now crowding 40, he won the master's age group.

Howard talked in interviews about maturing from pitting himself against others to competing against himself. In 1987, School of Champions expanded to a schedule of classes in 21 cities. Howard was sponsored by DaVinci, a clothing line, and Eucalyptamint, a rubbing ointment to relieve sore muscles. He also joined in warp-speed criteriums for the Nabisco Wheat Thins series that promoter Dave Pelletier organized around the country. Howard said he considered it a personal victory just to finish the races against the professional and Category I racers.

Competing against himself compelled Howard to try to break his 512-mile world record for distance in 24 hours. Jose Diaz of DaVinci suggested he try the Sunshine Speedway in Clearwater, Florida, which had advantages over Central Park. In May 1987, Howard traveled to Clearwater, where great white egrets and ospreys rode the air currents over the track. A coterie of riders helped pace Howard. One was his former Raleigh-CRC of A teammate, Bill Humphries, who promoted the ride.

They rode around the clock, piling up centuries—100 miles each. For most cyclists, riding back-to-back centuries would be grueling. Howard referred to them as peaceful. He improved the new distance record to 539.7 miles.

When he stopped and dismounted, he slumped into a chair. "I feel like I've been run over by a truck," he admitted. After he collected himself, he expressed satisfaction at raising the distance by 27 miles. "This record was important because it gave me a chance to test myself against myself. I broke my own record."

What John Howard was to American cycling in the 1970s, Frank Shorter was to running. Shorter, two months younger than Howard, won the 1972 Munich Olympics marathon and took the silver medal at the 1976 Montreal Olympics. But eventually, even Shorter had to make concessions to age. He cut back from running

100-plus miles a week and supplemented his workouts with cycling. After Howard and Shorter turned 40, it was inevitable that they meet in a competition in which they both ran and rode bicycles. At the Desert Princess Run-Bike-Run World Championship February 18, 1989, in a southern California resort called Cathedral City, the contest between Howard and Shorter in the master's division upstaged the 1,000-plus young triathletes and duathletes, including professionals George Pierce, Ken Souza, Paula Newby-Fraser, and Liz Downing.

The event was over a 10-kilometer run, most of which was in a riverbed of soft sand, followed by 62 kilometers (38.7 miles) over rolling hills, concluded by a repeat of the 10-kilometer run.

Shorter built up a lead of three and a half minutes on Howard over the first run, as expected. Then Howard quickly changed his running shoes for his cycling shoes and powered away on his bicycle like an express train. He overtook dozens of younger athletes. At the 20-mile marker, Howard blew past Shorter and used the rest of the ride to expand his margin.

When Howard reached the end of the cycling segment, the throng of spectators buzzed with excitement. His time of 1:30:51 was the second-fastest cycling time of the day. He had a lead of eight minutes on Shorter. "I stomped him on the bike," Howard said.

Back on the soft sand for the final run, Howard's legs started to cramp. He was running a minute-and-a-half per mile slower than Shorter, who loped along at a pace of 5 minutes and 30 seconds a mile. Howard struggled closer to the finish. He still led Shorter with a mile left when the course began the cement section that led to the end. "I died out there," Howard said.

Shorter, light as ever on his feet, caught Howard with a half-mile left. "That was so frustrating," Howard said. Both Shorter and Howard, 41, broke the master's course record. They placed in the top 20 of the event overall.

Although Howard had moved away from Missouri, he was still remembered in his hometown. On February 9, 1989, he was one of three inducted into the third annual Springfield-area Sports Hall of Fame. Presenting him his award were Wayne Stetina, his Olympic teammate, and Ned Reynolds, the sports director who had presided over Howard's first television appearance.

On Memorial Day weekend, Howard was invited east to Somerville, New Jersey, as part of the third annual round of inductions into the U.S. Bicycling Hall of Fame there. As Hall of

Fame President Frank Torpey read a summary of Howard's career before the dinner audience of 200, a previous Hall of Famer, Alf Goullet, 98, stood nearby holding the large wood-and-bronze plaque that Howard was to receive. It was an emotional moment. The Ironman's eyes started to water.

Goullet, legendary for his six-day victories on three continents, playfully waved the plaque in Howard's direction and asked, "How much are you willing to give me for this?" His quip brought welcome levity and delighted the audience. Goullet and Howard were two long riders who understood each other.

Another highlight of the year was returning that summer to the Bonneville Salt Flats with Freddy Markham, the California sprinter. At the national Human Powered Vehicle championships, Howard and Markham rode a tandem that was enclosed in a light, aerodynamically designed cover. They set a world record on the tandem by pedaling 60.5 MPH for the kilometer and 58.6 MPH for the mile.

Drawing from his quarter-century of competing as well as from what he had learned from coaching, Howard worked with film producer Mark Schulze to produce a 55-minute video, *John Howard's Lessons in Cycling*. Howard wrote the script and directed the production. The video was awarded a silver medal in the 1992 New York International Film Festival.

Critical success with the video is an extension of the commentating that Howard has done for CBS Sports, ESPN television, and assorted radio and cable television broadcasts on cycling and triathlons. He also has delivered lectures before health-care professionals and educators, and motivational speeches to civic clubs and trade organizations.

Behind Howard's accomplishments lies his driving tenacity, derived in large part from the work ethic he grew up with. His parents showed by example that hard work pays. In May 1992, a year after they celebrated their golden wedding anniversary, they were awarded their degrees from Drury College.

"I flew back to Springfield to attend my parents' commencement," Howard said. "I was really proud of what they had done. My brother and sister flew in with their kids. We celebrated with a family reunion."

Howard, 46 in 1993, looks like a composite of three periods of his life. He still has the over-developed cyclist's legs of his prime

years. His knees are covered with so much scar tissue that looking
for a single scar is impossible. A photo would show how the skin
can be scraped to the bone, gouged, cut, pounded and bruised,
yet still continue to grow back.

Moreover, his knees still carry their load gallantly. In 1991,
Howard returned to age-graded national championships and has
since won a variety of titles on the road and in off-road mountain
bike races. The U.S. Cycling Federation noted in its tabloid, *Cycling
USA*, that Howard in 1992 became the first in American cycling
to win road, time-trial, and off-road national championships in
the same year.

His torso still has the lean promise of adolescence. But from
the neck up, decades of sun and physical strain register on his
wind-carved face. His hair, still curly, has faded from blond to
gray. The lines on his face deepen like worn leather when he
smiles, particularly the crow's feet around his eyes. They show
the dues he paid on his way to becoming a senior statesman in
cycling and triathlons—sports that put a premium on youth.

When he started going to bicycle races in the late 1960s, he
told his mentor Ray Florman that he didn't want to work a
regular 9 to 5 job. He has avoided that treadmill. From racing, he
segued to a coaching career. Through 1993, he conducted some
200 training sessions for more than 5,000 athletes around the
United States and seven nations, including Australia and China.
He writes regularly for magazines like *Bicycle Guide*. He continues
to endorse KHS bicycles, and rides them to national titles.

Howard also wrote a historical novel based on the life of Major
Taylor, generally regarded as the first black athlete to cross the
color line in professional sports. Taylor was one of America's early
international superstar athletes. Howard is circulating the
manuscript.

Howard has made dreams into goals that he then accomplished.
The same can apply to nearly everyone else, he points out. "It
doesn't do any good to sit around and wish for things," he said.
"It's essential to connect what you want to do with the will to do
it. Having the will is a key issue. Another key is breaking the goal
down to parts that lead directly to achieving that goal, without
distractions. It's building those parts that has always been exciting
for me. Watching them come together is progress. That creates a
sense of momentum, which is what has kept me on track."

With age-graded competition flourishing and cycling
broadening from road racing to mountain biking, Howard sees

new opportunities. Mountain biking over rough trails out in the country, removed from traffic, favors his style of riding—allowing him to use his power, handling skills, and tactical experience. As long as he knows Alf Goullet, who turned 102 four months ahead of Howard's turning 46, he can say he hasn't reached his middle years.

"I view sports as a creative process, like sculpture," he said. "Sculptors work with wood or metal or plastic. I work with a training program, tactics, and races."

Part of his creative approach is to adapt cycling to boats for what he calls an aquacycle. He pedaled the aquacycle he helped design 37 miles through rough Pacific Ocean water from Dana Point in southern California to Catalina Island in 6 hours, 37 minutes to show what can be done with an aquacycle.

"With roads so crowded with traffic, I see great potential for aquacycles," Howard said. "It's great exercise. Doesn't jar the joints the way running or some aerobics do. There are plenty of rivers, streams, lakes, and ponds all over to use. With the right marketing and product line, aquacycles could be really popular.

"I'm still in the first half of my life. Recently, I finished second in a professional mountain bike race. I was on the podium with the winner, Greg Marini, who is 22. He said it was an honor to be on the podium with me. I said it was an honor to be on the podium with him. I've still got a lot left to do."

A MESSAGE FROM THE PUBLISHER

I first met John Howard nine years ago shortly after he finished competing in the Race Across America. He had numbness in his hands from nerve damage suffered during the grueling race, and I made some special gel-padded gloves for him. Over the years, we have become friends and worked together on numerous sports-medicine products for cyclists. While I can't stay on the same road with John on a bicycle, I can keep up with him running—which just goes to prove that even the best of champions can't always win when they get out of their own sport.

W. R. Spence, M.D.
Publisher

*A*t WRS Publishing, we are only interested in producing books we can be proud of—books that focus on people and/or issues that enlighten and inspire, books that change lives for the better, either through the celebration of human achievement or the revelation of human folly. **Call us at 1-800-299-3366 for suggestions or for a free book catalog.**

WATCH FOR THESE RELATED TITLES:

RACE ACROSS AMERICA tells the agonies and glories of the world's longest and cruelest transcontinental bicycle race.

LIFE ON THE LINE is the story of all-pro lineman Karl Nelson, who came through the cancer that ended his football career with the New York Giants.

YOUNG AT HEART outlines the running career of 85-year-old Johnny Kelley—who has answered the starting gun at 63 Boston Marathons—and of long-distance running in America in this century.

CLIMBING BACK, The story of Mark Wellman, Yosemite's incredible paraplegic ranger, who climbed El Capitan and Half Dome.

WRS
PUBLISHING
A Division of WRS Group, Inc.
Waco, Texas